Saudi Arabia

With an Account of the Development of Its Natural Resources

Saudi Arabia

With an Account of the Development of Its Natural Resources

THIRD EDITION

By K. S. Twitchell

WITH THE COLLABORATION OF
EDWARD J. JURJI AND
R. BAYLY WINDER

GREENWOOD PRESS, PUBLISHERS
NEW YORK

To the memory of

CHARLES R. CRANE

*the great American whose practical philanthropy
was the foundation of the present development of
the kingdom of his esteemed friend,*

the late King Abdul Aziz ibn-Saud

Preface to the Third Edition

THE purpose of this book is to give the Western world some idea of a country which is still one of the least known in the Middle East, and of the late King Abdul Aziz ibn-Saud, who founded the kingdom of Saudi Arabia, and his son, King Saud, who has succeeded him. I should not have thought of writing it had I not been urged to do so by Dr. Philip K. Hitti, Professor Emeritus of the Department of Oriental Studies of Princeton University, and by Mr. Datus C. Smith, Jr., former Director of the Princeton University Press.

Through a combination of circumstances which are explained in Chapter 4, "The First Agricultural Mission to Saudi Arabia," and Part III, "The Position of Saudi Arabia in World Economy," I was probably more closely associated with King ibn-Saud and his country than any other American up to 1946 (subsequently Mr. Fred Davies, Mr. Floyd Ohliger, and others of the Arabian American Oil Company were in closer contact with the King). In those early days there was much of Saudi Arabia which had not been previously visited by non-Moslems and through which I was able to travel in connection with various work done at the request of His Majesty and of Shaikh Abdullah Sulaiman, then Minister of Finance.

The amazing changes in administration, education, and general welfare, as well as the tremendous developments in oil, transportation, and commerce that have taken place during the eleven years since I wrote the first edition of this book are the reasons for preparing a revised third edition. The position of Saudi Arabia in being one of the world's greatest oil producers, as well as in having one of the greatest of oil reserves, makes this country of vital importance to America and to Europe. The attitude of King Saud and his government toward the menace of Communism is of great interest to the free world. Finally, the fact that Saudi Arabia has great influence in the

Moslem world of some 360,000,000 people is an exceedingly important factor in Middle East diplomacy.

ACKNOWLEDGMENTS. I wish to acknowledge the advice of the following friends and thank them most sincerely for their assistance: Dr. Philip K. Hitti, Mr. Shukry E. Khoury, and Mr. Farhat Ziadeh of the Princeton Department of Oriental Studies; Dr. Edward J. Jurji, collaborator on the first edition; Mr. Datus C. Smith, Jr., and Miss Jean MacLachlan of Princeton University Press for editorial assistance on the first edition, and Miss R. Miriam Brokaw, Managing Editor, for the present edition. I wish also to thank Mr. J. G. Hamilton and the late Mr. A. L. Wathen for much information gained while we were on the U.S. Agricultural Mission to Saudi Arabia during 1942 and 1943. I also thank Col. Gerald de Goury, M.C., for the use of information from his book *A Saudi Arabian Notebook*, Cairo, 1943. I am grateful to Capt. H. C. Armstrong, author of *Lord of Arabia*, for data concerning the life of King Abdul Aziz. I wish to express my appreciation of the services of, and information given me by, the late Ahmad Omar Fakhry, my companion, secretary, and interpreter during most of my travels in Saudi Arabia.

Especially do I wish to thank His Excellency Shaikh Hafez Wahba, many years Ambassador of Saudi Arabia to Great Britain, for much valuable data; as well as His Excellency Shaikh Asad Al-Faqih, first Ambassador to the United States, and his successor, His Excellency Shaikh Abdullah Al-Khayyal, present Saudi Ambassador in Washington, Dr. Omar Abu Khadra and his colleague, Jamil M. Baroody, Saudi Delegates to the United Nations, for numberless courtesies and varied information. The Division of Near Eastern and African Affairs of the Department of State has been most kind in assistance, as have ex-Ambassador J. Reeves Childs, Esq., and ex-Minister Col. William A. Eddy.

PREFACE

The extensive and valuable data on the oil operations would have been impossible to obtain without the assistance, courtesy, and generosity of the Arabian American Oil Company, headed by my esteemed friend Mr. Fred A. Davies, Chairman of the Board; Mr. Gary Owens, Vice President; Mr. Gordon Hamilton, Chief of Public Relations, and his secretary, Miss Lonergan. The latter went to great trouble in gathering data, maps, and photographs. I appreciate the information and details given me by the American Smelting & Refining Company concerning the operations of the Saudi Arabian Mining Syndicate, Ltd.; also various facts from the International Bechtel Corporation, Burns & Roe, Inc., Michael Baker, Jr., Inc. (Mr. Fred Awalt, representative), and Gellatly, Hankey & Co., Ltd.; as well as valuable data from Major H. St. J. Armitage and Mr. R. LeB. Bowen. I greatly appreciate the extensive data regarding the bibliography given by the Middle East Institute through the courtesy of Mr. Rothe, Jr. and Mr. Sands. I am deeply indebted to Professor R. Bayly Winder for detailed and valuable criticism.

And, finally, I wish to record my greatest appreciation for the assistance of my wife.

Many others have been most kind in suggestions and in giving data. I thank them all and ask their pardon in not mentioning them individually.

K. S. TWITCHELL

Spring, 1958

ix

Contents

xi

Illustrations

Aerial view of Jidda

Two views of the City of Learning. *Courtesy of the Arabian American Oil Company*

Beit Baghdadi, Jidda

Ministry of Foreign Affairs, Jidda. *Courtesy of the Arabian American Oil Company*

Street widening in Riyadh. *Courtesy of the Arabian American Oil Company*

Government tuberculosis hospital between Jidda and Mecca. *Courtesy of the Arabian American Oil Company*

Pilgrim caravan en route to Mecca

Signposts on the route to Mecca. Photograph at right, center, *Courtesy of the Arabian American Oil Company*

The Ka'ba in Mecca. *Courtesy of the Arabian American Oil Company*

A street in Medina. *Courtesy of the Arabian American Oil Company*

Islamic inscription near Taif

Mortar in ruins near Najran

The Hijaz railway

Fortress near Wejh

ILLUSTRATIONS FOLLOWING PAGE 210

Dhahran in 1933

Dhahran today. *Courtesy of the Arabian American Oil Company*

Homes in Dhahran. *Courtesy of the Arabian American Oil Company*

Hospital at Dhahran. *Courtesy of the Arabian American Oil Company*

Passenger train. *Courtesy of the Arabian American Oil Company*

ALL PICTURES NOT ACKNOWLEDGED WERE TAKEN BY THE AUTHOR

MAPS

I. Characteristic Features
of Saudi Arabia

His late Majesty, Abdul Aziz ibn-Saud, founder of Saudi Arabia, with his son, King Saud al Saud, the present monarch

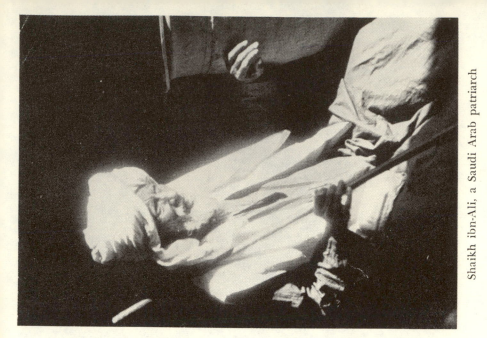

Shaikh ibn-Ali, a Saudi Arab patriarch

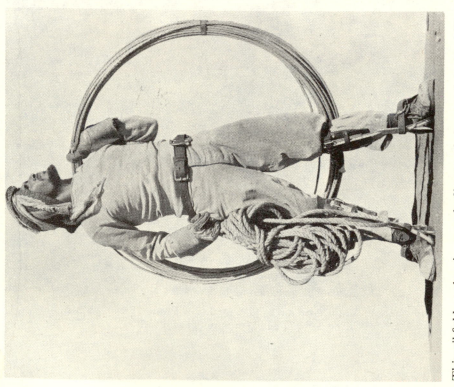

This oil-field worker is an embodiment of the amazing transition from camel driver to industrial worker

Primary school in Jidda. One of the older buildings of the new regime

Government school in Dammam

His Royal Highness, Prince Faisal ibn-Abdul Aziz, Prime Minister and Minister of Foreign Affairs

1. The Geographic Setting

SAUDI ARABIA comprises the bulk of the Arabian Peninsula. Due to some still undetermined boundaries, the area estimates vary from 618,000 to 870,000 square miles. Extending northward beyond the latitude of Alexandria, Egypt, the northern frontier reaches approximately that of Jerusalem. Jordan, Iraq, and Kuwait are its northern neighbors, while the Persian Gulf forms its eastern boundary down to the Trucial Coast, including Qatar and Oman. On the south lie Oman, Hadramawt, Aden Protectorate beyond the still undefined boundary of the "Empty Quarter" (*Rub al-Khali*). A part of the southwestern frontier is the unsurveyed portion of the Empty Quarter lying to the east of the Yemen. The southern boundary of the Saudi province of Asir contiguous with the northern end of Yemen has been surveyed and marked by the eminent British Arabist, H. St. John B. Philby, a boundary agreed upon by both the Arab governments. From this line northerly to the tip of the Gulf of Aqaba, the Red Sea washes the western shores of Saudi Arabia at the provinces of Asir and Hijaz.*

With regard to boundary lines, the following is quoted from a statement provided in 1945 by His Excellency, Shaikh Hafiz Wahba, Saudi Arabian Ambassador at the Court of St. James: "The boundaries between Najd and Transjordan were settled according to the treaty of Hadda signed in 1925. As to those between the Hijaz and Transjordan, the negotiations were broken off because of disagreement over Aqaba and Maan. The British government considered these two regions part of Transjordan, whereas the Saudi Arabian government insisted that

---

* For the convenience of the reader unfamiliar with Arabic, popular forms rather than the classical spelling of place-names have been used. A glossary of the classical equivalents of names which occur frequently will be found on p. 257. There is considerable variation in the transliteration of Arabic names in different sources. Thus "Hijaz" may be "Hejaz," etc. The reader should not be disturbed and should make his own inferences.

the two regions, until 1925, belonged to the Hijaz and that all their officials were appointed by King Husain. The question is still standing as it was before. As to the boundaries between Saudi Arabia and Qatar and Oman, negotiations were taken up in the years 1934, 1935 and 1937, but the two parties arrived at no solution."

However, in 1951 negotiations were resumed between Prince Faisal and the British government. The Qatar boundary is now settled but the decision regarding Oman is still pending.

1. *Hijaz*, which may be translated as "boundary" or "barrier," is the most well-known province of Saudi Arabia. It consists primarily of a 700-mile coastal plain lying along the Red Sea reaching from the southern side of Asir to the entrance to the Gulf of Aqaba. Varying in width from 10 to 40 miles, this plain extends to a massive, rugged mountain wall of igneous and metamorphic rocks on its eastern edge which towers over 8,000 feet above the sea. The western slopes of this range are especially precipitous at the southern end, abutting on the province of Asir. South of the Mecca-Taif-Riyadh route no motor road traverses the mountainous region, though two roads are found to the north, one from Jidda to the Mahad Dahab Mine, thence northerly to connection with the Medina-Hail route, as well as easterly to the Eshaira-Muwaih-Riyadh road; the other, a recently relocated, graded, and paved highway, runs from Jidda to Medina.

A third east-west road links Yenbo with Medina, joining the Jidda-Medina highway at Al Musaijid. The lowest pass traversed from the coast over the mountain wall is 2,200 feet in elevation but the ridge line in general varies from 3,800 to 7,000 feet. On the eastern side of this wall lies the tableland of Najd after a gentle slope easterly from the mountains.

2. *Asir*, meaning "difficult" or "dangerous," is the name of the second province. It lies to the south of the Hijaz and extends down to the boundary of the independent kingdom of Yemen. Including a coastal plain (Tihama) along the Red Sea

4

—200 miles in length and up to 40 miles wide—the area is densely populated in the river-flooded regions. In such localities as Ragaba, Gahama, and Khor al-Birk, lava flows have reached the sea. And as in the Hijaz, the mourtains on the eastern side of the Tihama are extremely rugged, rising to an elevation of over 9,000 feet. There are not many trails in Asir, and on these even a donkey finds it hard to ascend the plateau. The traveller is made only too aware that "difficult" is the proper designation for this province. Gently sloping to the east, the mountains are extensively terraced to prevent soil erosion and permit cultivation.

The Asir landscape is akin to certain parts of Yemen to the south, and to some regions in Cyprus and Italy. Its rainfall, exceeding the 4-inch average of most of Saudi Arabia, attains an annual amount of 10 to 12 inches, as judged by the first American Agricultural Mission from the condition of the vegetation. This comparatively heavy rainfall is confirmed, moreover, by the prevalence of a unique ("multiple eave") type of building at the capital, Abha, where the countryside of Asir begins to level off at 7,000 to 6,000 feet. Good-sized farming areas, parallel to the mountains, extend down the river valleys, reaching Najran and the Empty Quarter. This eastward inclination of the mountains slopes down to about 4,000 feet at Najran and to 3,600 feet at Bisha near the northeastern corner of Najran.

At the edge of the great desert below Najran, the aneroid barometer recorded 3,500 feet. It should be borne in mind that all elevations are those recorded by the author from his aneroid, and, being subject to weather conditions, are not absolutely accurate.

3. *Najd*, or "highlands," is largely a sedimentary plateau, composed of limestones and sandstones, except for occurrences of igneous metamorphics up to 200 miles wide in places along its western side. There are hills rising a few hundred feet above the general surface like islands. The altitude varies from 600

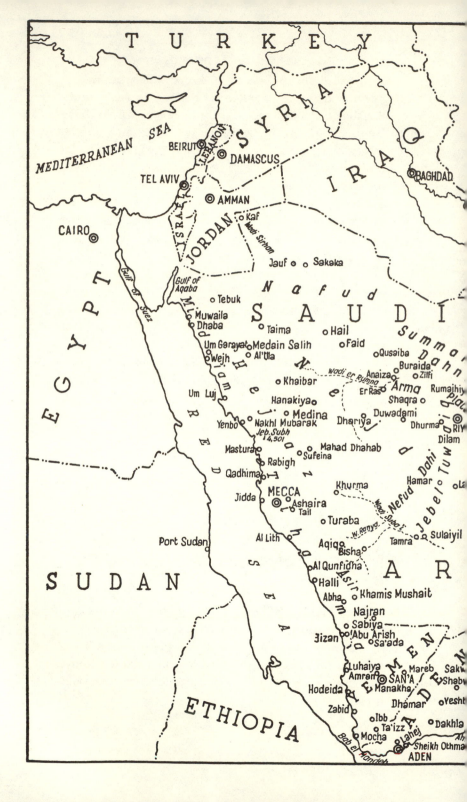

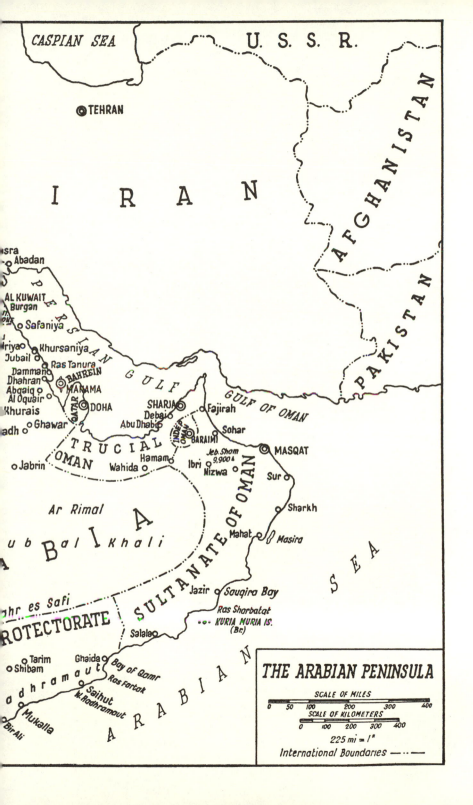

CASPIAN SEA

U.S.S.R.

◎ TEHRAN

I R A N

AFGHANISTAN

PAKISTAN

sra
○ Abadan

AL KUWAIT
Burgan
ou ○ Safaniya

P E R S I A N   G U L F

riya ○ Khursaniya
Jubail
Dammam ○ Ras Tanura
Dhahran ○ BAHREIN
Abqaiq ○ MANAMA
Al Oquair
Khurais
adh ○ Ghawar ○

QATAR

◎ DOHA

SHARJA ◎
Debai ○ ○ Fajirah
Abu Dhabi

GULF OF OMAN

INDEP
OMAN
○ Sohar
BARAIMI

TRUCIAL

OMAN

○ Jabrin

Wahida
Hamam ○

Ibri ○
Nizwa ○

Jeb.Shom
9,900 ▲

◎ MASQAT

○ Sur

○ Sharkh

SULTANATE OF OMAN

Ar Rimal

ub B al A Khali

Mahat ○ ○ Masira

hr es Safi

Jazir ○ Sauqira Bay

Ras Shorbatat
•• KURIA MURIA IS.
(Br.)

Salala ○

ROTECTORATE

A R A B I A N   S E A

○ Tarim
○ Shibam

adhramaut

Ghaida ○ Bay of Qamr
Ras Fartak

Saihut
w.Hadhramaut

Mukalla ○
Bir Ali ○

A R A B I A N

THE ARABIAN PENINSULA

SCALE OF MILES

0   50   100   200   300   400

SCALE OF KILOMETERS

0   100   200   300   400

225 mi = 1″

International Boundaries ——·——

feet at Sulaiyil on the Wadi Dawasir and 780 feet at Jabrin oasis on the south to 1,800 feet at Riyadh, 2,800 feet at Hail, then to 1,000 down to 300 feet along the Iraq frontier.

Najd is the heart of Saudi Arabia. In it lies Riyadh, the original home of King Abdul Aziz ibn-Saud and his son, the present ruler, King Saud ibn-Abdul Aziz. Riyadh is the political capital of the country. Najd is the cradle of Wahhabism, a Puritanical Moslem sect that began in the eighteenth century.

In this province are located the cities of Anaiza and Buraida, which have reared many an official of the Saudi regime, governors (*Amir*) of towns and districts, members of the police force, and the bulk of the standing army. The plateau extends eastward to the Hasa, the province lying east of the Dahna. Southward Najd merges into the Empty Quarter. As a province Najd is furthermore distinguished today as the scene of a flourishing agricultural development whose nucleus is at Kharj, 54 miles south of Riyadh.

4. *Hasa,* now officially called the Eastern Province, is the eastern province of Saudi Arabia. In this book we refer to it as Hasa, which an eminent Arabist, Dr. George Rentz, has translated as "sandy ground with water close to the surface." This is an accurate description of the province, which stretches from the state line of Najd, along the Dahna, to the Persian Gulf. It meets the Empty Quarter in the south, and in the north borders Kuwait and the Neutral Zones. Geologically, it is formed of sedimentary rocks. Since the first commercial oil field (called the "Dammam") at Dhahran in 1934, seven others have been proven and more are probable. Yet even prior to the discovery of oil in this province, it had already ranked as an important asset to Saudi Arabia, largely through the celebrated Hofuf oasis with its seven enormous water springs, of which the largest discharges 22,500 gallons of water per minute; and its more than two million palm trees which produce the highly prized *khilas* dates. The oil company equipment as well as petroleum produced here go through the ports

of Dammam and Ras Tanura, joined with the Dhahran oil field by pipelines. Formerly, however, the trade of Najd passed through the ports of Oqair, Qatif and Jubail.

It was a fortunate day for the whole country, with its four provinces, when according to a royal decree promulgated in 1932, it came to be known as "Saudi Arabia" instead of "Najd and Its Dependencies." The new name bore witness to the constitutive role of the Royal House of Saud, a ruling family like the Tudors and Stuarts of British history. As ranking member of his clan, and chief architect of the new state, King Abdul Aziz ibn-Saud was remarkably successful in consolidating the tribes and provinces under one sovereign and independent government.

2. Geology, Topography, and Climate

Geology

IT IS a source of immense economic advantage to Saudi Arabia that two-thirds of its eastern structure comprises what is normally known to geologists as a sedimentary formation—a variety of rock which under certain conditions becomes an ideal home for oil and coal deposits. These sedimentary formations are principally limestones, although at al-Ula, along the northwestern edge of the country, sandstone abounds in massive beds. The remaining western area, extending as far as the Red Sea, with the exception of sedimentary relics in the vicinity of the Farasan Islands, Jizan and Sabya in the south, and Umluj, Dhaba and Muwaila near the head of the Gulf of Aqaba, consists of igneous and metamorphic formations, favorable to metallic mineral deposits. A few metallic minerals are found in both kinds of formation but, with the exception of salt, lime, and gypsum, they are of little immediate benefit to the country. The sedimentary formations are, of course, the source of the important oil field developed at Jabal Dhahran in the Hasa, and of the newer fields of Ghawar, Abqaiq, Qatif, Fadhili, Khursaniyah, Abu Hadriyah, and Safaniya. It is not at all unlikely that still other commercial oil deposits may yet be discovered in this concession area of about 500,000 square miles.

Sandstone outcrops occur also farther south in Asir. South of the town of Khamaseen in Wadi Dawasir, at an elevation of 2,200 feet, a low mountain range projecting in a north to south direction seems to be entirely of coarse-grained aeolian sandstone, with large quartz pebble inclusions and sufficient iron oxides to give it a deep red color. Fragments appear in the form of slabs which resound when struck, with the bell-like ring of phonolite. Fantastic shapes, caused by erosion of wind and sand, fill the mountain ridges. Nevertheless, limestone fragments are found 58 miles south of Khamaseen, in the ancient Himyarite ruins of Qarya in the Empty Quarter, where old wells of an estimated depth of 90 feet were apparently constructed in limestone, indicating that the sandstone layer was not very thick.

A distance of 133 miles separates Khamaseen from the next watering place, Bir Himaa, standing 4,000 feet above the sea, on the western edge of the Empty Quarter. These wells are in a basin consisting entirely of red aeolian sandstone. Another 35 miles southwest is Bir Husainiya and its 129-feet-deep well where granite holds absolute sway, with several igneous flows in evidence, and the most recent pink (feldspar) granite enclosing fragments of the gray granite. From thence to Najran, all the country rock is definitely granite. The headquarters residence and office of the governor are situated near the head of the Najran valley, encircled, save on the east, by mountains. Those to the south and west are capped with sandstone, rising more than 1,500 feet high above the valley floor, itself 4,000 feet high. These sandstones and sediments extend to and through an extensive section of the mountains of the Yemen.

The western area, already referred to, extending from the Red Sea eastward to the points of contact with sedimentaries, is composed largely of igneous and volcanic rocks, many of which have undergone a great transformation—that is, have been "metamorphosed"—by tremendous torsion and twisting, caused by the formation of the great mountain range, a thousand miles long, which rises in a line parallel to the Red Sea. In Saudi Arabia, its peaks soar to a maximum height of over 9,000 feet, and to 11,000 in the Yemen. Scattered along the plateau east of the mountain summits are numerous geologically recent volcanic cones and lava flows and to the west a tongue of lava may be observed east of Abu-Arish close to the frontiers of the Yemen; while in several other spots, between Shuqaiq and Khor al-Birk, the lava reaches out into the Red

Sea. Then at Gahama, to the north of Shuqaiq, there is a volcanic cone which forms an island a short distance offshore.

Some 12 miles from Mecca, at Jabal Nura, there is an excellent quality of burned lime, obtained from sedimentary fragments which have been metamorphosed. Similar "islands" are to be seen on the road from Jidda to Mahad Dhahab, about 40 miles beyond Jidda, as well as at Kharne Aybad—or "White Goat's Horn"—approximately 100 miles from Jidda. Similar occurrences, though considerably smaller, have been noted in Najd 100 miles farther due east. At Mahad Dhahab Mine, the mine hill itself is a felsite and highly metamorphosed sedimentary overlain by a basaltic flow. The mine mountain is andesitic, cut by quartz veins and partly overlain by a rhyolite flow. Most of the exposures to the east of the volcanic and metamorphic mountain are granite. At Taif, the granite shows many intrusive dikes to the west as the mountains become higher. Close to the southern end of this massive mountain range—in the Yemen—there are stratified deposits of volcanic ash, or "tuff."

Topography

In order to visualize the general topography of Saudi Arabia one must again recall the coastal plain fringe along the Red Sea; then, the steep mountain wall rising to over 9,000 feet at the southern end of Asir, 8,000 feet behind Mecca, 4,000 west of Mahad Dhahab, 3,000 near Medina, and continuing northerly at about this same elevation, with Wadi Hamdh and other valleys cutting through at 2,000 feet. To the east of this mountain wall is the great Najd plateau, varying from 6,000 feet to 4,000 feet between Asir and Taif, thence descending to 2,200 at al-Ula. This whole tableland slopes gently eastward to the Persian Gulf. Granite hills lift their heads above the plateau in the western third, and the Tuwaik mountains, the Awanid Scarp and the Kharj rise to the north and south of Riyadh, above the general level. Lengthy folds and faults also appear along the Dahna, and there are many erosion-formed hills in the Hasa.

On the west side of the mountain range is the great coastal plain, known as Tihama, bordering the Red Sea. Its width, as we have seen, varies from 40 miles, at Hodeida in the Yemen, to an approximate average of 30 miles from Jizan northerly to Lith, then 10 to 20 about Wejh, and finally it shrinks to nothing at the Gulf of Aqaba. The mountain wall, behind this coastal plain, is dotted throughout with foothills, and there are great valleys (*wadis*) reaching far to the east, the largest of which is Wadi Hamdh, south of Wejh. One terminus of this valley comes close to Medina, while the other branch reaches the vicinity of al-Ula. Other important valleys are the Wadi Yenbo, Wadi Rabigh, Wadi Ghoran, Wadi Fatimah; and in Asir, Wadi Itwad and Wadi Bisha. At times they carry large amounts of water and also vast quantities of silt. The scarcity of vegetation on most of the mountain slopes that form the drainage basin of these valleys results in an almost 100 per cent run-off. The deposit of silt, on the other hand, forms many fertile arable lands in places where the river beds are nearly level, on the backwash of river bends, at the emergence of streams from the mountain walls and at the confluence of the rivers with the sea.

On the east side of the mountain wall, the slopes are much less precipitous, graduating to the great inland plateau which lies largely within the confines of the Najd province. At Asir in the south, the eastern mountain slopes are intensively terraced for cultivation. They reach the more level areas at elevations of from 6,000 to 7,000 feet. The general inclination is east by north until the edge of the Empty Quarter is reached. The immense Najd plains extend 900 miles to the north through Hail to the Iraq-Jordan frontier. The following elevations of points I visited confirm the statement that the Najd plains are fairly level. They also make it clear that along the eastern side of the Hijaz mountain range, the terrain slopes

13

gently to the North. The level areas at Taif average 5,000 feet above the sea; at Ashaira 3,700; at Birka 2,800; at Hafira, on the old Hijaz Railway, 1,740. Sixty-six miles to the north, along the railway line, at the old Turkish pilgrim fortress called Qalat al-Sura, the elevation is 2,200 feet. This fortress lies at the junction of the motor route leading to Khaibar, 104 miles southeast, which also has an elevation of 2,200 feet.

For the points lying on a line north from Sulaiyil, at the northern edge of the Empty Quarter, the following elevations have been recorded by an aneroid barometer:

	FEET		FEET
Sulaiyil	2,210	Anaiza	1,910
Laila in Aflaj	1,700	Rass	2,000
Kharj	1,360	Fawara	2,350
Badia Palace at Riyadh	1,800	Samira	2,700
Bir Rumah	1,760	Hail	2,800
Marrat	2,190	Faid	2,550
Buraida	1,820		

There are hills protruding through these huge plains, and long cliffs, 100 to 200 feet high, are formed by the fault scarps running in a general north-south direction near the Awanid mountains and also between Riyadh and Kharj. The Tuwaik mountains are in a similar parallel line but to the west of Kharj and Aflaj.

Another topographical phenomenon is the Nafud, the land of sand dunes. The Great Nafud or "Nafud Dahi" extends north from the immense desert of the Empty Quarter up to Jauf near latitude 30° north, where it merges with the Dahna. The width varies from 100 miles, west of Sulaiyil, to 25 miles near Marrat, and similarly near Anaiza and Buraida; then north and northwest of Hail it terminates in a great waste, 250 miles long. The greatest width is roughly 170 miles, lying south of Jauf. Its length from Sulaiyil at the northern edge of the Empty Quarter is about 800 miles. In the Nafud there are numerous great parallel ridges of sand interspersed with wind-swept exposures of the underlying rock—generally flat beds of

14

limestone. The dunes are like a sea and show the direction of the prevailing winds by huge crests and combs of sand, like breakers. These crests may reach a height of 500 feet but are usually 20 or 30 feet high. In many instances there are long gradual slopes like swells on the ocean and along these are cross ripples which, incidentally, are extremely hard on car springs.

The Dahna is a great ribbon of folds and faults, 25 to 60 miles wide, in the limestone which starts southeasterly from the Iraq border down to the Empty Quarter, forming a crescent-like figure. The general elevation is 1,200 feet at Maagala, on the eastern side of the Dahna, and 1,700 feet at Bir Rumah on the western side. From the eastern side of the Dahna the ground slopes gradually to sea level along the Persian Gulf. There are many slight faults and folds in this huge area "but as yet there have not been sufficient investigations to determine all its potentialities. However the Arabian American Oil Company issued a statement dated October 21, 1957, that "Wildcat" Khurais Well No. 1 had struck oil in indicated commercial quantity, so it is possible—even probable—that an entirely new oilfield may be developed.

Conspicuous in this great easterly sloping sedimentary area are many "islands" of limestone, capped with segregations of ferruginous chert or chert sediments. In many instances the underlying softer beds are eroded, leaving an overhanging yellowish brown "roof." I dubbed this the "thatched roof formation," and found these islands make excellent landmarks in a region where milestones are few.

Along the shore of the Persian Gulf as well as inland there are level plains, known as *sabkhahs* (mud flats), varying from a half mile to 15 or more in length. Their crust varies in thickness from a few inches to eighteen. In most places they will support cars and trucks, but travellers never forget the troubles entailed when motor transport breaks through this crust. The deeper the wheel sinks, the more liquid the bot-

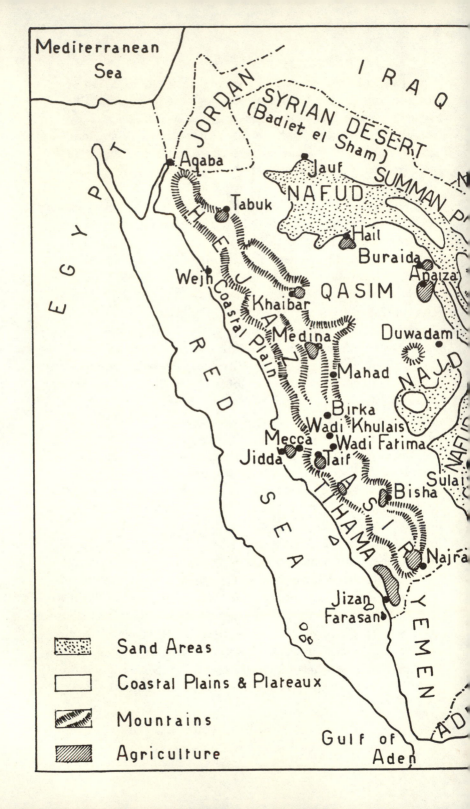

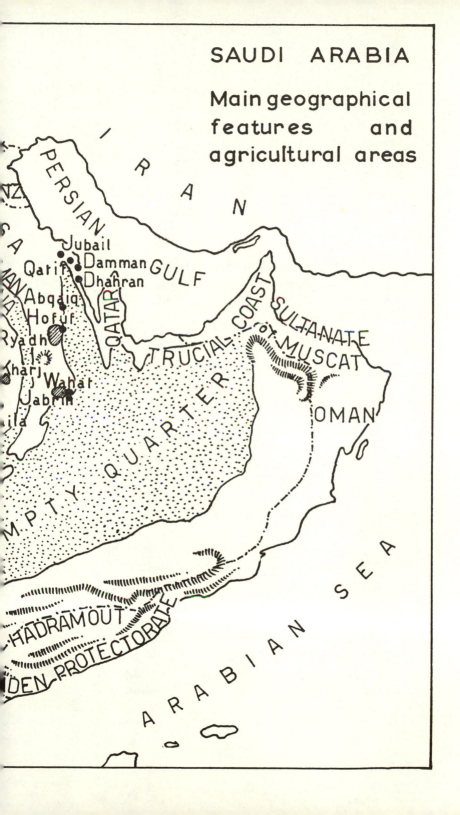

SAUDI ARABIA

Main geographical
features   and
agricultural areas

IRAN

PERSIAN

GULF

Jubail
Damman
Qatif
Dhahran

Abqaiq

Hofuf

Ryadh

harj

Wahat

Jabrin

ila

QATAR

TRUCIAL COAST

SULTANATE

of MUSCAT

OMAN

EMPTY QUARTER

HADRAMOUT

DEN PROTECTORATE

ARABIAN SEA

ARABIAN

tom. A broad-bearing surface of brush, mats, corrugated iron and boards to sustain high lift jacks, is the general method of moving a stranded vehicle, if a truck to tow the victim is not available. For hundreds of miles parallel to the coast lie a band of sand dunes, similar to those of the Nafud, varying in width up to more than 40 miles. In most places light cars with low-pressure 9″ x 13″ tires, light trucks with 10.5″ x 16″, and heavy trucks with 12″ x 24″, can traverse the sands.

Climate

In a vast country such as Saudi Arabia, with many fluctuations in elevation, wide divergence in climate is to be expected. In the Hijaz and Asir, the summer climate along the seacoast is hot and damp. The temperatures are seldom above 100° F. but the humidity is usually over 85 per cent, which, accompanying temperatures of 99° F., creates a mist like a Turkish bath. At Jidda during a sandstorm the mercury may cling to 119° F. The air then becomes so dry and heavy-laden with sand that visibility is but a few feet. On board ship in the Red Sea, during such a storm, poor visibility makes the use of the foghorn necessary. The lowest temperature I recorded at Jidda was 54° F. Generally a northwesterly breeze makes the summer weather bearable and the winter delightful. When the wind turns southerly, heat, humidity and storms are likely. From October to May is the "rainy season," with the promise of an occasional shower.

At a distance of five miles inshore the humidity is low, and it is generally less inside the line of foothills. As altitude is gained in climbing the Hijaz and Asir mountains, the air is still drier and more bracing. Along the southern end of the range, in Asir and southern Hijaz, the higher mountain slopes tend to condense the moisture. They also receive the influence of the monsoon, and rainfall attains its peak of 12 inches, according to an estimate based on topography and vegetation, made in November 1942 by J. G. Hamilton, a U.S. Department of Agriculture agronomist, and A. L. Wathen, Chief Engineer, Indian Office, U.S. Department of the Interior. That the rainfall is much heavier than farther east is demonstrated by the fact that the mud walls of buildings here are protected by multiple eaves of schist slabs.

In the highlands the temperature varies from 115° F. in the summer to occasionally freezing weather in the winter where the elevation is 5,000 feet or more. The nights are comparatively cool throughout. In all the Najd tableland uniform climate prevails. The nights are comfortable, even during the summer season, in the Nafud, Dahna and the Empty Quarter. They come as a welcome relief from the withering furnace heat which begins within one or two hours after sunrise and lasts till sunset. In the U.S. Agricultural Mission camp at Laila in Aflaj, Najd, we rested during midday, taking turns pouring glasses of water over ourselves and our cots, to draw some coolness from the rapid evaporation.

The great Hofuf oasis in the Hasa has a somewhat humid climate in summer, but its winter weather is crisp and invigorating. The surrounding sands tend to reduce the humidity, although at an average elevation of 680 feet, on July 2, 1942, during the U.S. Agricultural Mission trip, a temperature dry bulb registered 114° F., the wet 72° F. determining a humidity of 11 per cent. Along the Persian Gulf coast, the spring, summer and autumn climate is hot and damp, and on Bahrain Island, 22 miles off the Saudi Arabian shore, the humidity is even higher. No rainfall records have been made in Saudi Arabia save those of the British Legation and the oil and mining companies. These available findings, supplemented by those of H. St. John B. Philby and my own, make it seem clear that the average annual rainfall is 3.5 to 4.5 inches, except in the Asir mountains and southern Hijaz, where, as previously noted, it fluctuates between 10 and 12 inches. The average precipitation of about 4 inches may fall in three or four showers, mostly in December, although at

Mahad Dhahab Mine the heaviest rain I witnessed fell on May 11, 1935, but in November 1954 a rainfall of four inches occurred at Jidda. March 1958 reports from Aramco showed no material changes in rainfall or climate. The Saudis had no data available.

3. Agricultural and Pastoral Wealth

SAUDI ARABIA is arid except in a few portions of the Hijaz near Taif, Yenbo, and Medina; the Anaiza, Hail, Riyadh, Kharj, and Aflaj districts in Najd; and the Hofuf, Dammam to Qatif areas in Hasa; and the highlands of Asir.

The Food and Agriculture Organization of the United Nations ("F.A.O.," N. A. Lateef report of 1956) estimates that only 12 per cent of the population of Saudi Arabia are settled farmers, and 66 per cent nomadic Bedouins leading a pastoral existence. The remaining 22 per cent are urban. This last figure is much larger than it was in 1933, when the first oil concession was signed, and it is bound to increase with the growing small industries as well as the huge enterprises of the Arabian American Oil Company (Aramco).

Evidences of ancient larger areas of cultivation are seen by outlines of former fields and gardens in Hijaz along the Tihama plain, in many of the *wadis* or river valleys in Hijaz, Nejd, Hasa and Asir, and the numerous ruined dams in the vicinity of Taif and Khaibar. In most instances the outlines of field boundaries and irrigation ditches can be seen from the air. The areas in the vicinity of Kharj and Aflaj were extensive but the lowering of the water table as evidenced by successively lower discharges from the great water pools at Aflaj proves one of the reasons for the decreasing cultivation. Unfortunately, the wooded areas to the west of Aflaj have been almost destroyed by the demands for building timber and charcoal in the Riyadh area.

The F.A.O. estimated that at present less than 2 per cent of the entire country is under cultivation. Of this about 80 per cent is entirely under irrigation; the remaining 20 per cent, lying in the mountains of Asir and slightly to the north in Hijaz, is rain-fed. Nearly all sections of the country receive occasional rains, usually torrential cloudbursts. The amount of grasses which spring up after such downpours is miraculous, and furnishes the grazing for the Bedouin livestock.

There are three types of irrigation: (a) perennial from pits and wells, the water being obtained by donkeys or camels hoisting the water in skin bags as well as by turbine and centrifugal pumps; (b) by tunnels from springs; (c) by earthen diversion dams which direct the occasional flood waters (*sayls*) through ditches onto prepared bordered or diked areas. In the American West this is called "bolsa" irrigation.

The Saudi government allocated in its 1957 budget the sum of $67,980 for the completion of Akramah Dam and $636,570 for the Riyadh Dam Project.

In his F.A.O. report Mr. N. A. Lateef states that crops are irrigated generally every two days in summer and four or five days in winter. This is about $2\frac{1}{3}$ times as much as in American practice and causes the eventual waterlogging now in evidence in Hijaz, Nejd, and Hasa. It is of interest to note that the first U.S. Agricultural Mission to Saudi Arabia in 1942 found the same conditions and strongly recommended that adequate drainage be immediately undertaken exactly as later recommended by F.A.O. It is to be regretted that fifteen years passed before action was taken, with the consequently diminished amount of crops and cultivated areas. Only on the royal farms of Kharj and Khafs Daghara and those of Shaikh Abdullah Sulaiman has drainage been installed. It is hoped that the increased production on these will influence other Saudi Arabs to follow suit.

In 1954 King Saud ibn-Abdul Aziz gave his consent to having four plots granted for tests to be made with Reynolds aluminum mulch and portable overhead irrigation piping. I requested this in the hope that the results might be beneficial to Saudi Arabian agriculture. The following report was received from the Reynolds representative: "Our sprinkler system . . . can save 85 per cent of the irrigation water and 30 per cent of the farm land. . . . Ditches and borders not only use up land but curtail the use of machinery for cultivating and harvesting. . . . The aluminum foil mulch increased production 40 per cent . . . believe it will do better." This seems to be a valuable and promising possibility but much depends on the cost of equipment.

Salt crusts are produced by excessive irrigation. Examples of this condition can be seen in the areas of Kuseebal in Qasim, Khaibar north of Medina, Jabrin in southern Hasa on the edge of Rub al-Khali, and spots in Kharj.

In Jabrin so many anopheles mosquitoes breed in the pools of excess water that malaria has made this oasis practically uninhabited. The Bedouins who own the date palms occupy the land briefly twice yearly, to pollinate the dates in the spring and to harvest them in the fall. In the Khaibar oasis nearly the same conditions prevail except that a sparse population of Negroes has grown up who seem to be able to withstand the various illnesses of the region.

In general, farming is conducted in the same manner as in the time of Solomon. The same type of crooked wooden stick with the point or plowshare shod with a beaten iron shoe and drawn by oxen—or, rarely, by donkeys and camels—is used. The harrowing and smoothing is done by the farmer standing on a plank drawn by the draft animals. The seeding is broadcast by hand and harvesting is by the sickle. As a step forward in 1942 the U.S. Agricultural Mission demonstrated the scythe and "cradle" at Kharj.

Dams and Irrigation

Centuries ago the Arabs were competent farmers. The outlines of ancient gardens and irrigation ditches now partly covered by drifting sand are evidence. In addition, there are the many ancient dams, especially those in the vicinity of Taif. These were important both for flood control and for irrigation. In a land of such sparse rainfall as Arabia, one might smile and be incredulous of the phrase "flood control." Although the precipitation may average six inches annually, three or four cloudburst showers may constitute the rains for the year. Thus it can be readily understood that there are floods and that dams to control them would be, and have been, extremely valuable.

Every dam which I have seen except one is ruined. In several cases the damage is in the spillway; in others, the main structure. The design as well as the method of construction have been faulty. The exception which I have mentioned is a rough rock dam about twenty miles easterly from Taif. This was built not to store water but to impound the silt and erosion products brought from the higher country to the west by *sayls,* or floods. It is about 25 feet high and perhaps 200 feet long. Locally it is called "Say-Sudd." Dr. George Miles has translated the Kufic inscription on the cliff at the crest and side to read as follows: "This dam belongs to Abdullah Muawiyah, commander of the Believers. Abdullah bin Sakhr built it, with the permission of Allah, in the year fifty-eight (A.D. 677/78). Allah, pardon Abdullah Muawiyah, Commander of the Believers, and strengthen him, and make him victorious, and grant the Commander of the Believers the enjoyment of it. Amru bin Janab wrote it." Dr. Miles believes this is the oldest of all Islamic inscriptions. It is surely a great contrast to the inscriptions on the Hoover, Coolidge, and other American dams.

This type of dam represents a very efficient means of soil conservation. Mr. J. Guy Hamilton of the U.S. Agricultural Mission in 1942-1943 stated that Americans could teach the Arabs nothing regarding soil conservation.

Some years ago I wrote reports and in the past few years Dr. Glen Brown and Mr. Roy Jackson in collaboration with the Point Four program have made recommendations to repair as well as construct new water storage and soil conservation dams.

The Saudi Ministry of Agriculture, under its chief, Amir

Khalid Sudairi, is bending every effort toward developing larger water sources and consequently more food production. Recently, as a result of the activity of the geologists under Point Four auspices, an important discovery was made near Riyadh of a water-bearing bed having an estimated area of 80,000 square kilometers (30,880 square miles) at a depth of 400 feet. The reported discharge near Riyadh is 1,000,000 gallons per day, or approximately 700 gallons per minute. (My information is from *The Kingdom of Saudi Arabia,* by Omar A. Khadra, p. 12, Saudi Arabian Embassy, Washington, D.C.)

Crops

It is obvious that with only 2 per cent of the total area being arable, agricultural products are not sufficient to support the population, so large imports of food stuffs are required. At the same time, great efforts are being made to increase domestic production, of which dates are the most important.

The date palms are grown below an elevation of 5,000 feet and comprise the staple article of diet for all except the urban population. The propagation is by off-shoots if the same type of date as the parent tree is desired. Palms grown from seeds do not usually have the same characteristics as the parent. Date palms commence bearing fruit after eight years and continue to do so possibly eighty years or more. The harvest months are August and September.

Dates are packed in "mats," baskets of woven palm leaves. The filled mat usually weighs 200 pounds. In 1953 a modern date-processing plant was established by the government with the aid of the Food and Agricultural Organization in Hofuf and another in Medina. Both are operating at present and an export business is anticipated.

In western Saudi Arabia the finest types of dates are produced in the Medina vicinity. Fifteen excellent varieties were sent to me from Medina but there are undoubtedly several more. Yenbo is a date-exporting port.

The district of Bisha in Asir is famous for its dates, exporting quantities to many sections of this province, including the sea coast.

In Najd the Kharj project is now noted for this same fruit. Many thousands of date palms have been planted since 1937; during 1946 to 1948, some 3,000 in addition to the original groves were planted.

The Hofuf oasis in Hasa has long been an exporter of its renowned *khilas* dates. This variety is small in size but unusually sweet. The firms of the Qusaibi brothers and the Ajajis maintained a profitable business in these dates between Hasa and Bahrain for many years preceding the oil industry.

The crop of perhaps equal importance is the grain sorghum, of which there are five varieties, three white and two brown. Since these sorghums require about 180 days to mature, the U.S. Agricultural Mission of 1942 recommended the testing of American types, which require but 95 to 115 days to ripen. A staple food for most Bedouins and farmers and adapted to thriving in sandy areas such as are prevalent in the broad *wadis* or valley beds, the sorghums comprise a vital item in Bedouin life.

Millet is a general name for seeded sorghums, and this valuable grain is grown in nearly every place I visited. Most districts raised one white type of sorghum with one of brown or red. There are stunted types grown in the sands, having small heads and stalks only three feet high but in the Tihama flood plains of Asir and southern Hijaz the sorghums grow much larger heads and stalks reaching to 17.7 feet—as measured at Darb—competing with the famous corn of Iowa.

Wheat was formerly the staple article of diet, after dates, but some years ago enterprising merchants imported rice in quantities and at a price which induced practically the entire population to substitute it for wheat. The curtailment of shipping during World War II brought about a return to wheat. In many parts of the country the planting of wheat was therefore reintroduced, yielding substantially in 1944 and 1945. In 1942 many hundreds of tons of it had been produced at Kharj, and, 28 miles southeast, at Khafs Daghara. There are innumerable small plots raising wheat but, aside from Kharj and its vicinity, the largest amounts are grown on the terraced mountain slopes of Asir, in the eastern highlands toward Najran and in those plantations of the north toward Taif.

An interesting experiment has been made at Kharj, where considerable areas of ground had—by repeated and excessive irrigation—become too salty to yield anything but dates. In a plot of this land, two inches of the surface were scraped off, then heavily fertilized with animal manure and planted with wheat. A first-class quality was produced. A source of guano was discovered in the Persian Gulf which promises to cost a fraction of the commercial fertilizer and which analyzes 8 per cent nitrogen and 20 per cent phosphorus. It is hoped this will prove to be a very important plant stimulant. Another experiment was the selecting and planting of the best heads of native Saudi wheat. A yield of 60 bushels per acre was taken from the plot.

In addition to wheat, there are certain amounts of rice, barley, oats, and sesame grown. The latter is crushed to produce its highly prized oil. Alfalfa has become an extremely valuable cattle food crop. In Hasa it is grown in the date groves and is cut monthly.

Rice figures as an important product in the great Hofuf oasis of the Hasa. The large volume of water flowing from the seven huge springs in this spot makes possible the necessary flooding of rice fields. Most of the rice paddies lie in the date groves, and the entire crop is consumed locally. While the red variety of rice now prevails, tests with the higher-priced white grain are under way.

Minor agricultural products consist of a small and excellent supply of coffee from Asir, of the same Mocha variety for which the Yemen is justly famous. This is grown in small quantities in the terraced areas of Asir and consumed locally. These areas are on the Jabal Faifa at altitudes between 4,000 and 5,000 feet.

Qat (catha edulis) is also a lucrative cash crop; it grows at elevations above 4,000 feet. This is a green succulent plant with varying widths and tenderness of leaves. Freshly cut, these leaves are chewed and have a narcotic effect. The quality and price vary directly with the position—the leaves at the tip being the most tender and bringing the highest price.

Among the fruits raised are bananas, apricots, pomegranates, figs, peaches, citrons, oranges, limes, mulberries, prickly pears, pears, quinces, melons, papayas, crab apples, and grapes. Of vegetables the best known are potatoes, eggplant, okra, squash, radishes, onions, tomatoes, watermelons, cantaloupes, cucumbers, cabbages, carrots, lettuce, peppers, and beans. *Hiwar* is a plant raised here and in the Yemen, yielding the indigo dye which is made at Baish and other Tihama towns. Almonds and peanuts are produced in small quantities. The most important crop furnishing livestock feed is alfalfa. It is also employed in the making of a green stain for interior house decoration in Asir. The growing of cotton remains in the experimental stage at present.

Chemical fertilizers are not used in much of Saudi Arabia, but sheep and goat manure is almost universally applied by the farmers. The first recorded shipment of chemical fertilizers was sent to Saudi Arabia in 1942 on the recommendation of the U.S. Agricultural Mission. This was authorized and paid for by the then Minister of Finance, Shaikh Abdullah Sulaiman, and consisted of 90 tons of ammonium sulphate. King ibn-Saud was eager to increase his food production since World War II was curtailing the shipments of food supplies. This fertilizer was used entirely at Kharj and subsequent amounts have been imported and used in this project. It is reported that the application of 200 to 500 pounds per acre increased the yield of wheat from 900 to 2,700 pounds per acre. This same type of fertilizer has been used on the farms of Prince Abdullah-al-Faisal in Wadi Fatima and of Shaikh Abdullah Sulaiman near Jidda and near Dammam. On the other hand, fertilizer samples distributed to Wadi Fatima farmers prior to 1953 were not used and were allowed to go to waste.

The matter of the manufacture of fertilizer from waste gases of the Qatif, Dammam, and Abqaiq oil fields has been investigated and is under study. A rough estimate that $80,000,000 is required to build such a plant and the fact that these gases may be used to facilitate and prolong oil production make this project a subject of careful consideration.

New Farming Centers

There are several important agricultural areas and development projects in Saudi Arabia. The best known is the Kharj-Khafs Daghara, which stems from the initiative of the first Minister of Finance, Shaikh Abdullah Sulaiman Al Hamdan although King ibn-Saud of course had to approve the proposals, since nothing of importance could be done without royal sanction.

Kharj. The name may be derived from "Kharaj," which means "taxes," according to an eminent Arabic scholar, Dr. George Rentz. This project lies 54 miles southerly from Riyadh, with which it is now connected by railway and a paved highway.

With royal authorization Shaikh Abdullah had all kinds of appropriate modern agricultural equipment purchased in the United States and engaged well-qualified Americans—the majority from Texas—to direct operations. Subsequently Aramco was requested to take over the management of this important enterprise. It did so with admirable results until July 1955, when the Saudi government asked the company to withdraw

29

to allow its own nationals to assume control. Americans are now employed by the Saudi government to supervise this project.

The Saudi Arabian News of March 1957, published by the Saudi Arabian Embassy at New Delhi, India, stated that "King Saud just issued a royal decree commanding the government to distribute 1,400 plots of land to Saudi civilians and army men in the Al Kharj district south of Riyadh. It is hoped that these, 1,400 plots will make a new town named 'The New Saudiah.' "

The following is a brief history of the Kharj project.

About 1936 the Finance Minister had two agricultural engineers from Iraq plan and execute the initial reclamation of approximately 2,500 acres in the Kharj district and 800 acres in the Khafs Daghara. One of these men, Hassan Effendi, was still in charge under Shaikh Sulaiman Al Hamad, nephew of Shaikh Abdullah, when we of the U.S. Agricultural Mission visited Kharj in May 1942. The oil company engineers and geologists, Dr. R. A. Brancamp, T. C. Barger, and L. M. Snyder, made the water investigations and helped in much of the general planning while their field engineers, Brown, Perry, and Holbard, made the land and ditch surveys, directed construction and other technical work.

After our mission returned to Washington, the State Department sent a most efficient and able group of practical agriculturists loaned by the U.S. Department of Agriculture under the leadership of Mr. David Rogers. They directed an immense amount of construction along lines of the most approved American practice. This work included ditching for draining as well as for irrigation, and the introduction of the best methods of planting various crops including dates.

All these areas have to be irrigated. There are immense pits which supply this water; the largest ones, named Ain al-Samha and Ain Dhila, are each over 400 feet deep and about 300 feet in diameter. These are connected underground, so when pumping at the rate of 14 cubic feet per second the water level of both lowers 14 to 15 feet. It is estimated by Aramco engineers that pumps with a capacity of 100 cubic feet per second will make a drawdown of 100 to 120 feet. That amount would irrigate an estimated 3,500 acres. The turbine pumps are driven by Caterpillar Diesel engines; the water discharged from these fill the life-giving canals and ditches.

Crop production reached the goal in 1951 when the cash value of the harvest exceeded the costs of operation. For years the reverse was true—as is so often the case with government reclamation enterprises. In 1951 exceptional progress was made in the raising of poultry.

Primarily, the crops raised are for furnishing the royal family, the government, and people of the capital, Riyadh, with vegetables and fruits, but Kharj has now been developed into an agricultural demonstration and experimental center. It acts as a practical school for disseminating knowledge to farmers. Increasing numbers of farmers as well as large landowners are taking advantage of such an instructive organization.

The earliest written records seem to have commenced in June 1946. A June-July-August period of crops produced for three years gives an idea of the size of the Kharj project and its progress.

Although the Saudi Ambassador in Washington wrote (October 1957) that no further records are available, it is certain that a satisfactory production has been maintained and that the First Agricultural Mission of the American government has been of material benefit in agricultural studies and development.

	Tons of alfalfa	Lbs. of vegetables	Lbs. of melons	Bushels of wheat
1946	719	98,860	606,000	2,710
1947	1,720	123,450	720,800	7,591
1948	1,858	302,851	1,026,600	18,361

As stated previously, dates are the most valuable of all crops in Arabia. Many thousands of date offshoots have been planted from the very start (about 1938) by Shaikh Abdullah Sulaiman. In 1948, 242,040 pounds of dried dates were produced. Some 13,000 date palms were planted in the 1946-1948 period.

To further variety as well as production, improved types of apricot, orange, and tangerine trees have been imported from Baghdad, as well as grapes, pomegranates, crab apples, strawberry plants, and Irish seed potatoes from Beirut. The best varieties of American and native vegetables and melons are in production.

In 1949 a specialist in livestock started work on improvement programs, including sheep, goats, cattle, and poultry. As noted previously, the progress in the latter has been especially gratifying.

Since practically all agricultural production in Arabia depends on irrigation and water supply, the water wells drilled in connection with oil drilling, especially "wild-cats," and the forty wells along Tapline, are extremely valuable to the economy of Saudi Arabia. As a result of structure drilling, one well in Jafura and three wells in Rub al-Khali resulted in flowing water wells. During 1951 nineteen water wells were drilled in the vicinity of Riyadh and lately a great sub-surface reservoir has been discovered. Technical investigations with regard to water supply are being continued. All this water development is a proof of the tremendous benefit to the country by the operations of such an efficient and far-seeing organization as Aramco. The present Saudi Department of Agriculture has greatly profited by the oil company's work and is proceeding along the same lines.

Mechanization at Kharj has proved practical. In 1945 there were 1,452 workers on the farm; in 1949 this number was reduced to 742 but production was increased.

Wheat is planted by drills at the rate of fifty acres per day. Combines save up to 25 per cent of the wheat crop by less shattering, and loss by theft and spoilage by the "treading" by animals. The time for threshing a harvest is reduced to one month from the previous two or three months.

Such progress is of tremendous value as the country is still agricultural, not industrial, but the industry of oil has, and will, contribute to the progress in agriculture. (*Information by the courtesy of Aramco and by Kenneth J. Edwards, general manager of Kharj for some years*)

Taif. The Taif area, ranging from 4,000 to 5,500 feet above sea level, is excellent for the cultivation of grapes, peaches, apricots, pomegranates, and figs. Many of these are shipped to Jidda. At this altitude dates do not thrive.

North of Taif and about 1,000 feet lower, Prince Faisal has been developing many acres by cultivating citrus and other fruits as well as grains. Electrically driven pumps have been installed and offer an interesting contrast to the eight-donkey four-water skin type of well nearby.

A few miles east of Taif, Shaikh Abdullah Sulaiman has a productive fruit garden and attractive residence. Well water is raised by mechanical pumps and the buildings are lighted by electricity. This is one of many examples of progress without foreign financing. Shaikh Abdullah and other Saudis have welcomed and employed foreigners, mainly Americans, for technical management, aid, and advice.

To the northwest of Taif is a settlement called Ghaima, some hundreds of feet lower than Taif. Many abandoned areas have again been put under cultivation by the use of water from new wells as well as from renovated old ones. There is room for many acres of additional development. At one time this locality was discussed as a site for use as a hill station for foreigners resident in Jidda. Ghaima would be admirably suited for this since the climate is excellent, the elevation being generally 4,500 feet, and it is sufficiently distant to be entirely separate from the venerated city of Taif. This is the summer (May to October) Hijaz capital in place of Mecca.

Wadi Fatima. West of Taif and 3,000 feet lower, a large

farm has been developed by Shaikh Hamad Sulaiman Al Hamdan, brother of Shaikh Abdullah. This locality is called Sharia and has for centuries been a rest station for caravans, and lately for cars and convoys. Date palms should thrive there as well as fruits and crops since excellent water emanates through a "dibble" (tunnel) from the mountains. Additional water has been developed and the farming acreage increased. This is also a purely Arab enterprise.

At approximately 19 miles easterly from Jidda on the Mecca road in the Wadi Fatima there is an oasis called Hadda. Ancient ruins of walls and remains of masonry attest to extensive gardens here many, many centuries in the past. Shaikh Abdullah Sulaiman has devoted considerable funds for the establishing of an important agricultural project. Dates, vegetables, melons, fruits, and grains are being raised, in addition to poultry and livestock. This is one other independent Arab enterprise.

Hasa. There are two important projects in Hasa which can be undertaken as soon as the Saudi government desires, which would increase the productive area of the Hofuf oasis by nearly 50 per cent. Of course, the necessary surveys and topographical maps on which to base the layout and the irrigation—including drainage systems—should be made first. These projects consist of 5,000 acres in the Asfar district on the eastern side of the oasis and just north from the Hofuf-Oqair road and the adjoining village of Jishsha; and the Ayuna and Ayuna Jenubia area, at present estimated at 5,000 acres. However, there are in addition areas in the Ayuna and Jenubia district totaling 2,000 to 5,000 acres, lying in irregularly shaped tracts distributed among and around the date groves.

The present drainage water from the groves would be sufficient to irrigate these lands during the months of December through February. A development of an additional water supply would be required for operating during the entire year. The development by the government of a flowing artesian well

The Kharj reclamation project, showing the section which supplies most of the vegetables consumed in Riyadh

Poultry raising in the animal husbandry section at Kharj

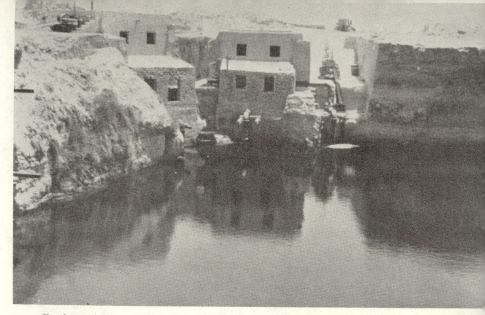

Reclamation project at Kharj. This pit, 300 feet in diameter by 420 feet in depth, called Ain Semha, is one of the principal sources of water for irrigating this great agricultural enterprise

A 6-camel-power 6-skin pumping plant at Yamama, near Kharj. This method of raising water for irrigation has been in use for many centuries. Each skin averages 12 gallons capacity

Farm in Najran, Asir, showing alfalfa fields and date palms

Typical buildings on Khamis Mushait plateau, Asir, elevation 6,000 feet

Ministry of Finance at Abha, capital of Asir. Projecting schist layers form multiple eaves for protection of mud walls against rain

Market day at Abha. This is the only area in Saudi Arabia where women are unveiled

at the western side of the oasis indicates that such supplemental irrigation water will not be difficult. This strike was made late in 1942, according to reports.

The soil is well suited for the raising of wheat; also much of it for rice, should there be sufficient water. Most of the ground surfaces in the above areas would require comparative little leveling. This project is a large and unusual asset. It could be productive after one season or more, depending upon the amount of equipment used and labor exerted. The yield per acre should be high, as the soil is virgin and of an excellent quality of sandy clay loam at Asfar, and good for wheat and rice in the Ayuna district. Here rice can be raised during the winter and other crops during the summer months. The soil is largely of shallow sandy loam underlain with impervious marl clay of varying depths. Here also there is evidence from ancient filled wells and water tunnels that formerly there was a more extensive civilization. The Ain Najm spring and garden of Shaikh Abdullah Sulaiman is one of these. When I first saw it in 1931 the spring was being excavated and walls repaired, but the present garden was entirely covered with sand. On the way to Ayuna Jenubia "homesteading" is progressing through bringing to life another ancient spring.

Incidentally, efficient archeological work in Hasa might throw light on a great deal of hitherto unknown history.

Jabrin. Another place of ancient history, present impoverishment, and future possibilities is the oasis of Jabrin. This lies 161 miles south from Hofuf at an average elevation of 720 feet. The area is estimated at 7,500 acres. It was reported that 400 families of the Murra tribes lived here only when the dates were to be pollinated in the spring and harvested in the fall; the rest of the year was spent in the adjoining desert, grazing the herds of camels, sheep, and goats. Their only crop was dates. The quality was poor in most cases, as the palms are planted so closely together that they now form clumps, and their offshoots are not removed to enable a better growth of

35

the parent tree. When better methods for care of the dates, as well as possibilities for raising vegetables, were suggested, the reply was that they, the Murra tribes, were not farmers and did not wish to become farmers. Therefore it is evident that no increase or progress in agriculture can be expected from the present inhabitants. By a well-supervised filling of the countless water pools in the oasis, the now prevalent malaria could be eliminated. It might then be possible to establish a settlement of *Ikhwan* who would follow efficient agricultural methods. A former *Ikhwan* settlement failed because of numerous deaths from malaria.

Qatif. The most important agricultural area along the Persian Gulf extends from Khobar to Qatif, and Sofwa, almost adjoining to the west. Of these the largest is the Qatif section, of an estimated 9,000 acres. Conditions are similar to those at Hofuf, except that the soil, being a sandy loam grading down to sand, is more porous and not so fertile. There are similar large springs furnishing irrigation water, but the drainage ditches should be deeper and the usual irrigation intervals increased by three to five days, lasting, that is, seven to twelve days in all. This would improve the quality of the dates and the growth as well as the production of all the fruit trees, the alfalfa and melons. As in most of the arable lands, fertility here would be improved by growing and plowing under green manure crops, such as cowpeas, soy beans, sisibanya, clovers, and alfalfa. Only actual tests will show which is, or are, the best types adapted for each region. Vegetables are being grown for the oil company at the Dhahran camp in a leased plot in Qatif where excellent results have been obtained.

At the Sofwa oasis a mile or so to the west of Qatif there are identical conditions. The flow of the largest spring, Ain Darush, was estimated by A. L. Wathen at 9,000 gallons per minute or 20 cubic feet per second. Much of the drainage from this oasis runs into the Persian Gulf.

Although the *khilas* and other Hofuf dates are considered

superior, those of Qatif and Sofwa are of good quality, many being shipped to Najd. Besides dates, bananas, papayas, pomegranates, mulberries, limes, grapes, alfalfa, sisibanya and peppers are grown.

On Tarut Island a mile offshore from Qatif there are again similar conditions of fair soil, large springs, and date groves. The same remarks regarding improvements by adequate drainage and green fertilizer are applicable here.

At a district called Ajam, lying 20 miles north from the oil village of Dhahran and west of Sofwa, there are large areas of good soil, some of it extremely rich, but swampy in places, watered by springs. Some are of unknown age but the moil marks of the ancients who cut down through the limestone to enlarge the mouths of some of the springs can still be seen. By adequate pumps and draining a valuable productive area could be reclaimed which might provide the staff and employees of the oil company with many fresh vegetables and fruits. It is being studied and investigated by the company.

Considerable benefit might be derived in gardens throughout the country by drying all surplus fruits and vegetables. They then last indefinitely and the cost of shipping them as compared to that of the fresh article is but a fraction. Since the nomads live largely on dates and rice they might welcome these additions to their diet. It is a matter which should be considered and investigated. J. G. Hamilton thought that this and a great increase in the culture of honey bees might aid food production and general health conditions, thereby increasing the country's prosperity.

Locusts are an annual menace to crops. The Saudi government is cooperating with the International Locust Mission in combatting this danger.

Livestock

A great source of wealth, surpassing even dates in value, is livestock. In order of usefulness the principal kinds of livestock are camels, sheep, goats, cows, donkeys, poultry, and horses.

The camel is the most important animal in Saudi Arabia, an indispensable part of every Bedouin family, whose status of wealth is commonly reckoned by the number of camels it owns. It provides the nomad with milk, meat, and transportation. A camel laden on one side with a portable wood and skin watering trough, balanced by a child and great black cooking pots on the other, is a sight frequently encountered in Saudi Arabia. Another is a tiny tot, perched on a tall beast plodding up and down an inclined plane, hauling up skin or leather buckets of water from the desert well. Indeed, much of the nomad's entire existence is devoted, with the aid of the camel, to procuring water. As a means of transport the camel is absolutely essential in pursuing the rains and fresh grazing areas. After the winter rains, the herds of camels, sheep, and goats are said to go for two or three months without visiting wells, getting their moisture in the meantime from shallow rain-water pools and cisterns, and from the heavy dews which lie on the grass and bushes during this part of the year.

Formerly there was a large export of camels to Africa, Egypt, Syria, and Iraq, but the advent of the automobile has put an end to this trade. Nevertheless, camels will always be essential to the economy of Saudi Arabia. Motor transport is increasing rapidly and may even become universal for long-distance carriage, yet it is doubtful whether it will ever be as cheap per ton-mile. Where the time element is not a factor, the companies operating in Saudi Arabia should use the maximum camel transport, since it contributes to the welfare of many people.

All camels in the land are of the single hump or dromedary type. Sheep furnish the greater part of the meat diet, goats supplement the camel milk, and only a few young camels are slaughtered for use as meat. Camel's hair is used but little, though the finest Arab gowns (*mashlah*) are made from camel's hair and wool.

Sheep rank next to camels in importance, and exist in considerably larger numbers, providing at present the bulk of the meat consumption. Invariably the Arab feast or banquet consists of a roasted sheep, cooked whole in a large pot and served, surrounded by boiled rice, on a great circular tray which is placed on a woven mat or black oilcloth. At Mecca, during the pilgrimage, each adult male is supposed to sacrifice at least one sheep. Thousands are thus consumed annually.

The Saudi Arabian varieties of sheep are peculiarly adapted to the semiaridity of the country. Sheep's milk is extensively used and a considerable amount of excellent cheese is made from it. All Arab sheep have fat, broad tails in which nourishment is stored as in the camel's hump. The fat from the tails constitutes an appreciable item of domestic commerce, as well as small export to Egypt. It is heated to form a kind of butter, corresponding to lard, known as *ghee* or *samn*, universally used in cooking, and quite palatable until it becomes rancid.

Of the several varieties of sheep, those with the best wool are largely from the Hasa, and, to a lesser degree, from Najd. A small fraction of the wool is sheared and woven into gowns, or the sleeveless, knee-length, heavy winter overcoats called *beedis*, for use in the highlands of Taif and Asir. Due to the natural oil in the wool, *beedis* shed water well for some time, but when thoroughly soaked after a day's rain, like a heavy sponge they become a burdensome load. Arabian wool is of the coarse type known as "carpet wool," used in carpet weaving. The United States imports this kind of wool from India and China, and there is an opportunity here for Saudi Arabia also to develop an export trade in this product. Very few sheepskins are exported as they are generally considered of poor quality. The black-headed Somali sheep has been introduced so further considerable export may be envisaged. Its skin is of a quality desired by American glove and pocketbook manufacturers. After the droughts of 1948 and 1949 in the Taif area, a large, hardy type of sheep from the Sudan was imported to strengthen the local flocks.

Goats are third on the livestock list. With camels, they furnish most of the milk consumed. Milk with rice and dates, as well as occasional mutton, constitute the standard Saudi Arabian diet. Goats, which thrive where sheep become emaciated, furnish the hair for the famous "black tents of Arabia." This hair varies in length, some coats being too short to shear. Since the vitality of one animal cannot produce at once the maximum of milk and hair, by selective breeding one type of goat could be produced to give maximum milk, and another superior length and amount of hair. Mixed with wool, goat's hair is also used for making rugs and carpets. The angora type of goat, used for producing mohair, probably is not hardy enough to endure the Arabian heat, though it may thrive in the heights of the Hijaz and Asir, where it could be tested at Taif and Abha. Some goat and sheep skins serve as jackets in the highland zone where *beedis* are too warm.

Dairy cows at Jidda supply the needs of some of the American and European residents. In other larger towns, though sufficient feed is available, very few herds are to be found, except the considerable number imported by Aramco in the Dhahran district. The only cattle range I saw was in the Hummaya district of southwestern Asir, close to the Yeman frontier. With an ample market for cattle products in Egypt, as well as in Jidda, Mecca, Riyadh, and the oil camps in Hasa, cattle raising could become a profitable enterprise, although at present transport considerations are prohibitive. With a good road from Jizan to Jidda, and shipping facilities at these two centers and at Suez, a lively cattle industry could be established, somewhat circumscribed, no doubt, by the limited range.

Up and down the land, donkeys are the ever-faithful, generally overloaded beasts of burden. Hasa produces a large type of donkey, 10 to 13 hands tall, almost invariably pure white.

A fast walker, this animal is used extensively in raising irrigation water by the hoisting of skin buckets from wells. A cross between this donkey and a strong Arab mare should produce an excellent mule to aid the development of local agriculture, and mules might in due course become an article of export. It is possible, though, that the affection and high esteem in which the horse is held by the Arabs might militate against any such cross-breeding. This breed of unusual donkey should also be perpetuated by mating only the best jackasses with good female donkeys. The castration of poor jacks would eliminate in the end the breed of small, weak, mouse-colored donkeys, of which at present there is an abundant number. An animal of inferior quality consumes almost the same amount of water and feed as a first-class one but yields infinitely less profitable service.

Najd has long been famed for its strain of Arab horses, but the outstanding ones, as in Europe and America, must be picked with painstaking care. The Arab horse is an extremely gentle and sensitive mount, quick on the start and of remarkable stamina. In my experience it is careless when traveling over smooth ground, often stumbling, but on a stony, strenuous terrain it is amazingly quick and sure-footed. Horses raised in the desert are usually nervous on mountain trails. The typical Arab horse has a beautiful, intelligent head with small ears, a thick neck, well-rounded hindquarters, is close coupled, carries the tail well out away from the rear, has clean, slender limbs and small feet. It is usually shod only forward, if at all. In Saudi Arabia the horse is primarily a luxury, used only for riding. It is treated as a pet, being almost a member of the family. In Jidda there are perhaps half a dozen horses employed for hauling carts from the customs quay to the various stores, but they are not used in plowing or the hoisting of well water.

King Abdul Aziz, his sons, grandsons, and most of the prominent Saudi Arabians enjoy riding, racing, and attending races.

41

The races at Riyadh, Taif, and other centers, in which the princes sometimes take part, attract considerable popular attention. At Yamama, near Kharj, King Saud has a large stable, and Saud ibn-Julwi, Governor of Al Hasa, has another at Hofuf.

But "the sport of kings" is constantly decreasing, probably due to the use of motor cars and airplanes. The horses in the stables at Taif and Yamama are little exercised. There has been only one day of racing in Taif during the past few years, that is, up to 1952, but since King Saud came to the throne there seems to be a revival of this interest. At Riyadh there is a royal racecourse which was being reconstructed in 1957 on the model of that in Bombay. The latest development is the transfer to Khafs Daghara of the stable of 800 horses belonging to the royal family.

Unlike Kharj this farming area is not under American direction. It is located 24 miles southerly and is irrigated from a similar great water pit.

The latest Saudi government estimates of livestock is as follows: sheep, 3,700,000; goats, 2,000,000; camels, 300,000; cattle, 60,000; donkeys, 40,000; horses, 3,000.

Estimates of poultry are not included by the government but practically every farmer and Bedouin has from one to perhaps five dozen chickens. They are seldom fed but thrive amazingly on foraging. As might be expected, both poultry and eggs are small and the average production per hen per year is estimated at 70 eggs.

Only at Kharj is there efficient poultry care. Here there are over 6,000 chickens consisting of the Leghorn, New Hampshire Red, and Rhode Island Red. It is reported that during 1953 they laid an average of 110 eggs per hen. In addition a few turkeys, ducks, and geese are raised at farms in this district.

At Kharj when it was under Aramco management new types of cattle were introduced in an endeavor to raise the best quality which would stand the climatic conditions. The following were imported: Jersey, Brown Swiss, Holstein, and Santa Gertrudis. Bulls were crossed with local Zebu cattle, and inter-breeding was made among these resulting breeds. In the Tihama area a livestock breeding station may be developed since pasture is relatively ample, but disease control should precede this development.

By 1957 the testing and experimenting settled on two types of cattle at Kharj as being the most valuable under the conditions prevailing there; these are the Texan "Santa Gertrudis" and the Indian "Sindha."

4. The First Agricultural Mission to Saudi Arabia

ONE of the earliest missions to Saudi Arabia was the United States Agricultural Mission to that country. It was authorized by the Department of State and financed by the Emergency Fund of the President. A brief account of this mission may be of interest since it was the forerunner of much subsequent agricultural development and since its report has been used as a reference for further planning.

During my stay at Riyadh in 1940, King ibn-Saud one day voiced his desire that interested groups or companies be found who might be willing to undertake a thorough examination of Najd's water resources and agricultural possibilities. He went on to express a wish for the introduction of drilling, pumping, and farming equipment. At my request a document embodying this oral commission was later handed me by order of the King.

Upon my return to America, and following conferences with representatives of the Departments of State, of the Interior, and of Agriculture, as well as with the directors of the oil and mining companies, I found it impossible to find the capital necessary to carry out the King's request. Nonetheless, the mining company for which I worked authorized me to travel over the southwestern states where conditions are somewhat similar to those of Najd. The Department of Interior gave me facilities to study the operations of the Indian Office among the reservations. Mr. A. L. Wathen, then chief engineer of the Bureau of Indian Affairs, U.S. Department of the Interior, introduced me to Vernon Edler, the president of the Peerless Pump Company, whose firm had made many pumping installations for irrigation. The amazing work done in Texas, New Mexico, Arizona, and California was brought to my notice.

When the 15,000-mile trip was concluded, it was decided that a message be sent ibn-Saud, informing him that companies ready to meet his request were not available, and proposing that he accept instead a mission sent by the American government. The mission would examine and report upon the agricultural and irrigation possibilities of all Saudi Arabia, and submit to him recommendations regarding methods of development. The exchange of cables led to the first official mission of goodwill, sent by the State Department of the United States to King Abdul Aziz ibn-Saud.

The personnel consisted of J. G. Hamilton, agronomist, Soil Conservation Service, U.S. Department of Agriculture, and A. L. Wathen. These gentlemen had many years of varied, extensive experience in the arid and semiarid areas of the southwestern states. As bearer of the King's request, and because of my knowledge of Saudi Arabia, I was made chief of the mission.

Leaving Washington airport on March 19, 1942, the mission traveled in the company of Admiral Standley, who was then proceeding to Moscow as American Ambassador to Russia; also of General Russell and Colonel Straum, who were going on special duty to India. The party landed at Cairo on the 26th.

Various matters delayed us in Egypt and it was not until May 9 that we left Cairo by plane. The party consisted of Mr. Alexander Kirk, United States Minister to Egypt and Saudi Arabia; his private secretary, Mr. Horne; the Second Secretary of the Legation, Raymond Hare; Colonel W. H. Crom of the U.S. Air Force; Major Towers, military attaché; Lieutenant Gerard, attaché of General Maxwell and representing him; and the Saudi Arab counselor of their legation at Cairo, Dr. Zerekli.

This was a unique occasion, for Mr. Kirk was to establish the first American Legation in Saudi Arabia. Appointed as Chargé d'Affaires, James S. Moose, Jr., was to organize the legation quarters and personnel at Jidda. He was promoted to the status of American Minister late in 1943. His tact, personality, and experience in Iran well qualified him for this position. The two other members of the U.S. Agricultural Mission had proceeded by sea to Jidda. They, with Mr. Moose and his secretary and our secretary-interpreter, Ahmad Fakhri, met us at the Najd airport where ibn-Saud had established his huge camp— a young city of tents.

The airborne party reached Bahrain in the early afternoon. We were guests of the Bahrain Petroleum Company for the night at Awali. The General Manager, the late Ward Anderson, was the host. He, with Floyd Oligher, General Manager of Aramco in Saudi Arabia, with his assistant, Roy Lebkicher, met and conveyed us to the oil camp. All the quarters were air-conditioned and furnished with American comforts and conveniences. The distance from Cairo by this route was 1,417 miles, taking eight hours, twenty-eight minutes flying time.

The next day all the party donned Arab costumes and, with the addition of Mr. Oligher and their chief geologist, Max Steineke, took off after lunch and landed at the camp of King Abdul Aziz ibn-Saud, 45 miles south of the famous watering place, Bir Ruma. The plane's navigation by Mr. Steineke was perfect.

The oil company engineers, Bert Perry and Merle Holbard, had done well to make a landing field for such a large plane in a stone- and brush-strewn *wadi*. They had a radio to keep contact with Bahrain and with the plane. Some of the King's soldiers asked what was in "the box"—the radio—and the engineers explained that the box had a voice which told them that a great bird would arrive there in twenty-five minutes, bringing guests from America to see Abdul Aziz. The plane duly arrived and about twenty men got out of it. The engineers at the radio turned to a Najdi soldier who had been curious and said, "What do you think of it?" He expressed awe and wonder both at what the box said and at what the "bird" had brought. However, the devout Moslem accepts everything as subject to the will of Allah and seldom is surprised, so he added critically, "The box was incorrect, for the bird arrived in twenty minutes, not twenty-five minutes, as it said!"

At the landing ground was a guard of honor. The Minister of Finance, Shaikh Abdullah Sulaiman Al Hamdan, welcomed Mr. Kirk and the party, and the captain and crew of the plane, on behalf of His Majesty. Tents were assigned to all, and after a meeting with our Jidda friends, arranging our baggage, and washing, we had an informal audience with the King. With him were the Heir Apparent Amir Saud, his brother the Viceroy of Hijaz, Amir Faisal, and four of his counselors, Basheer Magruby, Mohammed Goths, Rushdi Bey Melhas, and Khalid Bey Gargoni al-Walid.

On May 11, 1942, Alexander Kirk formally presented his credentials as American Minister to the sovereign state of Saudi Arabia. Shortly afterward he introduced the U.S. Agricultural Mission. The audiences took place in front of the great tent, in a square, about 75 feet to a side, covered with Persian rugs. Overstuffed chairs made in Egypt were lined up on three sides. All the American party sat at the King's right, the princes sat with their father, to their left were the Saudi ministers. As His Majesty expressed his pleasure in greeting the new American Minister and his friends, the ceremony of taking coffee was under way. Two tall Najdi soldiers, one in a brilliant scarlet robe and the other in deep vivid blue, with shoulder belts, automatic pistols, and cartridge magazines, plus a black *iqal* (head-rope) holding their *gutras* (head shawl), made an unforgettable picture. One poured about three-quarters of an inch of the Najd cardoman-spiced coffee into each small cup from the Najd type of brass coffee pot or *della*; the other followed at an interval collecting the empty cups. An incense burner was then passed to each guest as a sign that the audience was over.

All of the King's guests were charmed by his hospitality and cordiality, and the extraordinary scene left indelible impressions on all the Americans. Ibn-Saud asked Mr. Kirk if he would like to visit his capital and home, and a three-hour trip by car took us on May 12 to Riyadh. The American party occupied a part of the palace of Crown Prince Saud at Badia. Amir Saud gave us an enjoyable lunch of European dishes. Afterward we saw sound films given him by the British Legation, including views of President Roosevelt and Prime Minister Churchill meeting on the Atlantic and the return of the latter home via Iceland on *H.M.S. Prince of Wales.* The sound track was all in Arabic.

The next day we enjoyed a banquet at Muraba Palace with King Abdul Aziz. He sat at the head of a great table towering above the thirty-two guests. In contrast to the European lunch given by Amir Saud, this was a Najdi feast. There were eight great platters along the center line of the table, and on each was a foundation of rice interspersed with raisins, on which rested a whole sheep. Flanking these platters were dishes of chickens, meats, and vegetables. When we were assembled in the audience chamber before the banquet, an incident occurred which is characteristic of King ibn-Saud's great sense of loyalty to friends. When His Majesty entered the hall he took the central large seat which served as his throne. He motioned Minister Kirk to sit on his right with Secretary Hare and other members of the diplomatic corps; then Colonel Crom with the members of his military mission; last of all were members of the Agricultural Mission, who had lowest diplomatic status. The King directed that Mr. Wathen and Mr. Hamilton sit next to the State Department corps. I was still standing, curious to see what was coming next, when a large overstuffed chair was brought and set exactly opposite His Majesty. He directed me to occupy this, turning to Mr. Kirk, saying that this seat was for his old friend! By this gesture was protocol observed and friendship satisfied.

The next day Mr. Kirk with his party returned to Cairo by plane. Mr. Moose went to Dhahran, the Saudi oil town, by car. We of the Agricultural Mission proceeded to Kharj—54 miles south of Riyadh. Here was the great reclamation project initiated by the Finance Minister, the nucleus of the present agricultural interest and development. The oil company assisted by loaning its engineers and other staff members as advisers and by laying out some of the irrigation system, and the mining company advised and purchased considerable equipment on behalf of the Finance Minister. Much of the fresh fruit and fresh vegetable supply for Riyadh was being produced here. The King was intensely interested in this project and greatly appreciated the sending of the Agricultural Mission.

The report of the United States Agricultural Mission to Saudi Arabia was published in English and Arabic by the Imprimerie Misr in Cairo in 1943. At the request of the Saudi government, 300 copies were printed and sent to the Minister of Finance at Jidda.

To summarize briefly: by the kind cooperation of the Arabian American Oil Company, truck motor transport and supplies were furnished us for this Mission. Two Ford cars were provided by the Saudi government. We had to carry gasoline, lubricants, water, spare tires, spare car parts, as well as food and cooking equipment, tents for our soldier escorts, chauffeurs, mechanics, cook, and helper in addition to the several months' foods for ourselves. Aramco arranged all details most efficiently. The period of investigations was from May 15 to December 5, 1942. The distance travelled was 17,408 kilometers, or 10,793 miles. Although most of this distance was covered by motor transport, camels in extremely soft sand and sea-going dhows were also used.

All types of country, climate, soil, and living conditions were seen. Everywhere the Mission was received with greatest courtesy and hospitality by all Amirs, government officials, and Saudi Arab subjects of every class. Work was facilitated in every possible manner.

The report discussed each of the 74 areas investigated. First, details of present products and conditions were listed; then specific recommendations were made with a view to improving production and varieties of crops. It was emphasized that in respect to soil conservation by terracing of mountain slopes and dry wall dams, the Arab methods were equal if not superior to American practice. On the other hand, the experience gained by the United States in irrigation, the uses of fertilizers, and agricultural equipment could be of great benefit to Arabia.

The report has been of considerable value in planning agricultural developments.

5. Minor Economic Resources

Fishing

ALONG the Red Sea and Persian Gulf coasts of Saudi Arabia there are many men employed in fishing. The seaports are supplied with fish by fishermen who go out in *sambuks*, or dhows, and *khuris*, or dugouts, shaped like canoes. Some fishing is done with circular nets near shore in shallow water where the fisherman wades out to his waist to make the cast. Only small fish are obtained in this way, to be used as bait for the deepwater fishing in which hooks and hand lines are utilized. A unique method of baiting is commonly practiced, consisting in laying the hook with a handful of minnows between two stones of fist size, making a sort of sandwich. This sandwich is held firm by looping the fishline around the two stones in a bow half-hitch. With the stones acting as a sinker, the line is lowered to the desired depth, then given a sharp jerk which unties the stones and releases the minnows. They float around and reach the surface, whereas the hook, encased in a large minnow, stays down and catches the greedy fish which is after the largest meal.

The Arab who takes you out to fish generally knows the habitats of the different varieties. He will say, "At thirty fathoms we will get a sultana" and that means a vivid red fish will be caught. At sixty fathoms the catch may be some faras, a highly prized fish, toothless and difficult to hook but one that will make an especially delicious meal. Among the Red Sea reefs there are also barracuda, as at Port Sudan, nearly opposite Jidda.

It would seem reasonable that the fishing industry could be greatly increased by drying fish and sending them inland to provide an addition to the food supply. A proper investigation of this matter might also suggest the possibility of fish canning here and along the east coast of Arabia.

51

Sharks are abundant in both the Red Sea and the Persian Gulf. At the southern end of the former, a plant was established a few years ago to catch sharks on a large scale. The very tough skins are sold for special shoe leather, the fins have ready sale as food in China, and the oil is recovered for medicinal purposes since it is a chief source of Vitamin A. Equipment for the development of shark and other fishing was obtained but the work not prosecuted.

The *Saudi Arabian News* published at New Delhi, India, March 1957, reports that in 1952 several experts from the International Food and Agriculture Organization came to survey the Red Sea coastal area of the Hijaz and Asir. With the assistance of the government they made a report. The result of this was the formation of a stock company with a capital of 15,000,000 Saudi *riyals*. The company was granted a monopoly for 40 years.

This company bought equipment for catching and preserving fish, including fishing boats of 130 tons each and a plant with a daily output of 15 tons of ice. A storehouse has been built with a capacity of 200 tons. It also has equipment for rendering small fish into powder. This product is a cattle food which has a market in Europe. In addition, fish oil is extracted amounting to 10 tons daily. The company also supplies Mecca and Jidda with their food requirements of fish. The Ministry of Agriculture supervises this industry and encourages it.

Pearling

Although a few pearls have been found along the Red Sea, near Jidda and to the south, pearling has not yet become a successful commercial enterprise. On the other hand, the Persian Gulf has a historic reputation as the home of the finest pearls. The synthetic pearls and the Japanese cultured variety have done serious damage to the pearling industry, but the general increase in world prosperity in the past few years has raised pearl prices, with a decided benefit to this area.

Pearling methods in general use have followed the same pattern for thousands of years. The only exception was the use in 1935 of compressed air and deep-sea diving suits by some of the Italians in the employ of the Qusaibi brothers of Bahrain.

Diving for the pearl oyster is carried out in waters up to 60 feet deep. The pearling ships have large crews of divers who alternate between diving and opening and examining the oyster shells to extract the pearls. The ships are rigged with poles extending about five feet from the boat sides, with one diver to a pole, and one helper on board for each man in the water. As many divers as possible are crowded into each boat in order to cover the maximum area of pearl oyster sea bottom.

The diver is nude, save for a breechclout and a knife slung to one wrist for self-defense against sharks or the even more dreaded barracuda. He holds a weight, usually an ancient cannon ball or some stone of similar heaviness, attached to a light rope. Another light rope is attached to an open weave basket. When all is ready the diver signals his helper, who plays out the rope as rapidly as possible, the weight taking the diver down to the sea floor. There he puts all the oysters he sees into the basket, gives the signal, and comes to the surface, either hauled by the rope or under his own power. The basket is also hauled and dumped on the boat deck for opening and searching for the pearls. Some pearl divers use clothespins as clips on their noses, but their only equipment is the aforementioned knife. Ordinarily the crew and divers receive a proportionate part of the proceeds from the sale of pearls recovered, less deductions for food and expenses.

Between Yenbo and Umluj on the Red Sea coast there is a marine growth called "black coral," said to be peculiar to this region. Coral prayer beads set in rosaries of 33 or 99 beads each are sought throughout the Moslem world, and cigarette-holders, commanding high prices, are made of it at Jidda. This black coral is obtained by divers.

Weaving

Most Bedouin families weave from goat's hair, sometimes mixed with coarse wool, the heavy, carpet-like cloth of which their tents are composed. These tents are usually black and, save for one side, closed to the sun. The thickness of the cloth affords protection from the desert heat, and the temperature within is degrees cooler than outside. Strips, usually about 24 inches wide, are sewn together to give any desired size. The length varies, some great shaikhs' tents being 100 feet long by 20 wide, with partitions of the same material to separate the women's and other quarters.

Rugs of different colors are also woven and sold in the market places of larger towns such as Taif and Jidda. The best are of the natural white, brown, and black colors; the red, yellow, and other dyes are neither pleasing to the eye nor permanent. Usually a rug is made up of two pieces, each 20 to 30 inches wide, loosely sewn together and averaging a length of 9 to 12 feet. The Bedouin weavers fix small stakes in the ground, on which the warps or longitudinal cords are fastened, while a small wooden shuttle is used to weave the weft or transverse cords. A similar weave serves in the making of camel bags, indispensable to every family when traveling, for carrying small utensils, coffee equipment, and other household goods as well as small children.

Taif is the center of manufacture of the blanket-like coats known as *beedis*. White wool is commonly used, in the form of tightly twisted yarn matching that of the camel bags. Tighter weaving than that applied in the case of tent cloth produces a fabric which, as we have seen, sheds rain for a short time and provides an excellent cover from the heavy dews when sleeping beneath the stars.

Hofuf in the Hasa deserves credit as the principal manu-

facturing center of the gown which forms the universal costume of the Saudi Arabian. Everywhere known as *mashlah*,
except in Syria where its name is *aba*, this outer garment is
occasionally distinguished in its Syrian form by a specially
attached hood. The decoration about the neck is peculiar to
the *mashlah* of Najd, and there is no hood as in Syria.

There are several types of *mashlah*, the better ones being
woven of camel's hair, whereas the inferior grades are of wool
or wool mixed with camel's hair. Heavily woven thick types
are intended for cold weather, and loosely woven, light, transparent weights for summer temperatures. The generally preferred color is brown, the buff and black being less popular;
and in shape they approach the sleeveless academic gown of
the Western world, averaging 63 inches in width, and 44 in
length from the shoulder to the ground. The neckline is cut
square at the back of the neck, averages 8 to 9 inches across
the back, and is heavily embroidered with gold thread. This
gold embroidery, which is beautiful throughout and worked
with great skill, continues for about 20 inches down the front
of the gown in a tapering band. On either side of its neck opening the gown has gold cords, adorned with gold balls set two
inches apart and an inch in diameter each, terminating in three
smaller gold balls. Both the weaving and embroidery are executed by male artisans working with hand-looms at home.

Out of palm leaves there is almost universal weaving of
mats, used on house floors and ceilings. In Asir, baskets of all
sizes are expertly woven. Southern Tihama also furnishes some
especially attractive baskets, often serving as interior ornaments
in the houses and hung on wall pegs. In the vicinity of Abha
and the high plateau country, the baskets have stiff wooden
frames. Grass mats are woven throughout the realm. In their
rectangular shapes they are designed to serve as prayer-rugs
and beds, whereas circular ones are spread on the floor in the
place of dining-tables, which are still rare except in the royal
palaces, Jidda, and the vicinity of the oil and mining camps.

Baked Pottery

The chief pottery product is the water jar used by pilgrims on their journeys. Slightly porous, this jar permits the water to seep to the outside of the vessel, where the intense heat causes evaporation and cools the water within. A similar water container is known to the Mexicans, Portuguese, and other hot-climate peoples. Although Jidda makes most of this pottery, a variety of small pottery jars and vases, as well as tops of water pipes, are made in Medina and Asir. Other types of pottery jars and receptacles have been made for many centuries, as revealed by the fragments strewn over the entire country, especially at Jabrin, Aflaj, Najran, and along the ancient mine dumps scattered from Asir to Midian in northern Hijaz. Some of the green slip pottery found at Mahad Dhahab was assigned to the tenth century A.D. by experts of the British Museum.

The baked pottery industry is relatively small since clay and marl in sufficient quantities for pottery manufacture are available only at the seacoast. A strange sort of pottery, hardly thus to be classified, is that carved out of soft andesitic schist into various types of open dishes and lamps. There are large mines south of Taif and north of Duwadami which produced this material.

Boat Building

Boat building is an important industry in most of the seaports, especially Jidda and Jizan. The keel and ribs are of wood cut in the mountains of the interior; the natural curves of tree trunks, limbs, and crotches are skillfully fitted into the boat frame. There is no steaming or artificial bending of the wood. The side planking or skin, as well as the decking, is usually of the teak family, imported from India or Java. In many cases the iron spikes are made by the local blacksmiths, and driven into drilled holes, the large flat heads made water-tight by collars of local raw cotton twisted about them. In many instances, side planking is cunningly sawed to fit by overlaying one plank on another. Caulking is done with oakum soaked in oil or tar. Sesame oil and other imported oils are used to paint and to mix with paint. Locally made pigments of white, green and red are in general use.

It has been said that the graceful lines of the double-ended Red Sea fishing dhows are identical with those of the ancient Phoenicians which first traded between the eastern Mediterranean and Cornwall. The lines of the dhows used as lighters in the various harbors are different. Much broader in beam and with blunter bow and square sterns, they are not as pleasing to the eye. But the single mast, raked forward, with the large lateen sail, is common to both types. In the Persian Gulf the dhows are again different, except for the sails. Their bows are vertical and sterns overhang at 45 degrees. A large tank scow for fresh water is normally towed behind pearling dhows, for the crews are large, consisting of the divers as well as the sailors.

6. The Water Supply

THE water resources of Saudi Arabia, like those of almost every other part of the world, are dependent upon climate, geological formations, and topography. In this respect the country falls into four distinct divisions: (1) the southwestern region; (2) the northwest and central region; (3) the districts of the Ain al-Heet, Kharj and Aflaj water pits; and (4) eastern Hasa.

The Southwestern Region

This region consists of Asir and southern Hijaz. In the Asir mountains the rainfall, as noted above, has been estimated largely on the basis of vegetation at 10 to 12 inches. Many of the terraced fields on the eastern mountain slopes seem to rely on rainfall alone for crop production. Nearly all of the western slopes are too steep for cultivation. The stream beds, strewn with boulders, show that large amounts of water flow down them at times; in the Wadi Itwad many miles of perennial flowing water pass through one small stream. In the Red Sea coastal plain of Tihama, the rainfall seems to be similar to that of Jidda, that is, an average of 3 to 4.5 inches. The densely populated areas, from Lith to the border of the Yemen, are supported by the flood irrigation of the fertile silt brought down from the Asir mountains several times a year. Here the "bolsa" type of irrigation, common in southern Arizona and parts of Mexico, is used entirely. The red and white sorghum crops, observed at Darb and Baish, with stalks measuring as much as 17.7 feet in height, prove the fertility of this soil. Similar crops appear for approximately 300 miles along the Tihama coastal plain from the Yemen to Kunfida. To the north of Darb are the *wadis* supplying the water and soil for the districts about Wadi Hishash, Wadi Hamatha, Gahama, Dahaban, Khor al-Birk, Wadi Amk, Wadi Sherga, Hali, Wadi Yetha, Kunfida, Wadi al-Asiba and Lith.

There are at least two rivers between Darb and Baish whose floods, still unused, could be made available by suitable diversion dams. Those noted are Wadi Samra and Wadi Bedth. These flood irrigation areas extend for a length of 300 miles south from Lith to the Yemen border. The Tihama plains, varying in width, are far from being continuously fertile. As noted previously, several lava flows extend from the mountains to the seashore between Shuqaiq and Khor al-Birk. It is possible, however, that close investigation might reveal storage dam sites, also well sites, which might provide additional water for irrigation. There is sufficient suitable soil for extending arable areas considerably.

The Saudi government in cooperation with Point Four and the U.S. Geological Survey, contracted for water drilling by Michael Baker Jr. Gratifying results were obtained which can serve as examples for further development as well as immediately increasing a certain amount of cultivation by use of the new water.

At Lith five wells were drilled entirely in gravel. Two of these wells at 62 and 64 feet yielded 200 and 250 gallons per minute of good potable water.

At Kunfida two wells were completed to depths of 70 feet and 90 feet in gravel. Pumping tests showed flows of 300 gallons per minute. The quality of the water was good. Pumps and casings were set, and contracts for a pipeline given. At the present date, installation is probably completed. At Darb seven wells were drilled of which four showed capacities of 200 to 300 gallons per minute from a depth of 200 feet.

At Jizan a pipeline of 9.3 miles has been laid to convey water from two wells to the east of this city. The wells were drilled 250 feet deep and together discharge 300 gallons per minute. Formerly water was delivered to this important seaport by caravans of donkeys and camels carrying five-gallon kerosene tins which were the unit of transport.

On the eastern side of the Hijaz mountains the rainfall decreases rapidly until, within 50 miles or less, it is down to the general average of 3 to 5 inches. On the southern boundary of Asir, east of the mountain ridge and adjoining the Empty Quarter, lies the ancient area of Najran, where numerous evidences of the extensive and enlightened Himyarite occupancy appear. At the head of the Najran valley was the ancient dam called Mufija, though the basin above this ruined dam is of too steep a grade and too small an area to justify its rehabilitation. Four miles downstream is an excellent dam site called Jabal Raoum justifying careful recordings of flood and general water flow on which estimates for a storage dam might be based. Such recordings would include tests of bedrock and abutting rock formations. Should a dam prove economically feasible, many acres could be reclaimed near the mouth of the Najran valley.

The water table throughout the 15 miles from the dam site is indicated by wells, to be 12 to 15 feet below the present ground surface. The level is reported to vary little and the supply is ample. It was estimated that only one-fifth of the arable area is at present under cultivation.

The great springs at and adjoining Ain Husain show a plentiful supply of unused water close to the surface. Soil and climate make an attractive prospect for the production of more dates, sorghum, and alfalfa, besides the establishment of crops of sugar cane, wheat, cotton, with numerous vegetables and fruits. Some 200 miles north lies the great Wadi Dawasir, with its extensive branches. Great quantities of water flow through it, as evidenced by banks of silt, gravel, and boulders. Bisha has a stable water table at 30 to 50 feet, depending on the contour of the surface. The best dates in southwestern Saudi Arabia are raised here and exported to other districts. There are probabilities that sufficient water could be pumped from additional wells in the great Wadi Bisha bed and on banks parallel with it to increase substantially the productive area. The U.S. Agricultural Mission recommended the planting of many *athel* (tamarisk) trees in the river bed and along the banks in order to develop gas-producing fuel for the operation of pump engines. This is now being done in the vicinity of Medina.

The Wadi Bisha, for 170 miles down to its confluence 'with the Wadi Dawasir, has a great amount of subsurface water. On the way to Sulaiyil, some 55 miles beyond, one encounters many date groves and space for many more. Though brackish, the water is suitable for date culture, its depth being 2 to 4 feet at the wells and pits examined. Some new date offshoots have been planted recently, showing ambition and enterprise on the part of the Arabs. Ruins of buildings and small palm groves appear on the tributaries of the Wadi Dawasir. Those on the Wadi Tathlith, Wadi Hamdh, Wadi Bisha, and Wadi Ranya point to the existence of a larger population in the past.

The Northwest and Central Region

This region includes central and northern Hijaz, and all of Najd and western Hasa, excepting the great water pits of Ain al-Heet, Kharj, and Aflaj.

Because of the annual pilgrimage to Mecca, the water supply of Jidda, Saudi Arabia's foremost port on the Red Sea, is of vital importance. It is reported that in some years upwards of 125,000 men, women, and children land at this harbor and travel the 43 miles to the Holy City. Aware of the water problem thus created, the Turks some sixty years ago constructed a water system which drew a stream from the *wadi*, or river bed, at Ain Waziria, 6.8 miles east of Jidda. The stream of water runs through a "cut and cover" tunnel for the first third of the distance, and through a pair of 5-inch terra-cotta pipes the rest of the way to the city. The pipes employed were similar to the Roman system I uncovered in Cyprus. In order to help regulate the water situation at the city, the late Charles R. Crane of New York presented a 16-foot windmill and auxiliary gas engine complete with pump equipment and piping which, when I installed it late in 1931, raised an average of 40 gallons of water per minute. The city had two other sources of water; the one, its principal source of drinking water, consisted of condensing units producing 135 tons of fresh water in twenty-four hours; the other gave a precarious supply from cisterns and pits which preserved the run-off from rains.

In 1942 the U.S. Agricultural Mission investigated and reported upon an adequate fresh water supply which would lead spring water from the north side of Wadi Fatima to Jidda through 34 miles of pipe or covered masonry conduit.

The present population of Jidda is estimated at 200,000 and is rapidly increasing. Many fine residences have been and are being constructed. These have gardens which necessitate water in excess of that for domestic purposes. In accordance with suggestions by Aramco engineers and by the U.S. Agricultural Mission in 1942 water has been developed in the Wadi Fatima where many springs have been used during the past centuries for irrigation purposes. Each spring consists of an underground culvert, or water tunnel, which comes to the surface at the point where the water is used for irrigation. After the first five springs, the culvert has been tapped by constructing a small chamber at the point above which the water discharges into the open; the water is piped from this chamber to connect with the main line leading toward the city. At the last spring, named "Abu Sheib," settlement tanks are provided to catch the sand brought down from the six springs before this sediment passes into the trunk line running to Jidda.

The water is conveyed from Abu Sheib in a 12-inch diameter main to a reservoir of 1,000,000-gallon capacity. This was constructed on the north side of the Mecca road at 9.3 miles easterly from Jidda. From this reservoir a 15-inch main was laid along the north side of the highway to the city outskirts. From here various distribution lines were laid throughout the city. All the mains consist of imported asbestos cement pressure pipe. The total length from the most northerly spring to the center of the city is 50 miles and the entire cost was approximately $2,137,000. King Saud, then Heir Apparent, opened this project in late 1947. The above details were given me by the courtesy of the firm which contracted this enterprise, Gellatly, Hankey & Co. Ltd., Jidda and London.

Additional water sources are now being developed and planned. In 1954, a 24-inch diameter pipeline was added to increase the supply.

In the Wadi Fatima lying between Jidda and Mecca, there are several springs along the northern side and a large amount of subsurface water. The latter is derived from the spring-fed irrigation water, as well as from floods—or *sayls* (torrents)—coming down from the Hijaz mountains. An enormous amount of work has been done in excavating areas to bring them low enough to be irrigated by the springs. Since all the spoil was dug with a sort of hoe and carried in baskets—usually on the laborers' heads—the effort involved suggested that of ancient Egyptian enterprises. Many thousands of tons of spoil were handled to make those gardens. This same sort of sunken garden has been excavated near Anaiza in Najd.

Mecca is the political capital of Hijaz, and the religious heart of Islam, where non-Moslems are denied entrance. Its water supply is derived through a "cut and cover" tunnel from Ain Zubaida, about 9 miles southeast. Queen Zubaida, after whom the spring is named, wife of the Abbasid Caliph Harun al-Rashid, was both devout and generous. She made several pilgrimages from Baghdad to Mecca. It is said that she directed her engineers about A.D. 800 to make an ample water supply for Mecca. She also ordered the construction of watering places along the entire caravan route from Mecca to Baghdad at intervals of a day's march. These consisted of cisterns to catch the run-off from rains, and wells—whichever was the more efficient. Several of both types have been in continuous use for over a thousand years. The locations of these works, the types of material used and the methods of construction all show great skill.

63

A new source of water is by a 22-24 inch pipeline laid to tap the Wadi Fatima above the Jidda waterhead.

Other ports of importance are Yenbo and Wejh, situated 200 and 400 miles respectively north from Jidda. Yenbo is supplied with water by a condenser and a pipe line from a valley called Yenbu Nakhl, 26 miles to the east. The Baker company drilled four wells and completed two which together discharge 400 gallons per minute. Wejh depends upon cisterns and wells. One new well drilled 40 feet deep yields 100 gallons per minute, ample for this village.

The city of Taif, 138 miles from Jidda and 5,200 feet above it, is the summer capital of Hijaz. The gardens here are noted for grapes and other fruits, as well as vegetables. Barley and wheat also thrive. There are a few springs which emanate from the granite and gneiss, but most of the water for irrigation is obtained from wells. The average depth seems to be 30 feet, but some wells are 90 feet deep. Windmill, gas engine, and electric-driven pumps are in use, in addition to the time-honored skin buckets raised by camels or donkeys.

The Viceroy, Amir Faisal, and the former Finance Minister, Abdullah Sulaiman, have developed farms within a few miles of Taif. At Sharia, near Mecca on the road to Taif, another farm is being energetically developed by the ex-Deputy Minister of Finance, Shaikh Hamad Sulaiman. King Saud, like his father, is encouraging all possible water and agricultural development, for he, his ministers, and all the nation's leaders realize that the soundest prosperity is based on local production of sufficient food to support the population.

As non-Moslems can visit Taif only by special permission of the Saudi government, this district has not been extensively investigated by foreign engineers. Mr. Nils Lind, formerly of the U.S. Department of State, attached to the American Legation at Jidda, made the first, and a most excellent, report in 1945 on ancient dams and evidences of former reclamation projects in the region. Prince Mansour, Acting Viceroy in the absence of Prince Faisal, and the Minister of Finance wished a more technical report on irrigation possibilities; accordingly, during August 1945, I made an investigation of the local dams.

To sum up my findings very briefly: There are eight dam sites in the region, several of them already containing dams of ancient origin. Sud Saisid (*sudd* being the Arabic word for "dam"), about 6 miles east of Taif, possesses Kufic inscriptions on its rocks which read in translation: "This dam, belonging to Abdullah ibn-Muawiya Amir al-Muminin, built by Abdullah Ibrahim by Allah's instruction, 58 Anno Hegeira [A.D. 680]." The structure of the dam, in which no mortar or mud was used, is today in excellent condition, a magnificent tribute to the engineering skill of Abdullah Ibrahim. This was a flood control project to impound silt only. It was most successfully done, as is revealed by the fertile field now occupying the original dam basin.

Other of the ancient dams need reconstruction or reinforcement to obtain maximum efficiency. For instance, Sud Somalagi Dam, 19.4 miles southeast of Taif, might create very considerable additional crop production in the Somalagi valley if it were repaired. Sud al-Jabarjib Dam near Wadi Muhrim, 8 miles northwest of the city, though a new dam, was built too narrow in cross-section and has washed out several times. I gave the Director of Finance a rough, safe type of design, in hope that the next repairing might be permanent. This dam backs up subsurface water so that wells furnish irrigation water for the higher ground on the sides of the basin.

A further report on dams and wells was made by a team of three American experts in 1947. It was suggested that present dams be repaired and new ones constructed along the lines of my recommendation to back up subsurface water, thereby avoiding the rapid evaporation due to the intensity of the sun. Another suggestion was that wells should be deepened and "spidered" or fanned out horizontally at the bottom to tap greater areas as well as to provide larger water storage.

Shaikh Saleh Gezaz, Director of Finance in Taif district, 1946, wished me to see a possible site in the great Wadi Wejh, the largest river valley in the vicinity. We "jeeped" up the river bed for 14.5 miles and then walked a half-mile to al-Kharrah, at an elevation of 5,600 feet. Up to this point there are many benches and fields on both sides of the river bed, showing some present cultivation and evidences of considerably more farming in the past. At the bend of the river at al-Woohait, 9 miles above Taif, a great eucalyptus tree is growing, and a nut pine. Citrus fruits would thrive here. The valley narrows abruptly at al-Kharrah, and while there are excellent abutments for a 250-foot dam, the valley continues to be too narrow—it is more of a gorge than a valley—with too steep a slope, to justify such a high structure. However, three miles nearer Taif is a site called Shab al-Jeleed which, with the exception of that at Jabal Raoum in the Najran valley, is the most attractive one I have seen in Saudi Arabia. An appropriate dam (105 feet high, with a basin 6,000 feet long, an average width of 500 feet and water depth at the dam of 100 feet) would be of tremendous benefit to the gardens in the Taif district, as well as down the 11-mile valley to that city.

Among other potential water resources of the province, mention must be made of the extensive Wadi Hamdh, one of whose heads is near Medina. There are many arable areas similar to that examined at Malalia, approximately 50 miles north of Medina along the Hijaz railway line, where the water table is 8 to 12 feet below the surface, depending on the season of the year. Although slightly alkaline, the water is suitable for the irrigation of dates, alfalfa, and sorghums. In many parts of this valley ample soil and water are available for a substantial increase in population.

Similar conditions prevail in Wadi Jizal, a tributary of Wadi Hamdh, to the southwest of al-Ula, where signs of former occupancy are in evidence, although the only present inhabitants of this area are nomadic Bedouins. The efficient planting of tamarisk trees to protect the river banks, and to provide char-coal fuel for operating gas-engine driven pumps, should bring a considerable area into production and support a great num-ber of families. References to the fertility and richness of this district are found in the works of classical Arab historians and geographers. The development of the region offers opportuni-ties for settlement in small units of 5 to 10 acres.

Hail is the most important city in the great northern high-land area of Najd. The soil and water are efficiently used here and tapped to near their limit. Irrigation water, almost en-tirely obtained from wells, is at a depth of 30 to 80 feet, al-though in one small area it is but 8. The typical primitive method of raising water in skin buckets, hoisted by animals walking down inclined planes, is used exclusively. At Anaiza, excavations similar to those of the sublevel gardens bordering Wadi Fatima have been made, and are still in progress, bring-ing the gardens down to a level where the river bed of Wadi Rumma will irrigate the date groves and other plantations without the necessity of pumping.

There is another interesting water development in the Wadi Rumma, about 7 miles north of Anaiza, in a small, shallow flowing artesian water area. Locally handmade drilling tools are improvised to dig holes, penetrating an aquifer underlying a hard sandstone which in turn is overlain by the river-bed gravel. Several wells are yielding flowing water. Since flowing artesian supplies have had the sad experience of overdrilling in Utah, New Mexico, and California, the Saudi Arabian govern-ment was cautioned to regulate the number of holes in order to forestall depletion. All along the Wadi Rumma there were seen evidences of a large subsurface water supply. Numerous villages, with many gardens and cultivated fields, stretch from Buraida to al-Rass and Oglat al-Suqhour.

Another productive district is that of Khaibar, lying among the *harrahs*, or great lava fields, a hundred miles north from Medina. The general elevation is 2,200 feet above the sea. The extensive date groves, settlements, and the town of Khaibar lie between tongues of lava. There are numerous springs emanating from these flows. Too much water seems to be the case at Khaibar, for there is such a plague of the anopheles malaria-carrying mosquito that much of the land belongs to nonresident owners. Most of the present permanent inhabitants are descendants of African slaves. One of the greatest needs here is adequate drainage to prevent alkalinity, as well as to lessen mosquito-breeding areas.

There are inscriptions, records, and legends indicating that perhaps in early times this region was occupied by Jews. Six dams for storing irrigation water are reported, of which I inspected one called Sud Haseed. This dam is made of cut stone with lime mortar, and lies 15 miles southeast of Khaibar village. It is 182 feet long at its base, 270 feet along its crest, and 28 feet high above its stone pipe outlet. The capacity, as measured by A. L. Wathen, irrigation engineer of the U.S. Agricultural Mission, is 750 acre feet. The mud flood-line showed that the surrounding lava was so porous that the full capacity of the dam, greatly exceeding the figure given above, was never used. This dam could be cheaply rehabilitated, and the other five are said to be similar to it.

A description of the water resources of this section of Arabia would not be complete without one final reference to the form of drawing water which has perhaps been the most vital factor in the life of the nomad and Bedouin travelers. Hoisting of water by men, women, and camels from as much as 170 feet—the greatest depth observed, at Bir Rumah, on the western edge of the Dahna—is typical of many wells on the main caravan routes. The inflow of these caravan wells usually varies between 5 to 30 gallons per minute. Other watering places on the main caravan and motor route across Arabia, from Jidda on the Red Sea to Jubail on the Persian Gulf, may be of interest. It should be borne in mind that the depth at which water is reached often varies according to the season, so the following figures must be taken as approximate:

Birka	cistern
Muwai	20 feet to water
Dafina	80 feet to water
Afif	70 feet to water
Qaiaya	4 feet to water
Duwadami	9 to 20 feet
Khuff	12 feet
Marrat	surface
Awanid	20 feet
Jubaila	24 feet
Riyadh	50 feet
Ruma	170 feet
Maagala	flowing artesian
Uwainid	35 feet
Hinnot	12 feet
Jubail	flowing artesian

Districts of Riyadh, Kharj, and Aflaj

Saudi Arabia may well be gratified with the water potentialities now indicated. These developments are the result of the American Geological Survey (Dr. Glen Brown and Mr. Roy Jackson) working in conjunction with the Point Four program under Dr. Eden during 1952 to 1954 and continuing to the present.

The most important development is that near Riyadh. This is called Hayyir in the Wadi Hanifa and lies 18.7 miles distant. Steel pipe of 22 and 24 inches in diameter has been laid and pumps will shortly be operating. A French subsidiary of George Pott, International Water Corporation, Pittsburgh, Pa., drilled the initial well 4,201 feet deep and obtained a discharge of 2.5 million gallons per day (or 1,740 gallons per minute), but additional wells have now increased the water flow to 4,200 gallons per minute (March 1957).

A Belgian geologist mapped out the presumed course of this water north of Riyadh and terminating at Kharj. The total length is estimated to be 200 miles. The present water is suitable for irrigation but, due to the hydrogen sulphide and iron in solution, it is unpalatable, unless treated, for drinking purposes.

The water pits of Ain al-Heet, Kharj, Khafs Daghara, and Aflaj are similar, in that they are huge natural wells, ranging in diameter from 150 to 1,500 feet, and from 420 feet upward in depth. It seems that these pits have been formed first by a slight faulting or torsion which caused cracks in the sedimentary beds down to the main aquifer. The cracks were gradually enlarged by the ascending waters, which dissolved out the limestone but more especially the gypsum with which many of the sedimentaries are impregnated. Gradually the process formed caverns, the roofs of which finally broke when the span became too great, creating open pits.

As investigated and worked out by the oil company geologists, the source of the water is rainfall on the watershed of the Tuwaik mountain range, lying 150 to 200 miles west and running in a north-south direction for 500 miles. The western slope constitutes the main drainage basin.

Ain al-Heet is the first area containing these water pits, as one travels south from Riyadh, but Kharj has a larger group and lies 56 miles distant from the capital and at an average elevation of 1,500 feet above the sea. The two connecting pits of Kharj, called Ain Dhila and Ain Samha, are each about 300 feet in diameter and 420 feet deep. Another pit, named Umm Khisa, lies nearly a mile farther west, and is of about the same diameter but only 45 feet deep. It is probable that the source of water supply is the same as at the other two pits, although the caved-in limestone fragments have not as yet been removed by solution. An area of 3,500 acres is now under cultivation with the possibility, if the plans of the Ministry of Agriculture are put through, of an ultimate increase up to a total of nearly 8,000 acres.

The geologists and engineers of the oil company have accomplished much in studying water possibilities, drawing up reports, and laying out irrigation canals. The mining company assisted in recommending and purchasing various equipment on behalf of the government. The American government in 1942 sent the U.S. Agricultural Mission to study and report to King Abdul Aziz ibn-Saud on the water resources and agricultural possibilities of his country. They spent several weeks at Kharj working out some specific problems. The U.S. Lend-Lease Administration sent pumping equipment for Kharj to increase production at the earliest moment. Early in 1944 equipment also arrived in Arabia designated for testing the immense water resources at Aflaj.

The Khafs Daghara project, consisting of only one water pit, is 27 miles to the southwest. The water lies about 60 feet below the ground surface and is of unknown depth. The pit resembles those of Kharj in every respect except its diameter, which is about 150 feet. About 800 acres are now under cultivation, producing a higher quality of wheat than that of Kharj on account of superior soil.

A third group of water pits is in the district of Aflaj, 156 miles south from Kharj, 212 from Riyadh. The elevation of the largest pit, Ain Rass, is about 1,700 feet, and the water surface is some 27 feet below the general ground level. The depth of the water is unknown but the Governor stated that a weighted rope of over 400-foot length had failed to reach the bottom. The area is estimated at a length of 2,000 feet by a width of 800. From the rim are seen the remains of three large irrigation ditches lying side by side but at increasingly lower levels, indicating that the water level has receded a total of 27 feet during the last 2,000 years. Decrease in rainfall, increased evaporation, and the destruction of trees and vegetation might have caused the lowering of the water surface. The two fortresses and tunnels near here invite archeological and geological investigation in an area which only about half a dozen Westerners have visited to date. To increase the agricultural productivity, a British firm during 1950 and 1951 installed pumps here as well as at Kharj, Riyadh, and Hasa.

There are four other water pits in the Aflaj district: Ain Burj, Ain Heeb, Ain al-Botn, and Ain Shaghaib. The first three are connected together; the first two are estimated at a length of about 1,000 feet by a width of 250 and 350 feet, respectively. The third, Ain al-Botn, is about 100 by 50 feet. The fourth, Ain Shaghaib, lies about half a mile to the west; its surface is about 15 feet higher, and the diameter may be set at 200 feet. The depth of all these pits is unknown, but indications are that they approximate that of Ain Rass, which is over 400 feet deep. If the inflow is proportional to that of Kharj, an immense amount of water may be made available by pumping. To this end a pump, raising 4,500 gallons per minute, was shipped to Saudi Arabia by the Lend-Lease authorities. There are said to be seventeen villages in the Aflaj district, with Laila as the headquarters.

A broad area of sand loam, suitable for irrigation, lies to the east and north of these pits. Soil and climate favor the growing of wheat, barley, rice, alfalfa, *durra*, pomegranates, apricots, peaches, grapes, and vegetables. The present crops are dates, alfalfa, and sorghums (*durra*). The inhabitants are of the Bedouin pastoral and Murra tribes who care for little other than date cultivation and the tending of their herds and flocks. Since they despise agriculture, the farmers who are to cultivate this extensive and promising area would have to be brought from other parts of Saudi Arabia. From the Tuwaik mountains, rising to the west, a certain amount of timber is now obtained for use in the Kharj project. As elsewhere, the growing of *athel* trees here will further the irrigation project appreciably.

At Dthulm mine prospect in central Najd, a well located at 36 miles from the mine was drilled 200 feet in gravel and by pumping test yielded 100 gallons per minute. This well should benefit grazing tribes of Bedouins, but unfortunately the mining prospect proved valueless.

From 1952 to 1954 the American firm of Michael Baker Jr.

Inc. in cooperation with Point Four carried out an extensive program of water exploration. Six drilling rigs were used and 25 wells were sunk in various parts of the country.

Small water supplies for the Najd villages of Afif and Mu-waih were provided. These places were Bedouin water holes in 1932, but now have service stations and markets since they are on the main motor route between Mecca and Riyadh.

Eastern Hasa

Insofar as water supply in Saudi Arabia is concerned, the eastern Hasa region possesses the greatest potentialities. Prob-abilities of flowing artesian wells exist in a stretch of land extending a distance of over 100 miles west of the Persian Gulf and parallel to its coast. Bearing out this opinion are the wells drilled by Aramco at its Khobar, Abqaiq, Jubail, and abu-Hadriya camps, north and south from Dhahran; by the Saudi government in many localities at Jowia west of Abqaiq and at Hofuf; and by private interests, between Qatif and Khobar. The average depth of this artesian flow appears to be 200 to 300 feet, near the coast, but about 800 feet at Hofuf. Artesian well drilling was initiated in 1930 on Bahrain Island by Major Holmes.

In addition to these man-made water developments, a still larger supply, in the oases of Hofuf, Qatif, Sofwa, and Tarut, consists of immense flowing springs. The largest flowing spring at Hofuf, already mentioned as discharging 22,500 gallons per minute, is named Ain al-Hakl, in keeping with the practice, observable in many lands where a society has lived for thou-sands of years, of assigning a proper name to nearly every place of interest. The flows of three other springs in the Hofuf oasis have been estimated at 20,000 gallons per minute each. Five other springs show an estimated discharge of 800 to 4,000 gal-lons per minute. The Hofuf oasis, by far the largest in Saudi Arabia, has an average elevation of 500 feet. The oil company engineers have reported that the total area, in which more than two million date palms grow, measures about 25,000 acres.

There are in this neighborhood two other areas of about 5,000 acres each, which may be brought under cultivation if steps are taken toward their irrigation through the use of water now going to waste, plus a small supplementary amount of artesian flow. The crying need of Hofuf, and of the entire cultivated soil of Hasa as well, is for adequate drainage systems. Possibilities for a substantial increase in productive land in the eastern artesian-fed belt in Hasa are immense.

Among the other three great oases, Qatif, Sofwa, and Tarut Island, the largest spring, known as Ain Darush, is situated in Sofwa and has a per-minute flow of 900 gallons. Large springs, though with a lesser flow than that of Ain Darush, are Qatif, and Tarut on Tarut Island, as well as Bahrain, 22 miles off the Saudi Arabian coast. One of the submarine water springs in the Persian Gulf occurs a few miles north of Jubail where a spar buoy marked its location, by order of King ibn-Saud. Pearling boats are said to replenish their fresh water supply here. When we sailed past it in 1932, a sailor dove down from our launch with a skin bucket and brought up fairly fresh water. Plugging these submarine springs with cement, in order to conserve the great waste of water, has been recommended.

The last water resource to be noted in Hasa is that of the Jabrin oasis on the edge of the Empty Quarter. Lying at the junction of two ancient incense routes—from Oman to Mecca and Sohar to Baghdad—this oasis has an area estimated at 7,500 acres and an altitude of 700 feet. In July 1942, I recorded here a water table that was 8 to 20 feet below the surface, giving credit to Bedouin reports that in winter months most of the oasis was boggy, presumably due to diminished evaporation although it has a low rainfall of 2 to 4 inches. Throughout the area visited, pools of mosquito-breeding water were seen, which would account for the absence of permanent habitation.

Belonging to the four hundred families of the Murra tribe, this oasis is frequented by them twice a year—in the spring to pollinate the palm trees, and in the autumn to harvest the dates. An attempt, undertaken at the instigation of the King, to establish a permanent settlement of the *Ikhwan* in this oasis was later abandoned because of a heavy malaria death toll. An efficient drainage system might eliminate malaria and facilitate agricultural productivity. Listening to suggestions regarding improved living conditions, the local Amir said with unfeigned pride, "We are Bedouins, not farmers. We tend our camels, sheep and goats, coming here, only when necessary, to pollinate and to harvest dates." And the Murra tribe has the same attitude at Aflaj.

Nevertheless, the development of water and agricultural resources goes on despite Bedouin disapproval. Fostered by the King, the princes, and ministers, zeal for agricultural development has spread in the ranks of laborers in the concessionaire companies. While their rulers promote the reclamation of old as well as new acres, seeking the advice and assistance of friendly governments and locally operating companies, the laboring class, largely employed by the oil company save their wages with the hope of eventually purchasing small date groves and plantation lands. This movement has received an impetus since 1935 when oil and mining companies, engaging native workers on a large scale, helped to raise the living conditions and purchasing power of thousands of Saudi Arabians. The foundation of all progress was firmly laid when King Abdul Aziz ibn-Saud made life and property safe and secure within the borders of his kingdom.

7. Transportation and Communications

SAUDI ARABIA'S transportation and inland routes systems has hinged on the use of the camel, and to a lesser degree the ass, supplemented in recent years by the coming of the automobile, railway, and airplane.

With an average speed of two and a half miles per hour, the camel is the chief vehicle of transportation employed on the long caravan routes of pilgrims, traveling toward Mecca from Asir and Yemen, in the south; from Palestine, Syria, and Iraq, in the north; and from Najd, Kurdistan, Afghanistan, China, and India, in the east and north. The camel of Saudi Arabia is the single-humped dromedary, distinguished from the two-humped variety of Asia by its greater speed and size. Like the horse, the riding qualities of camels differ, ranging all the way from those of the type used in long-distance caravan travel, comparable thereby to the American draft horse, to the beautiful cream or white *dhalul* (riding camel) of Oman, which reputedly goes fifty miles in a day, a counterpart, as it were, to our best saddle horses or thoroughbreds.

Camels have a way of bucking—also a trick of dropping suddenly on their front knees, in the manner of a western broncho, though not nearly as quickly. For a novice, the sudden jerk could entail a serious fall on the head. The camel seems to take it for granted that the world is against him, for he usually grunts and groans whenever his master approaches him with the saddle and load. One rides sidesaddle, if he is wise, a leg curved around the forward horn, while another horn forms the back or cantle, each horn as a rule terminating in a ball with a sharp edge for ornament. The motion of the camel discourages one from leaning back, while any thought of sleeping or lolling seems out of the question. Stirrups are marked by their absence, and the single line to the bridle serves as a kind of halter without bits and is woven of many colors.

76

The wooden saddle frame is usually covered with a sheep-skin, and long bands of heavy woven wool, each about two inches wide, cover the camel on either side, reaching halfway to the ground. These bands keep off the flies when the camel is on the march, as well as ornament this highly prized animal. Additional dress may include a skin, or a woven or embroi-dered breastplate hung over the camel's chest from the horn of the saddle. A group of these camels, mounted by the char-acteristic soldiers of Najd, known as the *Hajjans* (drome-darists), is a magnificent sight, especially when the cavalcade comes charging over the sand. Although they 'run in a gro-tesque manner, the usual gait of a camel up to twelve miles an hour is a pace in which both legs on a side swing forward simultaneously. On a fine *dhalul* this gait is very pleasing up to six or seven miles per hour, but on the regular freight-car-rying stiff-legged camels, the motion can be irksome to the inexperienced. The pilgrims ride a kind of camel "pullman," equipped to carry two persons or a family, which is commonly known as a *shaqdaf* (camel-litter), with a light structure fitting over the camel's hump, having a woven rope bedstead about two and a half feet wide by four and a half feet long, on either side, and enclosed in a wicker canopy covered with grass mat-ting or Persian rugs, according to the wealth of the occupants. This serves as protection from sun and weather.

Due to their double joints, camels "couch" or lie down in a peculiar fashion of their own. A soldierly *Hajjan* will mount a young camel of the fast-riding *dhalul* type by climbing up its rump, using the tail as a handle, and thus onto its back, or by jumping up onto the neck. Except on wet surfaces no ani-mal is more sure-footed than the camel, which may be trusted to take the load of two mules down a steep trail. As a carrier it rates highest among beasts of burden, aside from the ele-phant, but when tractive effort is required it demonstrates poor quality. The average freight carried by an able-bodied camel is 100 kilograms (220 pounds), on either side, making a total of 440 pounds per animal. A quarter of a ton might be loaded on a camel, but more ordinarily the load is less than 400 pounds.

It was suggested previously that the famous breed of white donkeys from the Hasa deserves to be greatly increased as an adjunct to agricultural development. They operate like camels in hoisting the water-skin pumps, but they discharge their greatest function as carriers. The small type of oxen native to Arabia are good as draft animals and, though smaller than the Hasa donkeys, they contribute a distinct service in the cultivation of soil.

Only to a very small extent is the horse a factor in transportation. It is used only for occasional trips of short distance. Since King ibn-Saud outlawed the ancient Arabian practice of raiding, the chief use of the noble Arab horse has been limited to the national sport of racing.

Though an upstart means of transportation, the automobile now ranks above the camel in importance. First introduced in 1925, it is represented today by a large tonnage, with many passengers conveyed by car, bus, and truck. Back in 1931, the government busses, cars, and drivers were inspected by an able young British engineer, Cyril Ousman. Thanks to his training, the work is now performed by Saudi Arabian officers. The airplane is the latest entry in the transport field. Its importance is increasing with amazing rapidity.

Roads

The greatest travel is between Jidda and Mecca, a distance of 46 miles, on a road well laid-out by Egyptian government engineers. It has lately been repaved according to American practice by the International Bechtel Corporation. The road from Mecca to Taif and Riyadh, which attracts the next heaviest travel, has a natural surface and is subject to many washouts. The grades are not bad, and the same general routes could be followed in constructing a more permanent type of road, but realignments such as the projected detour between Muwai and Afif and Sharia via Wadi Muhrrm would be beneficial.

The road from Riyadh to Jubail, and thence to Qatif, Dhahran, and other points along the Persian Gulf, passes through stretches of difficult terrain. In the section stretching for a distance of 50 miles across the Dahna and 70 miles between Hinnot and Jubail, a type of asphalt "mix-in-place" might offer the best solution to the road problem. But the present route followed is far to the south, passing through Kharj, Hofuf, and Abqaiq. The sands on this route would be subject to the same "mix-in-place" construction. This variety of road was constructed across the Sinai Peninsula under the direction of the Shell Company engineers.

From Jubail to Dhahran, Aramco has made many excellent oil-surfaced roads. From Jidda to Mahad Dhahab Mine, a distance of 246 miles, the Saudi Arabian Mining Syndicate, Ltd., constructed a gravel-surfaced road, with a maximum grade of 7.5 to 8 per cent, with a 50-foot minimum radius of curvature, over which 15-ton White trucks with 8-ton four-wheeled trailers traveled satisfactorily. The usual type of truck which is employed by the oil company varies in tonnage between 10, 5 and 1.5 tons, but for special heavy service 15- to 20-ton crawler tread trailers are used. These are hauled by Caterpillar tractors. By far the greatest number of trucks and cars in the country are owned, however, by the government, which has a considerable fleet of army-type trucks; some are semi-armored and fitted with machine-gun mountings.

The various makes of American cars are represented in the country, with the ubiquitous Ford in the ascendancy, largely due to the fact that H. St. John B. Philby had the motor-car monopoly of the country for nearly ten years. Functioning under adverse conditions of climate and road, oftentimes without adequate care, these cars have reflected credit upon the sturdiness of the American automobile. The oil and mining

79

companies rendered through their personnel and engineers invaluable assistance to the government transport department, and the government in return provided the companies with fuel, lubricants, tires, and other supplies in cases of emergency.

King ibn-Saud long recognized the need for more and better roads. In 1939 he requested me to investigate the possibility of motor roads to connect Jizan with Abha, and Abha with Najran. Not till 1940 was the trip made and the reports drawn up, advising that routes for roads were found practicable in both cases. As the matter now stands, grades and curves on the Abha-Najran road have been laid out and marked. In the case of the main route from the Red Sea to the Persian Gulf it would be more practical at the beginning to construct only gravel-surfaced highways, except for the 40 miles across the Nafud, the 50 across Dahna, and the 70 across the Hinnot-Jubail sands, or those of Hofuf and Abqaiq where "mix-in-place" or similar oiled surfaces are suggested. The curves and grades should be carefully laid out, and a minimum width of 23 feet, or 7 meters, would make the passage of the largest trucks safe.

In 1956 King Saud opened a 350-mile, modern, paved highway between Jidda-Medina. That from Medina to Hail, and thence to Baghdad, as well as the Hail-Sakaka-Jauf road, requires investigation, and subsequent construction should traffic warrant the undertaking. Also, a road from Medina to Jordan, parallel to, or using the present railway bed, deserves consideration. As a service to the pilgrims hailing from Jordan, Palestine, Syria, Iran, Kurdistan, Afghanistan, and points east, a road connecting the Iraq-Palestine highway with Medina-Mecca was completed in 1950 and will be increasingly important. Another road, promising to become an artery of inland and international commerce, would be one that ran from Yenbo to Musaijid and Medina, and another from Yenbo to Umluj, Wejh, Duba, Muwailih, and Aqaba, whence it would join the routes leading to Egypt, Jordan, and Palestine. The opening of these new routes might increase the national income not only insofar as pilgrims and other travelers are concerned, but, to an even unexpected degree, through the attraction of tourists from America and Europe. Offered fair roads with adequate rest houses and accommodations, many motorists would undoubtedly be eager to travel through the hitherto remote lands of Hijaz and Asir.

The following statistics of the 1957 pilgrimage show how widespread is Islam, and how much use is made of the roads in Saudi Arabia through this one interest:

From	Number of Pilgrims	From	Number of Pilgrims
Aden	109	Libya	1,022
Afghanistan	2,494	Malay	4,273
Algeria	167	Mauritius	22
Arab Gulf States (Dubai,		Morocco	2,163
Oman, Sharjah, Qatar,		Nigeria	258
Sur, Muscat, Bahrain,		Northwest Africa	259
Maharah, Jalan Ku-		Pakistan	23,670
wait)	6,548	Palestine	4,783
Burma	163	Senegal	841
Capetown	70	Siam	1,686
Ceylon	115	Somaliland	132
China	95	Sudan	6,874
Cyprus	22	Syria	5,589
Egypt	32,109	Tunisia	964
Ethiopia	439	Turkey	3,199
Greece	3	United States	9
Hadramawt	6,407	USSR	128
Indian Muslims	13,166	West Africa	21,622
Indonesia	13,157	Yemen	43,773
Iraq	2,854	Yugoslavia	27
Iran	10,398	Zanzibar	274
Italy	1	*Total recorded*	215,575
Japan	1	*Saudi Arabs estimated*	800,000
Jordan	3,907	TOTAL OF ALL PILGRIMS	1,015,575
Lebanon	1,782		

Except for the paved highways between Jidda and Mecca and between Jidda and Medina, the best roads in Saudi Arabia are those constructed by Aramco in the immense oil-produc-

81

tive province of Hasa. Well-graded and oil-surfaced roads connect all the various oil fields and the important Hofuf area.

As may be noted in the 1957 budget, 700,000 *riyals* or $259,300 have been assigned for surveying the projected highway from Dammam to Jidda, a distance of approximately 900 miles.

There is under consideration a project for connecting all the capitals of the states of the Arab League with a Pan-Arab highway. This would be quite feasible and, as previously mentioned, might be of considerable financial benefit to the several nations because of tourist expenditures. But adequate hotel accommodation would be a vital necessity.

The following budget allocations decreed by Royal order Bo 3/10/1336, dated January 1, 1957, are concrete evidence of the great importance King Saud and his Council of Ministers attach to road construction:

	Saudi riyals	U.S. dollars
1. For account of Jidda-Medina road	7,000,000	1,890,000
2. For account of Riyadh-al-Dir, yah-al Shumasi road	4,000,000	1,080,000
3. Al-Kobar road	1,574,575	425,135
4. For account of Yanbu Medina road	2,500,000	675,000
5. Roads outside Riyadh	5,855,500	1,580,985
6. For account of Medina-Tabuk road	1,000,000	270,000
7. For account of Riyadh-al-Kharj road	6,000,000	1,620,000
8. For heavy road construction equipment	500,000	135,000
9. For surveys of Jidda-Dammam automobile highway	700,000	189,000
TOTAL	29,130,075	7,865,120

The following data about roads completed, under construction, and projected were given by the Saudi Ambassador Shaikh Abdullah Al-Kayyal in June 1957.

ROADS COMPLETED

FROM	TO	DISTANCE Kilometers	Miles	WIDTH Meters	Feet
Jidda	Medina	425	263	8	26
Jidda	Mecca	73	45	8	26
Mecca	Arafat and Holy Places	37	23	12	40
Yenbo	Badr	90	56	9	30
Taif	Howia Airport	20	12	7	23
Riyadh	City and suburbs	78	48	7	23
Riyadh (Under Construction)	Kharj	37	23	9	30
		50	31		
Khobar	Dammam and Dhahran	39	24	9	30
Medina	Tabouk	740	459	7	23
Mecca	Taif	120	74		

Bids Published

Arafat	Taif	71	44		

Roads Proposed and Under Construction

Riyadh	Kharj Haradh Station on Railway	190	118		
Riyadh	Taif	820	508		
Jidda	Jizan	750	465		
Haradh	Hofuf	150	93		

As a result of my trip in 1940, made at the request of King ibn-Saud, I suggest the following be added to this category:

FROM	ELEVATION	TO	ELEVATION	DISTANCE Kilometers	Miles
Abha	7,000 feet	Jizan	Sea level	283	175
Abha	7,000 feet	Najran	4,000 feet	317	196

Although it is obvious that great progress has been accomplished in road construction, the following brief history of the Jidda-Medina road will provide evidence that there are difficulties. This highway construction was initiated by John Howard, a British company, which lost so much money that it withdrew from Saudi Arabia and turned the work over to Brathwaite, another British organization. A total of 64 miles of paved road was completed when this firm threw up its contract, so the work lapsed in 1953. Some time thereafter, a Saudi

Arab, Shaikh Mohamed bin Ladin, took over, after purchasing much of the British equipment, and completed the project. Back in 1935 I instructed Bin Ladin how to use an engineer's level and bought an American instrument for him. In 1956 King Saud opened this important highway to Medina—the second holy Islamic city—from the pilgrim seaport of Jidda.

Next in importance to the trans-Arabian highway from Jidda through Riyadh to Dammam is a road to connect Jidda with Jizan. The distance of the route traveled is 527 miles, but an efficiently surveyed and located road would doubtless decrease this distance. No provision for this work seems to have been included in the January 1, 1957 budget. The present road conditions are terrible. One almost weeps to watch the cars climb over the jagged lava flows. The route now lies along the seacoast; investigation should be made to determine if a better route could be found along the eastern side of the Tihama coastal plain and at the foot of the mountain wall. There are difficult sands in the vicinities of Shuqaiq, Amk, Sharga, Hali, Kunfida, Shuwaik, and Lith, lava flows near Gahama and Khor al-Birk, and *sabkhahs* or mud-bridged swamps near al-Asaiba, southwest of Lith, and along the seacoast to the north of Lith, which might be avoided if inland route were practicable. The possibility should be thoroughly examined. If it were feasible, spur roads could then lead westward to the seaports. The whole Tihama would greatly benefit from good roads. Fish and seaborne imports could be traded for the better fruits and grains raised in the plains and mountains.

The richest agricultural part of Saudi Arabia is in Asir, except for the Hofuf and other Hasa oases. The King and the government are eager to develop this province and make it more accessible by the construction of adequate motor roads connecting the capital, Abha, with the Red Sea port, Jizan, to the west, and with the valley of Najran, near the edge of the Empty Quarter, to the east.

To emphasize the inaccessibility of Asir it may be stated

that when I made my first trip there in 1940, no American and few non-Moslems had even been in the interior of the province. At that time, ibn-Saud requested me to make a reconnaissance and advise him as to whether or not a road for motor transport could be constructed to connect Abha with the Tihama seaports which lie 7,000 feet below. The westward slopes of the mountains are bare rock and precipitous; they average thirty degrees and are, in places, steeper. There are few trails on which camels, mules, or donkeys can carry any appreciable load. After several weeks of strenuous traveling, two possible routes were found for road construction, but one had twenty-three hairpin bends and an average grade of 9 per cent to negotiate a vertical distance of 2,850 feet, so it might be said that there is only one practical route. A 6 to 8 per cent grade with probably only eight hairpin bends could be worked out on this route. The total distance from Abha to Jizan would be 175 miles and the maximum elevation 7,150 feet, just to the west of Abha.

The other necessary road in Asir is one to connect Abha with Najran. The latter town and valley are 196 miles to the east along the plateau. There are many villages along the whole route. The rainfall is judged to vary from 10 to 5 inches. The floor of the Najran valley at the government headquarters is 4,000 feet altitude. The road route I laid out tentatively comprises seventeen *agabats* or grades which average 8.5 per cent. Much of the route follows the ancient *hajj* or pilgrim way from the Yemen. Some of it is even older and is still called *tariq al-fil* ("road of the elephant"). There are many remains of good stone-paving, like Roman roads. The alignment is well done, but many of the grades are too steep and the curves too sharp to be incorporated into a motor road. The name suggests that this road was built during the attempted conquest of Mecca by the Abyssinians, with elephants, in the sixth century A.D.

Subsequently it will be of great benefit to construct a motor road from Najran to Bisha; thence one branch to the Wadi Dawasir extending up to Laila, Kharj, and Riyadh, the other branch to go through Turaba to Taif and Ashaira.

Railways

For many years Saudi Arabia was a nation without a railway. Now one has been built and is in operation between Dammam and the Persian Gulf and Riyadh. In the 1957 budget 2,000,000 Saudi *riyals* ($540,000) have been allocated for additional locomotives.

An extension was surveyed and engineered as a Point Four project in 1951 by International Engineering (Morrison-Knudsen). Nothing has been actually done yet, although a construction contract was given, in late 1956 to Morrison-Knudsen. But a letter from the Saudi Ambassador, Shaikh Kayyal, dated March 5, 1957, states: "The government is now in the process of constructing a railway 1,540 kilometers (955 miles) long between Riyadh and the Red Sea, linking the cities of Riyadh, Medina, Jidda, and Mecca." The estimated cost is $125,000,000.

The main line, American standard gauge, trackage of Saudi government railroad was completed in October 1951, surveying having commenced in 1946. A celebration was held to commemorate the arrival in Riyadh of the first freight and passenger train completing the 357-mile run from Dammam, the principal Persian Gulf port. Regular trains are now in operation, carrying passengers, oil products, agricultural produce, and various types of goods and materials to the interior. The time for this initial trip was 10 hours.

The railroad received its first regular passenger equipment in 1951. These modern air-conditioned cars provide first- and second-class passenger service. Twenty suburban-type passenger cars provide third-class service. When the roadbed is completely finished, runs from Riyadh to Dammam may be scheduled for about 8 hours.

The roadbed was designed to handle traffic at maximum

speeds of 62 miles per hour. It is built to American standards for first-class railroads, and the rail used is 80 pounds per yard. Drifting sand handicapped operations, but the sand problem is being brought under control by installing sand fences and oiling critical areas. Specially designed maintenance equipment, including sand-oiling cars, are in use. A 70-ton Jordan spreader for moving large volumes of sand, profiling the road-bed, and spreading ballast has been added to the maintenance equipment. This machine aids considerably in the program for developing a first-class railroad.

Facilities completed during 1951 included 115 miles of main-line track, the main wharf office building, a garage, and an oil waste house. Work is completed on the communications building and housing facilities at Dammam. The 7 main stations are Dammam, Dhahran, Abqaiq, Hofuf, Haradh, Kharj, and Riyadh. In addition there are 12 secondary stations. Design is nearing completion on the stations and supporting facilities at all locations. A modern railroad shop and related facilities for maintaining railroad equipment have been constructed at Dammam.

Marked progress was made on the radio communications system, and the automatic radio-telephone exchange was placed in service. Radio-telephone equipment was installed in all 15 locomotives. The communication and control system includes terminals at Dammam and Riyadh, 4 intermediate attended stations, and 5 unattended relay stations. The system provides: (1) voice contact between all operating stations; (2) voice contact between the central dispatcher at Dammam and trains moving anywhere on the system; (3) voice contact between trains within a radius of 5 to 10 miles; (4) a complete Dammam network covering shop, storage, and operations area; and (5) 3 direct voice circuits between Dhahran and Riyadh.

As the railroad traffic has become greater, the Dammam wharf and small craft pier handled increasing amounts of cargo. The tonnage is also increasing steadily, and the trestle and wharf are operating at or near capacity. A new all-steel, 380 H.P. tugboat is used for towing barges from vessels unloading at the main wharf to the small-craft pier. Efficient cargo-handling facilities are in use. Dammam pier is 7 miles long, and the pier head is in 45 feet depth of water.

At the end of 1951 personnel employed on the railroad and port project totaled 805, including 385 Saudi Arabs, 98 Americans, 203 Palestinians, and 89 Italians. Daily classes are held for the training of Arab personnel for supervisory and operating positions. In December 1951 a group of 11 Saudi Arabs was being processed to be sent to the United States for two months' training in maintenance, operation, and repair of equipment and rolling stock. In addition, service representatives of the equipment manufacturers were brought from the United States to instruct Saudi Arabs in equipment operation. It seems probable that the personnel has not altered greatly since then. The Saudi Ambassador wrote me in October 1957: "No statistics are available on the personnel on the Dammam-Riyadh Railway at present."

To emphasize the developments since the railway was inaugurated in 1951, Aramco has kindly furnished the following data:

The number of passengers carried during 1956 was 474,617, or over nine times the estimated initial number of 50,000.

The revenue productive freight handled during the above year totaled 574,658 tons. A considerable proportion of this, naturally, consisted of supplies for the oil fields. Near the railway line are the oil camps of Haradh, Al-Hawiyah, Uthmaniyah (now being replaced by Udhailiyah), Shedgum, and Abqaiq. The former capital of the province of Hasa, Hofuf, is the most important government station between Dhahran and Riyadh.

The rolling stock of the railway utilized at the end of 1956 consisted of the following items.

88

Locomotives,	17	{	2—1500 HP EMD locomotives 6—1000 HP Alco Diesel electric locomotives 6—380 HP Int. GE Diesel electric locomotives 3—150 HP Int. GE Diesel electric locomotives
Rail cranes,	2	{	1—50 ton Brown-hoist 1—80 ton Brown-hoist
Freight cars,	430	{	275—50 ton flat cars 35—50 ton gondola cars; including 2 second-hand 78—50 ton box cars 40—10,000 gallon tank cars 2—mechanical refrigerator cars
Work cars,	2	{	2—Jordan spreaders
Passenger cars	30	{	19—100 seat second-hand passenger coaches 2—dining cars, re-built, second-hand coaches 2—crew cars, re-built, second-hand coaches 2—baggage cars, re-built, second-hand coaches 1—work diner, second-hand dispensary car 4—Budd self-propelled rail cars, stainless steel

TOTAL ROLLING STOCK—481 pieces.

The railroad continued and expanded its Advanced Trade Training Program at Dammam. Employees took intensive three-month courses in railroad operation, maintenance, and administration. The courses are given on a rotation basis, with employees returning to their jobs for a year or more of practical application in between training periods. Permanent training facilities were completed and additional training specialists recruited.

Hijaz Railway. The name, Hijaz Railway, immediately conjures up pictures of Colonel T. E. Lawrence repeatedly wrecking parts of it during World War I. Very wisely he did not destroy the railway but did sufficient damage to prevent large-scale troop movements and to keep a large number of Turks repairing and guarding it. This considerably decreased the number of men available to fight against Allenby in the Palestine campaign.

Since the 1918 armistice no repairs have been made south of Maan, Jordan. The dates of 1907 and 1908 are still evident on the twisted steel ties and rails, which were manufactured in France. In many cases the culverts are blasted or washed out. Along the railway line and at some of the stations are wrecks of locomotives and steel frames of cars. The Bedouins undoubtedly used the wood for their camp fires. It is all a sad sight.

The railway, with a length of 840 kilometers, or 522 miles, in the Hijaz, was built by contributions from Moslems throughout the Islamic world. The title still remains with the "Waqf" (the Islamic treasury for gifts, bequests, and investments). King Abdul Aziz tried to get the nations who destroyed this religious railway to restore it to use, but he met with no success. During World War II, I proposed to the Saudi government that a road should be made over the railway roadbed in return for selling the badly needed steel, as scrap, to the Allies. The reply was that this was the property of the "Waqf" so the Saudi government did not have the right to dispose of it.

During the years since World War II there were sporadic talks regarding making a preliminary survey of the line with a view to its rehabilitation. Such a survey was finally made under the auspices of Point Four during the spring of 1954. Subsequently a Tripartite Commission was set up in Damascus to administer the proposed reconstruction. It invited combined engineering and construction bids and selected a Polish group in 1955. But when the initial survey team entered Saudi Arabia early in 1956, King Saud ordered them out of the country and caused the contract to be cancelled because they were Communists. Subsequently, an engineering contract was given to Brown & Blauvelt of New York City by the Saudi Arabian Ministry of Communications. They are now actively engaged on this enterprise. (I am indebted to Mr. Fred Awalt of Michael Baker Jr. Inc. for the above information.)

A letter of March 5, 1957 from Saudi Arabian Ambassador Shaikh Abdullah Kayyal, stated that King Saud had donated the sum of 2,000,000 Syrian liras ($400,000) to finance the surveys and had made agreements with Jordan and Syria regarding the construction.

Now that Turkey has lifted the ban against the pilgrimage to Mecca, there should be a large passenger traffic from that country as well as from Iran, Iraq, Syria, Lebanon, and Jordan but freight will be a minor item.

The American firm of Brown & Blauvelt, New York City, consulting civil engineers, has completed a survey of the Hijaz Railway from Medina to Maan. Their report was made and sent to the Hijaz Railway Committee for their decision. It stated four alternatives as follows:

1. Rehabilitation of the original 105 centimeter (41 inches) gauge track of 21.5 kilograms per meter (43.2 pounds per yard), and ties at 70.6 centimeter (27.5 inches) spacing.

2. Using the existing rail but adding ties where necessary, to make all spacing at 54 centimeters (21 inches).

3. Using existing acceptable rail, but all new rail to be 29.76 kilograms per meter (60 pounds per yard) and use of wood ties at 61 centimeters (23.8 inches) from center to center.

4. Replacement of all rail with new 29.76 kilograms per meter (60 pounds per yard) and installation of all new wood creosoted ties at 61 centimeters (24 inches approximately) spacing.

Personally, I would emphatically recommend the fourth alternative, unless the following proposal is adopted. This additional proposal seems to be of even more importance than the four listed. It would cost more than any of the original four alternatives but should give much greater ultimate benefits to Saudi Arabia and to the adjoining state of Jordan. This suggestion is to make all the Hijaz Railway of standard gauge, with the same type of 80-pound rails as are in use on the Riyadh-Dammam line. Although the initial cost would be greater than the existing narrow gauge railroad, the upkeep, the cost per ton mile of freight, and the units of equipment would all be less. The reasons are that a car of an average narrow gauge train would carry about 15 tons and there would be usually between 30 and 40 cars per train, or a maximum of 600 tons for one locomotive. Standard gauge cars have capacities of 50 to 70 tons and trains of 100 to 125 cars. Taking 100 cars would make 5,000 tons per locomotive and train crew, or 8 to 10 times as much tonnage as the narrow gauge unit. The number of passengers transported per train is not in the same ratio but is still greatly in favor of the standard gauge cars.

Diesel engines would naturally be used, since they are so much more efficient than steam locomotives as well as easier on the track and roadbed—thus lowering the maintenance expense. The fuel would be obtained from the Saudi Arabian oil fields.

Another factor is the development of the phosphates in Jordan. These are excellent fertilizers which would benefit many of the Hijaz, Najd, and Hasa farming areas. The cost of this fertilizer would be materially increased if it had to be transferred at Medina from the narrow to the standard gauge cars. The small gauge, being very limited in its distribution, necessitates specially manufactured equipment more expensive than standard size.

If the 60-kilometer (37 mile) railway is constructed from Maan to the head of the Gulf of Aqaba, sea transport would be available, but the line to Medina and Jidda would be a safeguard against the Gulf of Aqaba being blocked.

Aviation

Aviation has had an astounding record, as well as development.

The January 1, 1957, budget approved the amount of 40,-000,000 *riyals* or $10,800,000 for the Ministry of Defence and Aviation.

The air service (as of June 1957) consists of 5 Bristols, 10 Convairs, 13 Dakotas, 5 Skymasters and trainer planes, including Jets. The air service has been organized under TWA personnel but with General Ibrahim Al-Tassan in complete charge. The American personnel are continually training Saudi Arabs in maintenance as well as to be pilots. The record has been nothing short of miraculous, for there has *never* been a crash or serious accident, although millions of passenger miles have been flown. The airplane crews are now Saudi Arab, with the exception of the chief pilot, who is American.

Passengers, mail, and cargo are carried between the following towns according to the Saudi government statement: Riyadh, Hofuf, Dhahran, Medina, Jidda, Abha, Najran, Hail, Shakra, Anaiza, Majmaa, Yenbo, Wejh, Tabuk, Sakaka, Jizan, and others. Only Jidda, Riyadh, and Dhahran are first-class airports provided with lighting systems for night operation. The airport at Medina is being brought up to this status. The 1957 budget allocated 2,000,000 *riyals* ($540,000) for "Medina projects." Jidda, the initial airport, was first run by TWA but now entirely by the Saudi government. There are two paved runways, 6,000 feet and 6,500 feet long, ample for nearly all types of planes. There is an up-to-date control tower with adequate equipment and offices, as well as a terminal building with passenger, baggage, mail, freight, customs, and restaurant facilities. In addition, there are complete shops for maintenance, including main overhauls of engines. Regular external flights are made with passengers, mail, and freight from Saudi Arabia to Cairo, Beirut, Damascus, Amman, and Khartoum. The ultimate objective is to establish links with the important cities of the world.

Connections with Egypt, Syria, and Lebanon are maintained by Misr Airlines, Air Liban, and Saudi Arabian Airlines. The M.A.T.S. (Military Air Transport Service, U.S.) makes calls at Jidda as well as at Dhahran. Swissair has recently made arrangements to include Saudi Arabia in its calls.

Aden Airways, affiliated with B.O.A.C. (British Overseas Air Company), had flights from Cairo through Jidda and Port

93

Sudan to Aden, Massawa, and Addis Ababa up to the British-French-Israeli invasion of Egypt on October 29, 1956. It is probable these services will be resumed as soon as diplomatic relations with Britain are reinstated but to the present (May 1958) these have not been restored.

The oil company, Aramco, has 17 airplanes in active service. It maintains a service between Dhahran and New York City of two round trips weekly. Aerial photograph surveys are made. For keeping contact with the eight exploration parties, especially the seismic party in the central Rub al-Khali (the tremendous desert aptly named The Empty Quarter) and a gravity-magnetic party in the eastern section of this area, there was complete reliance on air transport for supplies. These included food, water, and gasoline, in addition to personnel. The light De Haviland "Beaver" aircraft proved excellent for use on the sandy areas. Planes have been especially valuable in patrolling the Trans-Arabian Pipeline and in many emergencies.

The foregoing facts are emphatic evidence that air service has made enormous strides since the first planes were delivered to the Saudi government by the British Air Force prior to World War II, the Bellanca "Sky-rocket" used by the Saudi Arabian Mining Syndicate from 1935 to 1937, and the folding wing Fairchild flown by Aramco at about the same time.

Shipping

In the maritime field, Saudi Arabia is planning great developments. It has already put into commission one of the world's largest tankers *Al Malik Saud El Awal* (King Saud I), with a stated capacity of 47,000 tons dead weight. The U.N. Delegate from Saudi Arabia, Dr. Omar Khadra, has stated "23 tankers were ordered constructed and they will soon join the Saudi fleet." But such a large program is subject to modifications and delays.

Jidda is an important seaport; 1,600 ships docked there in 1956. Among the lines which call more or less regularly in

Jidda are the Isthmian Line, Blue Funnel, Ellerman Lines, the Mogul Line, Holland Lloyd, Khedivial Mail, and formerly Lloyd Trestino, also coastwise vessels of the Ali Reza Zainal firm. In bringing supplies for merchants and government, the ships of the Isthmian Line, Roosevelt Pioneer Line, and Shell Company tankers call. The German Hansa Line made occasional calls in prewar days. Aramco tankers bring oil products from Ras Tanaura, in the Persian Gulf.

Dhows constitute the other means of coastal shipping. The lines of the sea-going dhows, such as those built at Jizan, as has been mentioned before, are thought to be the same as those which the Phoenicians used in their trade with Cornwall and the Mediterranean ports. The Saudi government commenced its merchant marine only a few years ago with four or five modified dhows equipped with slow-speed Diesel engines. These boats, which the Arabians call "lanches," have the usual great lateen mainsail besides the engine. These ships' capacities are up to 100 tons, and the *al-Medina* took thirty passengers from Jizan to Jidda. Most of the privately owned dhows are smaller and have sails only. They carry a considerable total amount of goods, since much of the overseas steamer freight entering Jidda is distributed to various ports by sail.

Formerly all deep-sea freight was lightered by sailing dhows to the old customs quay, but in 1951 the new government-financed pier was completed by International Bechtel Corporation. This pier is 1,845 feet overall length and the approach causeway and trestle is 1,285 feet carrying a roadway 24 feet wide. The pierhead is 100 feet by 500 feet and it accommodates two freighters simultaneously. There is a 30-ton crane for heavy lifts.

In 1937 a pier was completed by the Saudi Arabian Mining Syndicate Ltd. This extended 3,200 feet from shore and carried a 12-foot roadway. At the pierhead is a 15-ton capacity Diesel-engine-operated crane. At the pierhead the two fathoms depth of water provided for the berthing of two 50-ton steel lighters operated by a 60 HP tug. Supplies for the mine landed here and the gold ore concentrates and precipitates exported. Since the mine was worked out in 1954 and the company liquidated, this pier and installation have reverted to the Saudi government according to the terms of the concession.

Jidda is the most important port on the Red Sea in Saudi Arabia. Next in importance are Yenbo, 200 miles northerly, and Jizan, over 500 miles to the south. Wejh has a small harbor and lies 200 miles north from Yenbo. Formerly many pilgrims from Egypt and the north who were going to Medina were discharged in Yenbo, but in the past few years there have been very few, as practically all of them prefer to go first to Jidda and Mecca. About halfway between Yenbo and Wejh is the small but picturesque port of Umluj. Rabigh is another port, lying 96 miles north of Jidda, with an excellent small harbor. During World War I many supplies were landed here by the British for Lawrence and his troops. There is very little movement in this harbor now. North of Wejh about 90 miles is another small port called Duba. There are a number of fishing dhows here, also those which bring supplies from Wejh and Jidda. Still farther north is Muwailah. Near here are the dead oil seeps which have caused a certain amount of interest among the investigators of the country's resources. From Muwailah to the head of the Gulf of Aqaba there are no real ports. On the Saudi Arabian side of this gulf are few settlements or inhabitants. Between Jidda and Jizan the principal ports are Lith, Kunfida, Khor al-Birk, and Dhahaban.

On the Persian Gulf coast of Saudi Arabia, the Aramco ports of Dammam and Ras Tanura are the most important. Huge tonnages of supplies and equipment for the development of the oil fields pass through these two ports. At Dammam a pier has been constructed 7 miles long out to a depth of 45 feet of water at the pierhead. There are complete facilities for handling all types of cargo direct from ships to cars. The standard gauge railway extends to the end of the pier. In 1955 a total of 203 ships discharged cargoes here. Later figures are not available, but are larger, so much so that Ras Tanura has had to care for some 40 per cent of the supplies since the Dammam pier had become so congested.

The largest tonnage is of tankers at Ras Tanura. In 1955, 1,758 tankers and 66 freighters were handled, but less in 1956 due to the blocking of the Suez Canal, so 1,653 were serviced— an average of 148 monthly during the first ten months and 88 during each of the last two.

The marine headquarters of Aramco is at Ras Tanura and their transport in 1955 consisted of 17 tugs, 23 light craft, and 24 barges.

From Dammam the oil company runs a regular fast passenger service to Manama, Bahrain, daily. The oil tanker barges call at the oil docks a mile or two to the south of the main pier. Fifty miles to the south is Oqair, the former chief port through which most of the imports into Hasa and Najd passed. The ruins of an ancient town indicate that it has been a port for many centuries. Because of the facilities at the new ports of the oil company, the importance of Oqair has decreased to practically nil in the last few years.

Thirteen miles to the north of Dammam is Qatif. The extensive date groves of this oasis, and those of Sofwa just to the west, are the source of a considerable amount of freight in dates exported to Bahrain for consumption there, as well as some for trans-shipment. Tarut Island lies a mile or two to the east of Qatif. The space between Qatif jetty and Tarut is so shallow at low tide that the big sea-going Hasa donkeys form the transport instead of boats. To the north and east of Qatif is the previously mentioned oil port of Ras Tanura. King Abdul Aziz had long contemplated this as a deep seaport for eastern Saudi Arabia. He requested me to examine it and give an opinion regarding it in January 1932, before there was any oil company or concession. It looked favorable and it was so reported.

Approximately 40 miles north from Ras Tanura is the town of Jubail, which has long been used as another entry into northern Hasa and Najd. The harbor is shallow but there is protection for small boats. To the west at the edge of the sand dunes are springs and a flowing artesian well. About a mile northeastward out to sea occurs one of the great submarine springs. When I first visited it in early 1932, there was a large spar buoy marking the location so that the pearling vessels and others could obtain fresh water by letting down buckets. Nearly 60 miles north from Jubail and opposite abu-Hadriya oil field is the port of Manifa near which a new oil field is indicated. Northerly is the port for Safaniya oil field.

Both along the Red Sea coast and the Persian Gulf are numerous dangerous reefs. On the British Admiralty charts of the Red Sea Arabian coast, a warning is written which states that since the currents along here vary both in velocity and in direction, mariners should give extra wide berth to all reefs. In 1937 the Shell Company marine superintendent was sent to Jidda to inspect the harbor approaches and facilities for tankers calling to supply the mining company with Diesel oil to be used at the mine power plant. He came from Suez on an Italian ship of the Red Sea Line. About 20 miles north from Jidda the ship's captain disregarded the warning regarding currents, and his ship went aground on one of the reefs. The Shell superintendent was not well impressed with the Red Sea coast. It took a week of careful examination of all harbor beacons and buoys before he could overcome his initial prejudice and recommend Jidda and the mining company basin as safe for his ships to enter. As it happened, this was the only wreck that had occurred for many, many months!

Communications

The Director General of Posts and Telegraphs has charge of postal, telephone, cable, and wireless services. Early in his career King Abdul Aziz knitted his kingdom together by telephone and telegraph lines connecting Jidda, Mecca, and Taif and erected 14 Marconi wireless stations to connect Riyadh with all his other principal centers.

In these early days there was opposition by the extremist and puritanical Wahabis to anything not well understood, so their religious council, the "Ulema," questioned the King. He replied by having them assemble in one location and then went some distance away and read verses of the Koran which they clearly understood through the telephone receivers. They then agreed with His Majesty that if the word of Muhammad could be transmitted by this new equipment it could not be from the Devil! There was no subsequent objection to wireless or other rapid means of communication.

For communications abroad all messages were sent via the cable of the Eastern Telegraph Company between Jidda and Port Sudan, thence relayed to other parts of the world. This route was used until September 17, 1948, when the Mackay Radio and Telegraph Company Incorporated, an operating unit of the American Cable and Radio Corporation Inc., initiated direct service to New York from Jidda after having made a complete installation. The station was turned over to the Saudi government on October 15, 1951. The Saudi Arabs were so efficiently trained by Mr. Morgan (who made the installation) that he is now the only American employed.

The Saudi government has since inaugurated circuits between Jidda and Paris, as well as between Jidda and Rome.

Although messages are usually relayed via the Mackay Radio station at Tangier, Morocco, the service is practically a direct one and a great improvement in speed and accuracy over the former transmission systems. The Jidda station employs transmitters of 15 KW. There has been a tremendous growth of internal communications by radio, with installation and equipment of German radio equipment.

The following data indicate how important this system is

for communications between Saudi Arabia and the United States:

	NUMBER OF MESSAGES	
YEAR	*To Arabia*	*From Arabia*
1952	9,784	14,313
1953	7,359	7,261
1954	9,901	14,598
1955	12,553	16,725
1956	13,406	19,675
Jan.-June 1957	6,009	9,466

(Notes from W. J. Brennan, Manager, Business Department, American Cable and Radio Corporation, 67 Broad Street, New York City 44, N.Y.)

Telephonic communications are extensive. One can now talk direct from New York to Jidda and Riyadh, also from Riyadh to Egypt, Syria, Lebanon, Spain, and England. Inside Saudi Arabia there are lines connecting Jidda, Mecca, Taif, Riyadh, and Dammam. Some 4,000 phones of the dial type have been installed in Jidda. Riyadh is having similar equipment of German manufacture.

Broadcasting in Arabic is now being conducted in Jidda, Mecca, and Riyadh. Also to keep abreast of the times, two television stations are being erected in Dhahran. One is for Aramco and the other for the American Air Force.

The Press

Until the last very few years there were almost no local newspapers or periodicals published in Saudi Arabia. The following list indicates how rapidly the reading public has increased —naturally due to more widespread education.

	Published at	*Period*
Umm al-Qura	Mecca	Weekly, government
Khayrah	Mecca	Weekly, private
al-Manhal	Mecca	Monthly, private
al-Bilād al-Su'ūdīyah	Mecca	Daily, private
al-Ḥājj	Mecca	Monthly, government
al-Idhā'ah	Jidda	Monthly, government
al Zirā'ah (agriculture)	Jidda	Trimonthly or quarterly, government

TRANSPORTATION AND COMMUNICATIONS

al-Madīnah al-Munawwarah	Medina	Weekly, private
al-Yamāmah	Riyadh	Weekly, private
Akhbār al-Zahrān	Dammam	Biweekly, private
al-Shams wa-al-Wahīj	Dhahran	Weekly, Aramco
(in English by Aramco)		
Qafilat al-Zayt	Dhahran	Weekly, Aramco
Ḥajar	Hofuf	Monthly, private
al-Khalīj al-ʿArabi	Hofuf	Monthly, private

A total of twelve printing firms and presses are distributed among Jidda, Medina, Mecca, and Riyadh.

8. Important Centers of National Life

Mecca

IN ARABIC literature Mecca is often written "Mecca Al Mukarrama," meaning "The Blessed." It has for many centuries been the political capital of the kingdom of the Hijaz. Its fame, however, relates to its prestige as the foremost religious city in the Moslem world of some 350,000,000 people. The power and magnitude of this worldwide community has not adequately been understood in the West. Extending from the west coast of Africa as far eastward as the Philippines, and from Indonesia (formerly Java) lying about 10 degrees south of the equator to the Caucasus and Kirghis steppes at 40 degrees north latitude, the Moslem faith occupies a very impressive part of the earth's surface.

Birthplace of the Prophet Muhammad and home of the exalted Ka'ba, the destination of pilgrims from all parts of the Moslem world, Mecca is the first city of Hijaz and Saudi Arabia. Its outstanding feature is the great mosque which encloses the venerated shrine known as the Ka'ba, in one corner of which is the famous black stone—probably a meteorite—said to have been built by Abraham. It is obligatory for all Moslems to face this shrine when praying.

The five principal beliefs of Islam are: (1) There is one and only one Supreme Being. (2) Muhammad is his Prophet: and is the latest of the prophets. It is not believed that Muhammad was Divine. (3) Prayers are to be said five times daily. (4) Alms must be given and charity practiced. (5) The pilgrimage to Mecca must be made once during the lifetime of a good Moslem, but only if he or she is financially and physically able to do so. Alternatively, a proxy may be substituted.

Mecca lies at an elevation of about 1,400 feet and is 46 miles from the seaport of Jidda, an excellent asphalt road connecting the two cities. Like the hub of a wheel, its roads and trails radiate in all directions, although the only main highway is the one which passes from Jidda through the city, then proceeds easterly to Taif and Riyadh. Stone monuments—called in Arabic *alamat* (signs)—mark the limits of the Holy City beyond which non-Moslems may not go. Western travelers, Burton, Rutter, and Hurgronje, to name the three best known, have left us reliable descriptions of the Holy City, which need not be repeated here. The estimated population of 250,000 is doubled, if not tripled, during the pilgrimage season. During the "Hajj" or pilgrimage in 1956, the Saudi Consulate in New York City reported that there were 275,000 participants from abroad in this ceremony. To cope with this tremendous movement there are well-organized leaders called "Mutawafs" who take care of the reception at Jidda of groups of pilgrims, house them if necessary, at Jidda, transport them to Mecca, accommodate them there, and make the arrangements for their rituals including the trip to Muna and return.

A large quarantine station has been established at the south harbor of Jidda to care for the health of pilgrims. In the 1957 budget the sum of $167,270 was allocated for the completion of this station. At Mecca there are two large new well-equipped hospitals, modern as well as old-style hotels and guest houses. There are two royal palaces, schools, and a college, the latter of which teaches mainly religion. Moslem students of religion have studied during the past many years in the libraries.

It is not surprising that the sum of $16,200,000 was included in the 1957 budget for the item "Holy Mosque, Mecca," and that $1,080,000 was earmarked for "the Pilgrimage and the pilgrims."

Encompassed by rocky hills and subjected to intense summer heat, during the months of April to October the city which functions as the capital of Hijaz loses many of her leading citizens to Taif in the east, which serves as temporary capital of the province in the six hot months of the year.

103

Gravely concerned with the matter of water supply, which depended almost entirely upon Ain Zubaida about nine miles away, the Egyptian government sought to find a solution to the problem and went as far as to send a staff of engineers, some years ago, who made a thorough study of the situation, incorporating a specific proposal in their final report. An adequate supply is now being developed in the Wadi Fatima water-shed. When in residence at the Holy City, King Abdul Aziz in the past sent for his drinking water to a well several miles away known as Bir Joraina, at an elevation of 1,350 feet, where the freshest water of the neighborhood is found. Upon my suggestion, hand pumps were installed here and a cover was placed on the well to prevent contamination as the herds and sheep were watered. Considering the process of pumping too slow and onerous, however, the Bedouins broke the pumps and cast aside the cover. Resort might in the future be made to a small gas engine to operate the pumps, discharging into an elevated tank furnished with suitable valves. However, the water supply for Mecca has now been greatly increased, as have the number of electric and public utilities. Some streets, including the Muna road, have been paved. There is a five-year project to reconstruct the Great Mosque and to widen the streets of Mecca, at an estimated expense of $132,000,000.

It is to be expected that Mecca, the religious and cultural center of Saudi Arabia, would have the largest number of publications of any city in the country. The official government organ is *Umm al-Qura*, published weekly, which records government calls for bids, contracts, concessions, edicts, laws, and regulations. A privately published weekly periodical is called *Khera*. The only daily newspaper is *Belad El Saudia*, which is a private enterprise, as is the monthly *Al Manhal*. There is another monthly magazine called *El Hajj*, published by the government.

Medina

The burial place of Muhammad and scene of his temporal power, Medina is the second sacred city of the country and the Islamic world, wherein the entry of non-Moslems is also prohibited. It lies at an elevation of about 2,000 feet above the sea, is 239 miles north of Jidda, and has an estimated population of 60,000. Within the enclosure of its historic mosque stands the tomb of Muhammad. Noted for its beauty and simplicity, this mosque, the first sanctuary in Islam, was built by the Prophet upon his arrival from Mecca in July 622. Tradition has it that he let his camel wander unguided, despite many invitations to alight, until it finally stopped and knelt at the site which the Prophet forthwith designated for a house of worship. The original and ancient name of the city, Yathrib, was changed subsequent to his arrival therein to Madinat-al-Nabi (City of the Prophet), whence comes "Medina." Plentiful water permits cultivation of abundant fruits and vegetables, exceeding local need, but the inadequate transportation system offers little extension to the limited market. With the construction of good roads and the development of more mines, the prosperity of Medina has increased, its export of dates multiplied, and its general welfare advanced. A date-packing industry has been established. Since Medina dates are famous for their quality, it is probable that a lucrative and increasingly important export market will eventuate. Possibly other fruits as well as vegetables may be processed so that this industry may develop. The gardens of Medina have long enjoyed a great reputation for their excellence. Recently a rug factory has been initiated so another enterprise is potential.

The Saudi government's 1957 budget included $1,890,000 for additional work on the Medina-Jidda road; $675,000 for the Medina-Yenbo road; repairs and additions to the Prophet's Mosque, $1,080,000; and various projects for Medina, $540,-000. These allocations are further evidence of the widespread benefits of the great revenues from the oil development.

Taif

Delightfully situated at an elevation of 5,100 feet above the sea, Taif has an estimated population of 30,000 and is the summer capital of Hijaz where Prince Faisal ordinarily resides from April to October. He has a thriving farm at Howiya, 11 miles north of the city, where oranges, grapefruit, lemons, citrons, pears, and peaches are raised. Large fields of alfalfa and other grains are cultivated in the small farms and fields surrounding Taif. Many delicious grapes are shipped by camel and truck to Mecca and Jidda. The large area tributary to this city gives it the economic advantage of a large market. Its products include the characteristic woolen *beedis*, as well as woven wool and goat-hair rugs and carpets. The water supply is derived from wells and one fine spring.

The city boasts a comfortable, orderly, government-operated hotel, supplemented by a guest house with modern amenities for the more important visitors. A telephone exchange connects all government offices as well as many private houses. Its buildings are stone-granite, largely quarried in a spot to the southwest of the city. Of these the most remarkable is Shubra Palace, now an army warehouse, half a mile outside the former city wall, which was demolished in 1947, and had been built by the Turks when they ruled Hijaz. The palace consists of three floors, with spacious chambers about 16 feet high, and is surrounded by orchards. In the suburbs, smaller stone houses are beginning to rise, indicating an increase in the number of people from Mecca, Jidda, and elsewhere who seek this place as a summer resort.

Taif is recognized as one of the oldest cities in Hijaz. Of its several mosques, the largest is one at which the Prophet is thought to have worshiped once, although he had not been cordially received in the city at the beginning. A certain degree of sanctity attaches to the name of Taif today and non-Moslems are admitted only by special permission from the highest political authority.

About A.D. 627 the army of the Prophet Muhammad besieged Taif for forty days without success and then retired. Within a year the Taifites sent a delegation to Medina and declared that the Prophet was their spiritual as well as political leader. It was during this siege that Muhammad used catapults for shooting stones and also employed covered cars or hand driven tanks. (*The Battlefields of Muhamed* by Muhammed Hamidullah.) This action may be considered the forerunner of the American and British military missions at Taif in 1945 and following, for they trained the Saudi Arab army in the use of armored cars and mobile artillery.

The present city of Taif has a modern power plant which furnishes it with electricity. This company has Saudi Arab shareholders and the plant is operated by Saudis.

For telephone services, $10,753 was budgeted in 1957. There are good schools in the city, and a large modern hospital is nearing completion. The importance attached to this hospital, named "al-Sadad," may be judged by the fact that the sum of $319,643 was set aside for it in the 1957 budget.

Jidda

The main Red Sea seaport of Saudi Arabia, Jidda has an estimated population of 200,000 and is 190 miles from Port Sudan and 711 miles from Suez. Much of the drinking water supply was formerly obtained by condensing sea water in a plant that had a daily capacity of 150 tons. The desire of the government for a more adequate supply has been met by having the water resources of the springs above Hadda, up the Wadi Fatima, tapped by the use of a pipeline approximately 50 miles in length. A doubling of this line is contemplated. The present water system has been described in the chapter on "Water Resources."

Jidda was a walled city; the gate facing south was called the Yemen, the one facing toward the Holy City, the Mecca Gate, and that facing north was the Medina Gate. In 1947 the walls and gates were demolished. The oil company offices and all the legations are located along the waterfront between the

Medina Gate and the customs quay and post office. A telephone exchange connects the main public and private establishments in the city. A sum of $7,047 was budgeted in 1957 for work on the automatic telephone building. In the southern outskirts there is a walled cemetery for non-Moslems, whereas that of the Moslems is to the east. A mile southeast is the new palace called Kazam, to the south of which spreads out the village of Nazla. Northeast of the city are a government guest house, called Khundra, and a modern, air-conditioned hotel named the Kandara Palace Hotel, as well as many smaller places to accommodate pilgrims and travelers. To the east are large hangars and an air field, paved and lighted.

A new pier has been constructed at Saudi government expense by International Bechtel Incorporated. This is located a mile south of the old Customs and Quarantine Quay (a site I had recommended in 1947). It is operated by the old Saudi firm of Ali Reza Zainal, or "Beit Zainal," under contract with the Saudi government. The pier extends into 32 feet of water at low tide and at the pierhead, 100 feet by 560 feet, two deep-sea vessels can dock alongside. The causeway fill is 5,500 feet long and the steel trestle approach with the pier is 2,243 feet long. The roadway is 24 feet wide.

On the pier are the modern custom house offices. On the northern side are extensive warehouses and on the southern side ample accommodations for pilgrims. Offices of coast guard and passport officials are here also. There is a lighthouse tower in the center of the customs building to facilitate entering the port.

Pier facilities for handling cargoes include the following:

```
1 Stiffleg derrick (American Hoist & Derrick Co.)
  capacity    50 tons    at    60 ft. radius
     "        41   "      "    68 ft.    "
     "        35   "      "    78 ft.    "
4 Tow-motors and 7 trailers
2 Portable 5 ton cranes, "Loraine," 30 ft. boom
1 Portable 10 ton crane, "Bay City," 40 ft. boom
1 Tug, "Abdullah Sulaiman," reported to be 700 HP
```

108

There are ample facilities for fueling oil burning vessels of all types and sizes.

As the industrial center of western Saudi Arabia, Jidda is the natural location for banks. By far the longest established is the Netherlands Trading Society of Holland. For many years Gellatly Hankey & Co., Ltd., did an excellent business representing the British Westminster Bank, Ltd., but information recently received states that this service has been discontinued.

The American Express Company and the National City Bank of New York have offices in Jidda, as do the British Bank of the Middle East, the French bank of Indo-Chine, the Bank of Pakistan, the Bank of Lebanon, Bank of Egypt, Cairo Bank, and Arab Bank. There are thus appreciable foreign financing facilities. National banking enterprise is evidenced by the National Commercial Bank of Saudi Arabia. The Bank of Riyadh has been formed and located in that city.

The Saudi Monetary Agency was established June 13, 1952. Its purpose was to strengthen the currency of Saudi Arabia in relation to foreign currencies. This has now been accomplished. Mr. George A. Blowers, with long experience in Addis Ababa as chief of the Bank of Ethiopia, laid the foundations of this Saudi Arabian financial department; he was succeeded by Mr. John Standish. Dr. Samuel Stratton, chief of Point Four, was vitally interested in this work. The successful introduction of paper currency, called "receipts," was a real feat in a country which had always used only gold and silver coinage. Many transactions have been greatly facilitated by the transition from coinage.

A twenty-room building has just been entirely remodeled to house the monetary agency.

Jidda has been the home of all foreign embassies, legations, and delegations. The principal ones are the Embassies of the United States of America, Spain, Egypt, Syria, Lebanon, Iraq, Sudan, Pakistan, India, and Afghanistan. The following countries have legations—Jordan, Tunisia, Turkey, Indonesia, West Germany, Italy, and Switzerland. Until the Suez crisis, of course, there were also the British and French.

A telephone system containing 4,000 dial phones of German make greatly facilitates diplomatic, social, and business intercourse. Formerly most governmental departments were located in Jidda, but they are now being moved to Riyadh to make it the true capital of Saudi Arabia.

Since Jidda was the port for Mecca from time immemorial it has had quarantine facilities. These are on two islands in the inner harbor, some five or six miles southerly from the new pier. During the past few years these facilities have been improved and enlarged. The present capacity is 3,000 persons. In the 1957 budget the sum of $121,933 was designated for "the basic works of the quarantine station."

In Jidda 5.9 miles of street paving was installed by Michael Baker Jr., Inc. This firm also made a study for plans for a complete sewage system, including sewage disposal. It is most important that this be accomplished in the near future since many residences are located near the lagoon in the northern part of the city where there is no drainage, so serious disease from sewage is almost certain to occur. The numerous new buildings have modern European plumbing as well as electricity but, to be sanitary, it is vital that sewage disposal is adequate.

Power plants totaling 9,300 KW furnish light, air conditioning, and small power units for this rapidly growing city. In 1942 the population was estimated at 25,000 so one can imagine how remarkably it has developed to reach the present 200,000.

The old government hospital has been renovated and increased in capacity, and a new one built. Several privately operated nursing homes in addition to the old British Embassy Clinic have been established. At the airport an additional customs building has been constructed and a school for Saudi Air

Force instruction. Accommodations have been extended for the American personnel of the Saudi airlines. Facilities include water supply, electricity, and modern plumbing.

King Saud, his council of Ministers and Chamber of Commerce (the latter fostered by the Ali Reza Zainal), are eager to have various small industries established in Jidda and vicinity. An appreciable amount of success has crowned their efforts. One of the first productive enterprises was that of quarrying and processing of marble. This was entirely due to the initiative of Mohamed Bin Ladin and his brother. Italian equipment and personnel have been imported. Beautiful marble tiles, panels, and mosaics are produced in quantity. A soap factory of 900 tons capacity, sufficient for the country's needs, is in operation. Although the bulk of Saudi Arabs still wear sandals—very well adapted to a hot climate—there is a new factory which produces 700 pairs of shoes daily, together with travelling bags and ladies' handbags.

There are many garages and small machine shops which are kept busy in the repair and maintenance of motor vehicles. The dust and sand of this arid country cause excessive wear on all machinery, especially on automobiles.

Excellent brick and tiles have long been produced in Jidda but the output has lately been greatly increased. Medina, Riyadh, and Dammam have similar production.

For several years furniture of good style and quality has been manufactured. This industry had to develop slowly, for not many years ago, long benches—"rochans"—placed along the walls of rooms served in place of chairs. For dining, large circular mats, three feet or more in diameter, were laid on the floor. The dishes of the meal were placed on these, with the diners sitting cross-legged around the repast. Hands were used in place of knives and forks.

In addition to the furniture factory in Jidda, there is a branch at Hadda, some 23 miles up the Wadi Fatima toward Mecca.

111

With the advance in the technique of metal working in which oxygen is used so largely for cutting and welding steel and iron, a large amount of oxygen is consumed. A plant has now been established for furnishing this oxygen; it provides for some export as well as local consumption.

Limited cotton textile work is being commenced.

The Saudi Arabian News, published monthly by the Saudi Arabian Embassy in Washington, D.C., stated in its July 1957 issue that King Saud had laid the foundation stone of a plant of the Arab Cement Company. This is located 8 miles northerly from Jidda on the Medina road. No information was given regarding the number of barrels per day of cement output expected.

Yenbo

With an estimated population of 10,000, Yenbo ranks next to Jidda as an important seaport of Hijaz, possessing a well-protected and deep, though small, harbor, and a wireless telegraph station. Derived from condensed sea water and water impounded in cisterns, the drinking supply will be improved when the fresh supply, 26 miles distant, is piped into the town. Like most of the country's political administrators, the Governor of Yenbo is a man from Najd. He is assisted by a Director of Finance, a Chief of Customs, and a leader of religious matters.

Yenbo is the port of Medina, but the 131-mile-long road joining the two cities is far from being a motor highway, and trucks can carry only part load over it, but the 1957 budget included the sum of $675,000 for its reconstruction. Easterly from the city are the numerous villages dotting the Wadi Yenbo (better known as Yenbo Nakhl, "Yenbo of the palm groves"). Farther up are the Wadi Ais with date groves and villages, and the Wadi Jizal, with the ancient remains of a vanished civilization and agricultural activity. Only a very few nomads are seen today roaming the Wadi Jizal, and there are no fixed habitations. North from Yenbo is the small fishing village of Umluj, then the port of Wejh at a distance of 186 miles.

Wejh

Picturesquely situated on a bluff facing the sea, Wejh has a population estimated at 10,000 and a harbor of deep water which, however, is only large enough for the 1,500-ton ships of the Khedievial Mail Line. As at other ports, the cargoes are lightered between ship and shore. The roof of the Governor's house has a commanding view, and the edifice was immortalized by T. E. Lawrence, who set up headquarters in it during the Arab campaign in World War I. The water supply is derived from wells a mile inland with a new one drilled under Point Four auspices. About 9 miles to the east are the ancient mines of Umm Garayat, worked by King David, according to the accounts of antiquity. The Saudi Arabian Mining Syndicate gave serious thought to the possibility of reopening the ancient mines in this region but, after diamond drilling and careful sampling, it was proved that there was nothing of sufficient size and value here to justify the necessary investment. For examining the northern part of the Hijaz, the company decided to use Wejh as one of its airplane bases, and a satisfactory flying field was cleared. This was used during the two years of prospecting the mines concession, but it is too small for present-day planes.

A few miles to the east, an Egyptian fortress—one of the series of forts that have been built on the pilgrims' route at intervals of twenty to thirty miles—rises with its cut-stone buildings of medieval architecture, flanking towers, battlements, rooms along the walls, and central courtyard refreshed by a well. In the days preceding the Saudi regime, pilgrims in Saudi Arabia were at the mercy of highway robbers and could buy protection from the local shaikhs only at an exorbitant price. Hence, the deep concern of Egypt for the safety of her citizens

113

traveling with the pilgrim caravans between Suez and Mecca led to the establishment of these fortresses (*qal'ah*) for their protection.

Abha

The beautifully situated city of Abha, with an approximate population of 25,000, is the capital of Asir province. It stands at an elevation of 7,000 feet above sea level, a basin surrounded by terraced fields and villages, with mountains rising to a height of 9,000 feet in the haze of the west and northwest. A rainfall of 10 to 12 inches causes the mountain slopes to be covered with a carpet of green vegetation; some of the fields are cultivated without the need for irrigation. The Wadi Abha, a small stream carrying several floods each year, flows through the northern side of the city.

A former governor of Asir, al-Amir Turki Sudairi, was eager to increase the prosperity of his province. To that end, he was anxious to advance to construction of good roads and to further agricultural activity. He invited me to investigate the possibility of a dam to store flood waters of the Wadi Abha, and, with A. L. Wathen of the U.S. Agricultural Mission, I suggested in 1942 a suitable location for the dam, pending further action by the government.

The buildings of Abha are of the stone and mud brick multiple-eave variety, typical of Asir, with the exception of the fortresslike Governor's offices, residence, and barracks, which are entirely of stone. There are flat roofs everywhere. Two well-built stone-arched bridges cross the Wadi Abha.

Most of the hills and mountain tops surrounding Abha are crowned by stone fortresses built by the Turks. Under the rule of ibn-Saud and King Saud all but one of these forts are empty today; the one remaining in use commands the main route up from the Tihama plains, as well as Abha and the road to Abha coming from Khamis Mushait to the east.

114

The Jidda airport, with a Saudi Arabian Airlines plane

Aerial view of Jidda, taken shortly before the city walls were demolished in 1947

Entrance to the City of Learning in Jidda

A former royal palace now converted to a part of the City of Learning

Beit Baghdadi, in Jidda, typical of the older Arab architecture

The Ministry of Foreign Affairs, in Jidda, recently completed

Street widening in Riyadh, the capital of Saudi Arabia

Government tuberculosis hospital between Jidda and Mecca

Pilgrim caravan within a day's journey of Mecca after traveling sixty-seven days from Damascus. Pilgrims now also come by air, train, and motor transport

Signpost on the route to Mecca near the boundary of sacred territory

A further warning of off-limits for non-Moslems

The Ka'ba in Mecca, toward which the world's Moslems (approximately 300,000,000) bow five times daily in prayer

A street in Medina, the other sacred city of Saudi Arabia. In the background is the dome of the mosque where the Prophet Muhammad was buried

The earliest dated Islamic inscription, AH 58 or AD 680. This is chiselled in the rock wall at one end of a dam for soil conservation a few miles east of Taif

Mortar in the ruins of Dhat-al-Okdood, Najran, a city which is the locale of one of the earliest legendary Christian martyrs

The Hijaz Railway, financed by Moslem contributions, was wrecked by Colonel Lawrence in World War I. Surveying for its replacement has been accomplished

A fortress near Wejh, one of many built by Egyptians in past centuries to protect their pilgrims going to Mecca

Jizan

The capital of the Tihama region of Asir, and one-time seaport of the Idrisids, Jizan, with a population estimated to be 10,000, is located atop a promontory which the encircling high tides sometimes turn into a veritable island. A stone fortress rises on the most commanding hillock to a height of 100 feet above water. The Governor's residence is also made of stone, as are nearly half of the town's habitations, whereas the rest are of the straw-roofed, wooden frame type. The fire hazard incurred by the highly inflammable straw-covered houses moved the Governor, al-Amir Khalid Sudairi in 1942 to stipulate that hereafter none but stone buildings could be erected.

There is a considerable export-import business between the Yemen and the seaports along the Jizan coast. The shipwrights are extremely adept in the building and repair of dhows, using, as previously observed, the natural bend of timber to produce a seaworthy ship. In an open pit near the south edge of Jizan, another industry, the extraction of rock salt, thrives. Suggested improvements, involving the employment of modern methods for stripping and mining the salt, now await vigorous, efficient development. In view of its extensive commercial connections with the hamlets of the Farasan Islands in the west, with abu-Arish and Hummaya in the southwest, added to its vital contact with the centers of population in Sabya and Tihama, Jizan possesses a background favorable to growth. Formerly, caravans of camels, each camel loaded with an average of 8 5-gallon gasoline tins, transported water from springs a few miles inland to the city. This system of water supply has now been replaced by a pipeline recommended by Point Four.

Kunfida

Two hundred miles south of Jidda is another important seaport of Asir, Kunfida, with a population of 8,000 to 10,000 and a considerable hinterland in the foothills of the Hijaz-Asir mountain wall at a distance varying from 10 to 20 miles due east. Its two-story buildings are flat-roofed, with numerous large windows, and are whitewashed on the exterior and interior. The more modest dwelling places have straw sides and roofs, woven over a heavy wooden frame. The water supply is derived from pits about 2.5 miles inland. A pipeline is being planned. As with Abha, the development of Kunfida is considered essential to the general welfare of the entire region.

Najran

The Najran valley is at the southern end of Asir, with the Yemen boundary lying along the mountains just to the south of it. It is estimated that some 10,000 people occupy this vicinity. The valley has an average altitude of 4,000 feet and is 27 miles long from its head at the ancient dam, called Mufija, to its emergence from the hills onto the great plains extending eastward to the Empty Quarter. The average width of the valley is about three miles. There are several villages in the valley, but life in Najran centers around the Governor's fortresslike headquarters four miles from the head. The offices, the official residence, the barracks, guest and audience rooms and stores are located inside compound walls, as is the wireless station. Just outside, to the east, is the government hospital.

The Governor's buildings are two stories high, of sun-dried mud "bats," not bricks, a type of construction peculiar to Asir, so far as I have seen. These cylindrical "bats" are approximately 18 inches long by 12 inches in diameter. The farmhouses in the valley are surrounded by walled fields of alfalfa, date palms, and so forth, and are four or five stories high. They were originally built for defense against raiders as well as to afford more comfortable sleeping quarters. The livestock occupy the first floor, which serves as a barn; in the second is usually stored the harvested crops.

Riyadh

Situated in the Wadi Hanifa at an elevation of 1,700 feet

above sea level, Riyadh is the capital of Saudi Arabia. It has been expanding tremendously in the past few years. In 1946 the population was estimated at 60,000 people; in 1952, 80,-000; and in 1957, 350,000. The moving of most of the governmental offices to Riyadh, formerly located in Jidda, in addition to the greatly increased commerce with the Persian Gulf area, due to the railway, and the development of many branches of government activity in this city, account for most of the remarkable growth.

Discovery of an immense reservoir of sub-surface water has caused a great extension of the city limits because of the possibility of residences being surrounded by ever highly prized gardens. Details of this valuable asset are given in Chapter 5. The government is placing great importance on this matter as evidenced by its 1957 budget designating $464,022 for the Riyadh dam project.

For many years palaces have been built, first by the late King Abdul Aziz ibn-Saud and then for, and by, various of his princely sons. The largest one of the old style and type was called "Muraba," or square palace. This was built of sun-dried mud bricks two stories high with the usual Saudi Arab flat roof and crenelated parapet around its edge. This, as well as the other numerous royal residences, had the inevitable central courtyard which undoubtedly represents the original early Semitic house plan. This type of architecture was carried by the Arabs into Spain and from there introduced into the New World, where it persists in different forms, notably in the patios of buildings in Mexico, South America, and the Pacific coast of the United States. This construction is a great contrast to the present modernistic style prevalent in most of the newest buildings which are characteristic of Europe. The older type is pleasingly typical of Najd. The architect of the new building for the Ministry of Foreign Affairs in Jidda has achieved a happy blending of the old and the new. Tremendous efforts are being made toward developing Riyadh into a capital city worthy of a great Islamic country. It is reported that the immense sum of $200,000,000 is being spent to attain this goal.

King Saud has two palaces in Riyadh, as has Prince Faisal. There are several others for the older members of the royal family. For many years various palaces have been used as guest houses but now an elaborate guest house has just been completed. It is modern in every respect, including lighting and plumbing, which in the old days were conspicuous by their absence. But there was great charm in the old-time primitive surroundings. The gigantic figure of King Abdul Aziz with his ministers, advisors, and friends sitting on the floor around a great mat piled high with a sheep on top of and surrounded by rice, and many dishes of chicken, soups, vegetables, fruits, and sweets, make an unforgettable picture. Such an informal friendly atmosphere can hardly be duplicated at the modern tables with chairs.

The brochure produced by the Saudi Arabian Embassy in Madrid, Spain, in honor of the recent visit of King Saud states that he is daily host in Riyadh to a maximum of 10,000 and a minimum of 800 guests. I think these fabulous figures must include the large numbers of Bedouin chiefs and tribesmen who periodically visit the capital to receive their annual subsidies.

In addition to guest houses there are two new hotels, the Railway and the Airport. Both are reportedly completely modern and expensive.

Early in his career King Abdul Aziz installed a powerful Marconi radio station in Riyadh to keep him in close touch with all his principal cities and towns. This system has been greatly amplified by King Saud. Telephones are being installed through the city. In 1956 he inaugurated a new line by which he spoke to President Nasser in Cairo. Now there is direct contact with America and Europe both by telephone and telegraph.

The amount of $237,481 has been budgeted for 1957 to finance the Riyadh telephone project.

The present ruler is keenly interested in health and education. The huge modern government hospital is nearing completion. A sum of $551,923 was allocated for this account, while $177,750 is included in the 1957 budget for financing four clinics, also in Riyadh.

Parks and gardens are being greatly expanded and streets are being widened and beautified by having parkways along their centers. These, I believe, are being financed and included in the $6,210,000 set aside in the 1957 budget for Riyadh projects.

"Electreeks," or lamps using kerosene vaporized by air pressure produced by individual air pumps, were universally the lighting for the palaces when I first visited Riyadh in 1932. Electricity is now the general method of lighting. It also furnishes the power for the increasingly numerous pumps which provide the irrigation water. Formerly donkeys, oxen, and camels hoisted the water in calf or goat skins for the same purpose. The 1957 budget includes $1,080,000 to finance additional electric power. The new railway from the Persian Gulf employs many tank cars to bring the oil for the Diesel-engined power plants that generate the electricity.

The recently established Bank of Riyadh undoubtedly facilitates the handling of many government financial matters.

Modern buildings have been completed to house the Military Academy of Abdul Aziz. Quoting from *The Kingdom of Saudi Arabia*, by Dr. Omar A. Khadra, Permanent United Nations Delegate of Saudi Arabia: "This is modeled after the best institutions in the West and is provided with all the necessary equipment for the training of Saudi Arabian officers in the arts of warfare. It can train approximately 600 officers each year in the science of ballistics and the new weapons of war. Officers are dispatched annually to Egypt, the United Kingdom, and the United States of America, to study and receive training in all aspects of modern warfare. Saudi Arabia has entered into a contractual arrangement with the Department of Defense, in

Washington, D.C., providing for Saudi Arabian officers to study for periods ranging from six months to one year in the various military installations of America. Each year approximately seventy-five officers arrive here (U.S.A.) in accordance with the provisions of the above-mentioned agreement."

Several ordnance factories are already producing various kinds of arms and ammunition. Unfortunately there were two accidents in a plant at Kharj where serious explosions occurred. This operation was furnished by a French company and was under French supervision. It is reported that this plant has now been repaired.

Special attention is given by the Ministry of Defense to military hospitals, mobile clinics, and other medical facilities.

A University of Saudi Arabia has been projected by the order of King Saud. All departments of a modern university are contemplated. The Saudi Theological Institute with its extensive library has become the principal center of learning in the country.

Primary and secondary schools established for some time are being expanded and a school for girls has recently been established. The latter was the outgrowth of an orphanage sponsored by a wife of Prince Faisal and other members of the royal family.

Riyadh is the present western terminus of the standard-gauge, 357-mile railway through the main oil fields to the Persian Gulf port of Dammam. Surveys have been made to extend this railway through Anaiza, Buraida, Medina, and Jidda to Mecca. It is reported that a construction contract has been signed with the American firm of Morrison, Knudsen & Co., but there is no advice that work has been commenced.

Although regular air service has been established only a few years, there is now an excellent modern airport and paved runway north of Riyadh, constructed by the Bechtel International Corporation. The port is well lighted to provide for night operation. The transition from camels to motor transport and then to the airplane in the brief period since 1930 is amazing.

Motor traffic is heavy in and around the city but a program of highway construction is greatly facilitating it. For roads around Riyadh the sum of $1,580,985 has been set aside. To expedite the transport of fruit, cereals, and vegetable products from the famous agricultural enterprise at Kharj 54 miles to the south, a paved road is being constructed. The amount of $1,620,000 was included in the 1957 budget for this project.

Broadcasting in Arabic is being done from Riyadh, as well as from Jidda and Mecca. It is reported that the programs are being expanded.

Buraida

A city of about 50,000 inhabitants, Buraida lies in the northern part of Wadi Rumma's left bank. It is especially favored by the salubrity of the climate and by its proximity to the Wadi, whose water, though not very fresh to the taste, affords the city an immense means of agricultural development—hence the large-scale cultivation of the palm tree and the growing of many orchards, as well as plantations of tamarisk trees. Buraida is believed to be the world's leading camel market. Indeed it is one of Najd's foremost centers of population, and has acquired, largely due to its focal position in a region of fifty villages, a tremendous degree of wealth and prosperity, making it an economic asset to the country at large. As one of the busiest and cleanest marts in Najd, Buraida has won notoriety for its wide though characteristically winding streets, formerly excelling in this respect even Riyadh itself. The commodious quarters of the Governor are attractively set within the ramparts of the city's fortress which, but for the six unpretentious mosques, forms the chief architectural center of interest. A four-story building of impressive size, the fortress rises in the northeast of the city, has a wall 40 feet high, and is six hundred years old, with a tower nearly 50 feet in diameter from whose top one gets a splendid view of the countryside.

Anaiza

Eighteen miles north from Buraida, on a wadi that is tributary to Rumma, spreads out the city of Anaiza, long a competitor of Buraida. It has been acclaimed as the Paris of Najd, and it is a vital center in the economic life of the province, as a link on the long lines of commercial communication with Egypt, Iraq, and India. Moreover, the friendliness and courtesy of the Anaiza folk stand in marked contrast to the proverbial aloofness of Buraida. With an estimated population of 50,000, the city boasts over Buraida, also, its cleaner and more orderly houses of sun-burned mud brick. The streets are generally narrow and crooked, with not even space for a single car to pass through. Gardens are walled in, leaving no open space on either side of the street. Surrounded by sandy plains, beyond the ring of orchards that extend a distance of two miles north, Anaiza must cope with the encroaching desert by a system of dikes and windbreaks of tamarisk trees.

Hail

Between the twin mountain ranges of Aja and Salma runs the Wadi Uqda, its northern part the background of Hail, capital of the defunct Rashid dynasty, whose defeat at the hands of the Sauds brought their first city into eclipse. Hail is 280 miles northeast of Medina, at an altitude of 2,800 feet, and has a population of about 30,000. Rising on a slight bluff in the broad valley, the city is protected at the southern end by two fortresses, each built on a separate hill. The larger fortress is about 50 feet above the city, whereas the smaller, Jabal Ayarif, is 90 feet above it. Built of cut-stone and reminiscent of medieval fortifications, these defenses with their battlements and flanking towers are extremely picturesque. Not far from the wireless station, housed in the main fortress, appears the Governor's residence on the edge of the city. The water supply is inadequate, since some of it must be hoisted from a depth of 75 feet. It is remarkable, nevertheless, that much cultivation goes on in Hail despite the scarcity of water, proving the observation by U.S. Agricultural experts that far too much water is generally used in irrigation in Saudi Arabia. Dates are the chief crop, but pomegranates, citrus fruits, and vegetables are also grown today. The main market street of Hail is unusually broad and a surprisingly large variety of commodities, consisting of local products and imported goods, are normally on sale in the shops and stores.

Hofuf

Hofuf, located in Hasa, was the seat of the provincial governor, and home of the two wealthy merchant families, the Qusaibis and Ajajis. The oasis of Hofuf is said to have a total population of 150,000, of whom 60,000 live in the city itself. Hofuf is a walled city within which an inner wall encloses the Governor's palace, embracing a mosque, administrative offices, private residences, and stables. The formidable inner walls are of limestone and sun-dried brick, ringed roundabout by a dry moat. Circular flanking towers are located at numerous points adjacent to the main wall, and a batter imparts greater stability and strength to the entire structure. A product of white limestone erosion, the soil from which the walls and buildings are made dazzles the eye in the intense sunlight.

A marketplace of broad dimensions, with buildings of one, sometimes two, stories, faces the wide street along the moat and wall of the citadel. The numerous narrow and winding streets of the market district are covered for protection against the sun's rays. Of two or three stories as a rule, its houses are marked by flat roofs, commonly used as sleeping quarters. The city is growing to such an extent that there are now many shops and small stores outside the main market.

The four Qusaibi brothers, and the former Minister of Fi-

123

nance, Shaikh Abdullah Salaiman, have very attractive pavilions in the date groves in Hofuf. The one owned by the Qusaibis is a large structure, located partly over the discharge of their spring, about 75 feet wide by 85 feet long, and 20 feet high to the roof in back. It is open on three sides, facing the garden, and the floor is elevated two or three feet above the ground level, affording a better view of the pomegranates, figs, papayas, and citrus trees growing among the date palms. The back quarter of the building is the usual two stories high; the upper story is used for resting and siestas, while the lower is for bathing. The tepid water from the spring runs through the length of this room, in which there is a long wall serving as a seat along each side to facilitate luxurious bathing.

According to F. S. Vidal (*The Oasis of Al-Hasa*) the establishment of Hofuf in A.D. 570 is open to doubt but it seems from the Islamic pottery found in the vicinity of the city walls that it was inhabited during the tenth century A.D.

The name Hofuf has a root meaning of "to hiss, whiz or blow"; it was the "cool and breezy place," due to the springs and palm groves.

The father of Saudi Arabia, King Abdul Aziz, captured the town from the Turks in 1913. It was the capital of the province of Hasa until February 1953 when it was replaced by Dammam.

The present-day city is an important stop on the Dammam-Riyadh Railway. The station building is of attractive Arabesque architecture rather than modernistic. In addition to numerous passengers, large tonnages of supplies are handled for the oil activities in the immense Ghawar field. Supplies are also shipped through to Kharj and Riyadh.

King Saud has extended education so there are now eight schools in the adjoining villages, large primary schools in Hofuf and the adjoining city of al-Mubarraz, a secondary school in Hofuf and a mosque assigned for instruction of women in afternoon periods. There were four night schools in

Hofuf and two in al-Mubarraz in 1952 but with the present rapid development of education fostered by King Saud the number has doubtless greatly increased—no data are at hand.

There is an excellent airport south of the town with a paved runway and adequate terminal facilities. Here also the architecture is harmonious with that of Hofuf. To house the travellers there is the Hofuf National Hotel. This also acts as the bus station.

As in all Saudi towns there are numerous mosques with their characteristic minarets. In Hofuf there are 40 per cent of the Shia branch of Islam and in al-Mubarraz the Sunni sect is of an equal proportion. These groups are the two major sects; there have been bloody wars between them so it is heartening to know that in Hasa the two denominations are living peacefully together. There is no segregation in the schools.

There are seven immense springs, one of which discharges 22,500 gallons of water per minute; 20 to 40 smaller springs are reported. These are responsible for the two million date palms which make the Hofuf area famous. In many of the groves rice is grown among the trees. The *khilas* have long been a notable date export.

The markets of Hofuf have imports of every sort from the world over. Prominent are automobile spares and mechanics' tools. The railway has greatly stimulated business, although the foundation of the rapid growth and prosperity is due to the employment by Aramco and the supplies purchased by its employees as well as to a limited extent by Aramco itself.

The local production includes the heavy wool *beedis*, a sort of winter blanket-coat, the *mashlah*, or outer gown almost universally worn by Saudi Arabs. This may be woven of wool or of camel's hair and is made in light weight for summer and heavy for winter wear.

Hasa is also famous for the manufacture of the *della* or coffee pot peculiar to Saudi Arabia. This ware is of both copper and brass. Material woven of goat hair is famous in the making of the "black tents of Arabia." Pottery and basketry are also produced.

The formation by local capital of the Hasa Electrical Supply Company will stimulate manufacturers if its rates per kilowatt are not excessive. With oil so closely available this enterprise should be beneficial for both the inhabitants and the shareholders.

Hospitals have been established and are being improved.

Dhahran

The headquarters of the Arabian American Oil Company, Dhahran, with a population of 12,500, is an entirely new town, situated on the hill of that name which rises 300 feet above the Persian Gulf, about 5 miles from the coast. This hill is the "dome" which constitutes the first oil field in Saudi Arabia. At present there are 1,200 Americans living there, and the Saudi Arabian villages adjoining to the north and east have about 4,000 inhabitants. The oil company employed in 1956 19,632 people in its activities in Saudi Arabia which include operation of a 200,000-barrel refinery at Ras Tanura nearby.

Ras Tanura is the main port on the coast for the oil company, and a pipeline conveys oil from the Dhahran dome to the tankers or refinery there. Many supplies have been and still are transshipped to Bahrain Island offshore, but in the future use of Ras Tanura and even more the use of the port of Dammam will avoid much of the expense which this entails.

Dhahran seems like a bit of the United States transported to Saudi Arabia. In addition to its extensive shops, offices, and storehouses for the work of the company, it possesses a hospital, moving picture theater—the only one at present in Saudi Arabia—tennis courts, baseball park, golf course, swimming pool, and a modern steam laundry. The resident staff members live in air-conditioned houses.

Food for this thriving oil town is largely imported from

America, but fish, fresh meat, vegetables, and fruit are provided from the company's farming project and from the gardens of the neighboring towns of Khobar, Dammam, Qatif, and Sofwa. American agricultural methods are used with great success, and are being taught to the Saudi Arabians. Constant communication is maintained between Jidda, the field operations, and the Saudi government by radio, but with Bahrain by motor launch.

Qatif

Qatif, with a population estimated at 30,000, 36 miles northeast of Dhahran, is the largest market town on the Persian Gulf coast of Saudi Arabia. The amir or Governor of this section of the Hasa has his headquarters here, as do the Director of Finance, and customs and wireless officials. Large fresh water springs irrigate Qatif's thousands of date palms, papayas, citrus fruit trees, rice, and alfalfa. The city exports a large quantity of dates and is the chief distributing center for a very extensive area. Much of the business of Hofuf passes through, or is with, Qatif. Its prosperity has been very materially increased by the money brought into the country by the oil company, as has that of the whole region.

A unique type of alfalfa which tolerates a water table of only 2 feet below the ground surface has been developed in Qatif gardens. Seeds have been secured by J. G. Hamilton of the 1942 U.S. Agricultural Mission and sent to the U.S. Department of Agriculture in Washington. Some high-water table areas of the United States may be benefited by this type of alfalfa.

Dammam and Khobar

These two ancient ports on the Persian Gulf are in the vicinity of Dhahran—Dammam 16.5 miles away, and Khobar 5.5. Khobar lies just to the north of the new oil company pier from which continuous contact is maintained with Bahrain by fast motor launches and shallow-draft boats. Formerly but small villages, these ports are now credited with a population of 20,000 each.

At Dammam an ancient fortress guards a large fresh water spring which provides the village with domestic water. The building may be of Portuguese origin, like that on Darain Island off Qatif. At high tide the spring and fortress are entirely surrounded by the intensely salty water of the Persian Gulf.

There are many truck gardens adjoining the two villages, irrigated by springs and flowing artesian wells. Cultivation is being rapidly increased by drilling. However, the Saudi Government officials were cautioned by the U.S. Agricultural Mission to control the flows from the drilled wells by valves, as artesian water has very definite limits.

Dammam is rapidly growing to be a large port. A seven-mile pier was completed in early 1951. This reaches a terminus where deep-sea vessels come alongside. The standard gauge railway runs to the pier-head where modern cranes facilitate cargo handling. Saudi Arabia thus has the best-equipped pier on the Persian Gulf—except possibly Kuwait.

9. Architecture and Archeology

Architecture

IN A country equivalent in size to a third of the United States, there are bound to be many types of dwellings to meet the needs of a varied climate. Such coastal towns bordering the Red Sea as Jidda, Yenbo, Jizan, and Sabya show the influence of Turkish design. The houses rise four to six stories high, and have large rooms, many windows, high ceilings, and large verandas. Along the entire coast buildings are of well-cut coral, with clay mortar and with wooden ties in the walls. On the flat roofs, commonly partitioned and used for sleeping quarters, one also sometimes finds kitchens and servants' quarters. Among the houses that are free of Turkish influence, the ceilings are lower and the rooms, though well built, are smaller. Plumbing and sanitary fixtures have been introduced only recently. The building example set by the mining and oil companies has been followed by the legations and others, but since 1953 there has been a tremendous upsurge of construction of all kinds. Nearly all large buildings are of the most modernistic European design. The use of reinforced concrete is now almost universal.

In southern Tihama, also bordering the Red Sea, the building style is apt to derive from the African conical hut, with a frame constructed of branches skillfully embedded in the ground and interlaced above to form a strong building, averaging about 18 feet in diameter by 20 feet to the apex of the conical roof. The walls are about 9 feet high, and the roof is of coarse grass fastened to the frame by ropes of twisted grass. Both walls and floors of the interior are usually plastered with mud. Fancy woven baskets hang on wooden pegs in the wall for adornment. A group of huts within one enclosure corresponds to the several rooms of a single house. Kiln-baked bricks of soft texture are in some cases used to make one-story houses.

An entirely different type of architecture prevails at Abha, the capital of Asir. Here the "multiple eave" style of architecture .obtains, unique for its two- or three-story structure and flat roof. The first story is made of stone and the ones above are of sun-dried mud bricks. Protruding layers of schist—a slatelike rock—are built into the mud walls. These are the so-called "multiple eaves," placed in straight lines averaging 19 inches apart. Projecting 17 to 19 inches from the wall surface as a cantilever at a very slight downward inclination, they prevent the rains from running down the wall surface and causing erosion. This has proved helpful in an area where an average rainfall of 10 to 12 inches brings many heavy showers. Another architectural form, designed to resist the violent winds, occurs in the lofty mountain regions of 9,000 feet elevation. The buildings have walls entirely of stone. Small doors and windows facilitate heating, a low rectangular enclosure being built at one end of the room where the burning of charcoal provides enough heat and is incidentally used to boil the coffee.

Still another type of buildings is found in Asir, particularly in the area of 10- to 5-inch rainfall, lying east from the Abha district. With sun-dried mud brick walls, the buildings here are up to five stories tall and have a batter or slope to impart greater stability. A re-entrant corner on the flat roof forms the landlord's open-air sleeping porch. A high mud brick wall usually surrounds each group of buildings, and their external appearance is of a pleasing shape and color. Red mud is utilized as paint for parts of the walls, and also to form frames around the windows. White paint made out of lime is used to outline the top-story windows. An attractive and original style of interior decoration may be observed at Abha—the largest city in Asir's most fertile southern region—and Khamis Mushait. The floor and about three feet up the walls are covered with a light green stain made from the juice of alfalfa. Benchlike seats line the walls, equipped with cushions and lozengelike hard pillows forming arm rests and dividers at right angles to the wall. Painted in red, white, blue, and black by the women, a decorated wainscot rises above the pillows to an average height of 18 inches. The wainscot decoration consists of geometric designs presenting no curved lines, only lattice work, crosses, squares, and angles. In Najran one sees buildings similar in shape and size, but without any interior or exterior decoration. Here, as at Bisha, Khurma, and Ranya, the walls are built by forming mud mixed with straw into cylindrical "bats" about 12 inches in diameter by 18 inches long. These "bats" are laid on thick mud mortar and pressed firmly down as each course is laid.

In Najd the buildings are also of sun-dried mud brick, flat-roofed and seldom more than two stories high, except for occasional towers at one corner of the larger buildings, such as the Governor's residence at Buraida. The customary plan is to build around a central, rectangular, roofless court or patio. The walls extend some 3 to 6 feet above the roof and terminate in characteristic crenelations. Except for the decorations on doors, which are of heavy wood, bearing arabesque designs in red, white, blue, and black, there are only the simplest embellishments.

In Hasa, the towers of the Hofuf citadel and outer walls have a batter in a proportion of about one to ten. The buildings are generally two to three stories high, flat roofs being the order save for the few small thatched-roofed buildings. The windows and doors are numerous and spacious. As a rule, the stores, servants' and watermen's quarters are on the ground floor, whereas the master, family, and guests occupy the second floor. Geometrical designs are incised in the plaster before it sets, a most attractive type of decoration. Covered with a cheap grade of cotton cloth, the ceilings in many cases bear the words "Made in Japan" stamped in blue dye on the cloth.

Taif has some unique, spacious, stone buildings, including

the palace formerly occupied by the Viceroy of Hijaz, Amir Faisal. Many were constructed during the Turkish regime and carry the impress of that era. Of excellent stone workmanship and lofty rooms they are invariably cool during the summer, since the city stands at an altitude of 5,100 feet. Two to four stories in height, these dwellings have plain white interiors with little attempt at ornamentation, but the most recently built homes are showing more color and decoration.

Since 1953 many new buildings of modern architecture have been erected, including a palace for Amir Faisal. Reinforced concrete is used in the construction of the palace.

Archeological Remains

Saudi Arabia contains many traces of former civilizations which would be of keen interest to the archeologist. Of late the Saudi Arabians have come to realize the importance of preserving these relics of antiquity, but little study has been made of them as yet. While not pretending to a survey of the archeological possibilities of the country, I can mention a few of the interesting sites and ruins encountered on my travels.

As noted previously, there are miles of ancient ruins and marks of former cultivation in the Wadi Jizal, northeast of Yenbo. When I was traveling by plane north from Yenbo, between Umluj and Wadi Hamdh, strange circular walls of stone, with a single-line stone wall extending radially from the circle, were to be seen. The circles were judged to be 200 feet in diameter. South from Wejh on the south bank of the Wadi Hamdh are the remains of what seems to be a Roman temple. There are still some steps in place, but the finely carved gypsum stones have been largely used to mark the graves of men killed in a local skirmish.

Along the route north from Medina which follows the line of the old Hijaz Railway, the first station with a village of importance is al-Ula. This town is situated near and among cliffs of yellow and red sandstone, bordering flat *wadis*. Five and a half miles from al-Ula at Horaiba are the remains of a large settlement, containing some inscriptions and many fragments of pottery. In the 60-foot sandstone cliffs adjoining the ruins are many rooms or tombs cut out of the solid rock; in some cases the space is just large enough for one coffin. All the tombs have been opened and robbed, as far as I saw or learned.

Eleven miles from Horaiba, farther north along the railway, is the ancient Nabatean group of tombs called Medain Saleh, described in detail in Doughty's great *Arabia Deserta*. Here there are possibly 20 or 30 tombs cut out of the soft yellow sandstone hills. They vary in size and all have numerous niches to receive coffins. The largest tomb I visited measured 18'-9" by 13'. The roof was 7 feet above the floor which sounded hollow, so there may be an opening beneath. Niches are sometimes as much as 5 feet below the main floor level, and extend 5 or 6 feet into the room walls.

On the exterior of the Medain Saleh tombs, the face of the cliff is cut smooth in a vertical plane; the tomb entrance is a gabled door, usually at least 3 by 7 feet, surrounded by a finely carved casing. In many cases an eagle was carved at the apex of the gable and there was also one at each end in line with the sides of the door. The heads of these eagles, and often the bodies, have been destroyed by the zealous Wahhabis, who believe that since only Allah can make a living figure, any mortal who tries to depict one is committing sacrilege. Under the apex of one of the doorway gables is carved a flat, round, somewhat grotesque human face which is flanked on either side by a snake lying parallel to the slope of the gable and extending from the apex to the lower corner.

West of Taif, also in Hijaz, a number of angular Kufic inscriptions are to be found. They are mostly Koranic verses and devotional passages in praise of Allah, but there are also several pictures of animals etched into the granite rock. The period of Kufic writing extends in the history of Arabic epigraphy from A.D. 720 to 1120. There are many ancient dams, now in disrepair, a few miles southeast to west from Taif, evidence of an evanescent civilization.

Approximately 20 miles easterly from this city there is an ancient soil conservation dam called "Sud Say-Sud." It is built of huge boulders and is 25 to 30 feet in height by, roughly, 250 feet along the crest. It is quite pervious, letting the water through but confining the soil erosion products. When I visited it during 1945 there was a fertile field in the dam basin. On the granite cliff near the southern end of the dam is a Kufic inscription. Dr. George C. Miles, Curator of the American Numismatic Society of New York, has translated this and believes it is the "earliest dated historical inscription of Islam. The lines are written in Muawiyah's name and are dated in the year 58 of the Hijrah, A.D. 677/78." The inscription reads: "This dam (belongs) to Abdullah Muawiyah, Commander of the Believers. Abdullah bin Sakhr built it, with the permission of Allah, in the year fifty-eight. O, Allah pardon Abdullah Muawiyh, Commander of the Believers, and strengthen him, and make him victorious, and grant the Commander of the Believers, the enjoyment of it. Amru bin Janab wrote it." (Vol. vii, No. 4, October 1948, *Journal of Near Eastern Studies*.)

Eleven miles southeast of Khamis Mushait, in Asir, and 150 feet above the route to Abha, are the ancient mounds and ruins of Jabal Hamoona. Kiln-burned brick fragments, pieces of slag, and fragments of pottery cover quite an area. There are also two large granite grinding wheels, one measuring 4' 9" in diameter and 17" in thickness. These are the type called "Chilian mills," originating in South America and now modified and used in North America for the crushing of silver and other ores, as well as for olive and sesame crushing in eastern Mediterranean countries. There are faint inscriptions on the hard black basic dyke rocks of the mountain, which seem similar to but more primitive than the Himyaritic.

In the vicinity of al-Hamdtha on Wadi Tathlith, 183 miles from Najran, Asir, there are abandoned gardens, ruins, and gold-mine dumps, showing that there was in ancient times a large settlement here. It is said that the Shammar tribes, now living around Hail and to the north, migrated from this region.

In the Najran valley lies the great ruined city of Dhat al-Okdood, covering an area of 20 acres. The walled area itself contains 12 acres. The Governor of Najran, Amir Turki ibn-Muthdi, appreciated the archeological significance of Dhat al-Okdood, and he wisely prohibited any trespassing or random excavating. There are large Chilian mill wheels and a huge mortar to be seen there, besides many fragments of pottery and numerous Himyarite inscriptions. One block of stone measuring 9'-9" by 3'-3" by 2'-1" shows considerable engineering skill, also confirmed by large cut stones in the remnants of the walls.

For many centuries Bedouins and local farmers have been carrying away charcoal, bones, and other remains from Dhat al-Okdood, spoil which they use as fertilizer. There is a local legend connected with these bones, having to do with a king who ruled Najran about A.D. 300. His son, Abdullah ibn-Thamir, was converted from idolatry to Christianity, much to his father's anger. The old king tried to kill Abdullah by throwing him into the Wadi Najran to drown, but the son survived. Moreover, he failed to die when his thwarted father tried again by throwing him over a cliff. After the second attempt on his life, Abdullah declared in public audience before the king that he could never be harmed unless his father, too, become a convert. The crafty king pretended to become a Christian and then called his son before him. He struck him lightly on the head with a cane and Abdullah fell down dead. The crowd in the great hall were immensely impressed and all became converted. However, they were so angry at the king for using his power against his son that he became afraid for his life. He had many "large, long trenches" (*ukhdud*) dug, and ordered his soldiers to kill all the converts by throwing them in the trenches, heaping wood upon them, and burning them.

Thus, says the legend, come the layers of charcoal with bones intermixed at Dhat al-Okdood.

It was reported to me that vessels and trinkets of silver, gold, and copper have also been found. It is told that one Bedouin came across a bronze statue of a lion which was too large for any of his camel bags. He solved the difficulty by breaking off the head of the statue and so divided the load to his satisfaction. Amir Turki ibn-Muthdi gave me an alabaster Himyaritic head from the ruins.

II. Social and Political Development

10. The Saudi Arabians

Population

THERE are no verified figures on the exact population of Saudi Arabia. In the absence of official census reports, a number of contradictory estimates have been proposed, varying between three and six million. Perhaps one would come reasonably close to the truth of the matter if a figure were struck, halfway between the two extremes, at about four and a half million. The following estimates of population have been made in conference with Ambassador Shaikh Abdullah Al-Khayyal at Washington.

Abha	25,000	Kunfida	10,000
Abqaiq	10,000	Lith	5,000
Abu Arish	10,000	Mastura	5,000
Anaiza	50,000	Mecca	250,000
Ar Rass	10,000	Medina	60,000
Baish	5,000	Muwaila	5,000
Bisha	20,000	Najran	10,000
Buraida	50,000	Qatif	30,000
Dammam	20,000	Rabigh	5,000
Dhahran	12,500	Ras Tanura	15,000
Dhibba	5,000	Riyadh	350,000
Faid	5,000	Sabya	10,000
Hail	30,000	Sufaina	5,000
Hofuf	100,000	Taif	30,000
Jauf	20,000	Uthmaniya	10,000
Jidda	200,000	Wejh	10,000
Jizan	10,000	Yenbo	10,000
Jubail	5,000	Yenbo Nakhl	20,000
Khobar	20,000		

Total urbanites   1,455,000

If the Foreign Agricultural Service was correct in estimating that 78 per cent of the population of Saudi Arabia is nomadic and Bedouin, they would number 5,159,000, making the total 6,614,000. But I think it quite possible that both the town estimates and the present estimated proportion of nomads are higher than a census would reveal.

In keeping with the time-honored practice of Arabia, the people know no color line. It may be recalled that Islam's first muezzin was a Negro. Conscious of the fact that, together with the peoples of Europe and America, they are in the main representatives of the Caucasian family, the Arabians designate Americans and English as "red," referring to their ruddy complexion. To be sure, mixed racial strains abound in the country, and many of the inhabitants of the southern Tihama regions may be classified as black, being the descendants of African slaves. But in Najd and among the Bedouins in general, the brown Mediterranean type predominates. The coloring of the townspeople varies from white to light brown, and those with a Syrian strain range from pure white to almost pale. Irrespective of complexion and racial peculiarities, the Saudi Arabian is invariably proud of his family, his tribe, his king, his country, and his ancestry.

Government

Though outwardly autocratic in several respects, the government set over the Saudi Arabian peoples is patriarchal and shows certain attributes of democracy. At a given hour of the day, King Saud makes himself accessible to his subjects, following the custom of his father. Sitting as a supreme court of appeal, he hears the complaints brought before him by even the humblest members of society. A lowly Bedouin may thus appear before the mighty lord of the realm and ask that justice be established in his case. From the King's decision there can be no appeal.

Saudi Arabian law is governed by the Koran, much of which parallels the Mosaic code. Capital punishment is enforced by the ancient form of decapitation by the sword—the penalty for murder. If a man is found guilty of theft, the penalty for the first offense may be amputation of the left hand at the wrist. Eighty lashes of the whip are given for drunkenness. Should a woman be taken in adultery, she is liable to burial to the waist in a pit; stoning to death follows. Adultery, however, is not widespread, partly because of the Koranic injunction that a man may take unto himself as many as four wives, on condition that he cherish them all and provide for them equally.

No considerations of color or pedigree weighed with King ibn-Saud in carrying out his judgments. Usually humane and lenient, he could upon occasion be stern and harsh. Ibn-Saud was regarded, by the consensus of opinion among the people, as a man of wisdom and righteousness. The qualities of justice, generosity, and hospitality added to his fame and popularity, and his son King Saud is following in his footsteps. Quite probably, the policies of Heir Apparent Faisal will be similar, differing in but few respects.

Manners and Customs

Arab courtesy and hospitality are proverbial. In former times the protection of a guest was as obligatory as providing him with food and shelter. My first encounter with this code dates back to 1931, the time of my first visit to Saudi Arabia. Accompanied by my wife, I stopped at the Red Sea port of Rabigh where the Chief of Police, Sayyid al-Khurdi, offered us a hospitable dinner. After the meal the two guests were about to depart when Sayyid asked, "In your country how many days does the asylum of a guest last?" I was somewhat puzzled, but before I could reply, the host put the query in another form: "How far from you must a guest be before he may be killed?" It was a dark night, and the question did not suggest happy thoughts, especially as we were perhaps the only Americans within a thousand miles. I replied that in our country the protection of a guest lasted indefinitely both as to time and distance, but al-Khurdi seemed to have mental reservations about this answer.

There are innumerable anecdotes about Arabs who gave their last morsel to feed a guest. One story concerns a poor Bedouin shaikh who had endured the loss of his flocks and

141

herds until only one horse was left. A man who had long coveted the horse and offered to buy him arrived one day and was invited to stay for a meal. When served, the guest observed an abundance of meat and a scarcity of oats and rice. Having partaken heavily of the food, he tried once more to rescue his host from penury. This time he offered to buy the horse for a much greater price than it was worth. The shaikh listened attentively, then replied, "I thank you for your generosity, but we have just consumed my horse!"

At a Bedouin camp, and elsewhere, one is consistently invited to drink coffee. It is considered discourteous if the usual three cups is not taken. For each serving, the coffee is roasted, ground with a brass mortar and pestle, and after some seconds of pulverizing, the *gahwaji* (coffee boy) taps the sides of the mortar with the pestle to notify the company that coffee is served. In the case of a European or American traveling in Saudi Arabia, the authorities customarily assign to the foreigner an escort who performs the duties of a coffee boy, rising at an early hour to prepare coffee which he serves at stated intervals till late at night. Generally without handles, coffee cups are two inches in lip diameter by two inches in depth, and have small bases. In holding the quarter-to-half full cup, one uses the right hand. Pouring from a brass pot called a *della*, the server passes from one guest to another. Two or three cups are drunk, and unless one shakes the cup from side to side as a gesture that he wishes no more the cup is filled and refilled indefinitely.

On more formal occasions, small cups of heavily sweetened green or black tea are introduced after coffee. Mint is at times added, making a delicious drink. Teacups, usually of glass, about one inch diameter by one and a half inch in depth, are used, and it is the proper custom to drink only one cup. Following this, a retainer enters, bearing a small urn containing live charcoal on which a piece of aromatic Indian wood is placed by the host, producing a pungent white smoke. As it is taken around among the guests, the urn is placed by the servant or soldier under the chin of each guest, who holds his head shawl around it with two hands, in order to insure a thorough perfuming of his beard. With this pleasant ceremony the party comes to an end and the guests take their leave forthwith.

With few exceptions, the food is placed in receptacles on great mats, or oilcloth, laid on the floor. As previously mentioned, the customary main item in a dinner is the platter of sheep, cooked whole. The meat is surrounded by well-cooked rice in which are sometimes raisins. Dishes of chicken, soups, stews, vegetables, fruits, and sweetmeats are placed around the main platters, the servants and escort usually acting as attendants and holding bowls of milk—camel's, goat's, or sheep's —which is called *laban hamid* (sour milk). It is excellent for the digestion and priceless when one has an attack of dysentery. The guests kneel or sit cross-legged at the typical Arab feast. Although there are spoons, most of the food is eaten from one's hand, always the right hand if one observes Arab etiquette. This is to give evidence that the guest trusts his host, as his dagger hand is occupied. Before as well as after each meal, usually inside the dining room, one or more servants hold a brass pitcher of warm water which is poured over the guests' hands into a brass bowl underneath. Another servant holds the towel and soap. Thus are the requirements of cleanliness, stipulated by Arab courtesy and the Moslem religion, fulfilled.

In Hijaz it is customary for the sons of the host, sometimes even the host himself, to wait upon the guests. As a rule in Najd, however, the host sits at the head of the party, with the guest of honor at his right hand. In Asir and Hasa, the host, having received each guest and conversed with him, leads him to the dining hall and sees that he is seated; he then departs and is not seen again till after the meal. In certain instances, the host will take the guest to another room for a brief conversation before leaving, but more generally he is bade farewell directly after he has completed his meal and washed his hands. There are other matters of etiquette strange to a West-erner. When one enters a reception hall, one's shoes are re-moved, whereas one's head remains covered. When sitting on the floor with a group, one should take care that the soles of his feet do not face any of those present, as that would be con-sidered insulting; preferably, one should keep his feet hidden.

It was also a matter of courtesy to wear Saudi Arabian head-dress when traveling outside Jidda, Mahad Dhahab, and Dhahran. Formal dress, consisting of a Najdi costume, was usually required of all received in audience at Riyadh by King ibn-Saud. But King Saud does not make this a stipulation. Mr. Alexander Kirk complied with this formality, as did his party of twelve Americans, when in May 1942 he presented his cre-dentials at Riyadh as United States Minister to Saudi Arabia. The wearing of prescribed dress at court is not without prece-dent elsewhere; up to a few years ago it was obligatory for those presented at the Court of St. James in London to wear knee breeches conforming to certain specifications. Western cus-toms and etiquette are now tending to replace the strictly Arab in many of the larger towns.

An entirely Moslem country, Saudi Arabia observes Friday instead of Sunday as the weekly day of rest. The fasting month of Ramadan, in a broad sense a counterpart to the Christian Lenten period, is a season of abstinence from sexual inter-course, food, and drink during the daylight, unless one hap-pens to be ill or on a journey of more than three days. Strictly observed by the faithful, Ramadan closes in a three-day festival (*'id*) when all municipalities of larger size display their equip-ment for entertainment. The marked fondness of the typical Arab for children reveals itself at the festivals when every child, even the poorest, tours the amusement area of the town, wearing a new dress and accompanied by the proud father. The very few women who appear at such public gatherings are shrouded from tip to toe, with small slits in their veils for their eyes. The chief attractions for the children are swings, small Ferris wheels, and merry-go-rounds, entirely portable equipment made of wood. When one calls on government officials and friends during the festival, coffee and hard candy are served. On departure the guest is sprinkled with rose or other perfumed water.

With an inborn liking for sports, the Arabian takes readily to association football and basketball, although so far these games are chiefly confined to schools. Formerly banned, football is now encouraged and has become extremely popular in all sections of the country. A short time ago there was a league of eight teams in Jidda alone; now there are probably several more. Prime Minister Prince Faisal is patron. There are teams in Mecca, Taif, Riyadh, Hofuf, and the oil towns as well as in Wejh and other towns in the Hijaz. Horse racing, without the extra inducement of betting, is universally popular among all classes, and the Arabian seems to be a natural rider, whether on horse, camel, or donkey.

Falconry is still practiced extensively in Najd, and the hawks are carefully trained. On my first trip across Arabia, I visited the camp which the King had established for his favorite sport of hunting, where I was met by an officer carrying a falcon on its perch. Describing the way a hare, bustard, or gazelle is captured, he explained that the falcon alights on the prey's head and overwhelms it by pecking at its eyes. When a lesser bustard was spied stirring in the fields, the Najdi officer proceeded to demonstrate. He removed the little leather hood which covered the falcon's eyes, held up the perch until the bird caught sight of the bustard, whereupon the falcon made a neat take-off and spiraled up some distance. In vain did we watch for the falcon to dive upon the bustard, now quickly vanishing, for he had evidently changed his mind and had decided to regain his freedom, soaring to a height that lost him to sight. Embarrassed beyond words, the officer explained that the falcon was really too young to be trusted, but that surely he would be recovered and receive further training.

Until February 1952 it was the general custom for inmates of jails and prisons to rely on relatives and/or friends for their food. It is reported that now King Saud has ordered that henceforth prisoners throughout Saudi Arabia are to be fed and clothed at government expense. This is one of the many reforms being introduced by the new monarch.

Another advance was the decree by King Abdul Aziz ibn-Saud dated May 24, 1952, abolishing "Hajj"—pilgrim-dues amounting to £20 ($56) collected from each pilgrim to Mecca. The total average was estimated at £8,000,000 ($22,400,000) annually. This ruler was long famed for generosity and sincerity in his religion.

Slavery

In Arabia the status of slavery has been somewhat different from that in other countries. The word for slave is "Abd." Many proper names include this word. For example, "Abd al Aziz" means "Slave of the Beloved" (this word is one of the reported 99 appellations given in the Koran to God, or Allah). "Abdullah" means slave of God.

The owner of a slave is responsible for his entire welfare. There is no color prejudice in Arab states. Many slaves have been freed and have risen to prominent positions in their countries. For instance, the present Minister of Finance in Saudi Arabia is the son of a slave. He is universally respected for his great ability in the political field as well as for his literary gifts, and is a most popular member of all prominent social circles.

In a treaty of September 17, 1927, and in subsequent exchanges of letters in the early 1930's, the late King Abd signed an agreement with the British government prohibiting slave trading and the importation of slaves. This agreement has been, and is being, strictly implemented. However, there is a certain amount of smuggling. The Saudi laws are strictly enforced and include the punishment of smugglers and return of slaves to their countries of origin.

Due to the impact of economic and social developments during the last quarter century, slavery in Saudi Arabia has been dying a natural death, although there are still scattered vestiges of it.

The Prophet Muhammad tried to deter the then almost universal practice of slavery by making the following rules which are included in the Koran. (1) No wife can be sold into slavery. (2) No debtor can be sold into slavery. (3) No one taken in piracy can be sold. (4) Any slave owner who manumits a slave especially gratifies Allah.

11. The House of Saud

IBN-SAUD ranked among the foremost figures of this age. Not since the Arabian Prophet called a nation into being had so much of the Arabian Peninsula been assembled under one man. The present emergence of nation-states is the first eclipse of his vast power. It is the purpose of this chapter to describe very briefly the beginnings of the House of Saud.

The full name of the founder King is Abdul Aziz ibn-Abdul Rahman Al Faisal Al Saud. He was born in November 1880 in the palace at Riyadh. To most Arabs he was known simply as Abdul Aziz (servant of the Mighty). His father was Abdul Rahman, the Sultan of Najd; his mother was Sarah, daughter of Ahmad Sudairi, a member of the Dawasir tribe which inhabits a region in the southern parts of Najd toward the Empty Quarter. His ancestor, Saud the Great ($+$1814), headed the martial and inflexible forces which swept the Arabian Peninsula, proclaiming the puritanical Islamic doctrine of the great reformer Muhammad ibn-Abdul Wahhab, with whose rise in the middle of the eighteenth century the history of the House of Saud is closely related. Saud's military campaigns were finally checked by Ibrahim, the son of Muhammad Ali, the eminent Viceroy of Egypt.

The Sauds trace their ancestry, in accordance with the genealogical practice of the Arabs, to Bakr ibn-Wa'il ibn-Rabi'ah ibn-Nazar ibn-Ma'add ibn-Adnan. Though vague, and sometimes fictitious, the genealogies of Arabia are not without significance. They rest upon the assumption that an original, now defunct, stock, that of Qahtan, and a more recent one, Adnan, form the two parent stocks of the land. The children of the former grouping—Qahtan—presumably inhabited the south. Theirs was the opulent ancient civilization of the Yemen, Hadramawt, and the neighboring coast, that of the Sabaeans and Minaeans. The Adnanites, from whom the Sauds are ulti-

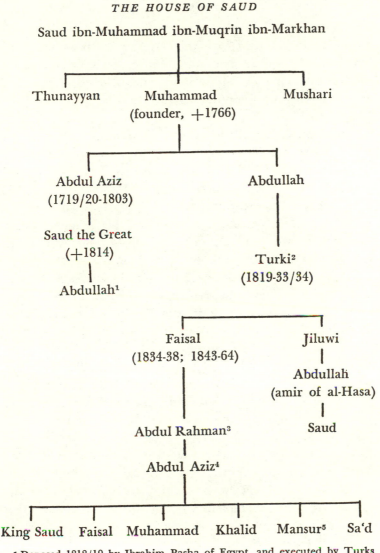

Saud ibn-Muhammad ibn-Muqrin ibn-Markhan

Thunayyan   Muhammad   Mushari
(founder, +1766)

Abdul Aziz   Abdullah
(1719/20-1803)

Saud the Great
(+1814)
           Turki[2]
Abdullah[1]   (1819-33/34)

Faisal   Jiluwi
(1834-38; 1843-64)
          Abdullah
          (amir of al-Hasa)

Abdul Rahman[3]   Saud

Abdul Aziz[4]

King Saud   Faisal   Muhammad   Khalid   Mansur[5]   Sa'd

[1] Deposed 1818/19 by Ibrahim Pasha of Egypt, and executed by Turks at Constantinople.
[2] Founder of Second Saudi state.
[3] His two brothers, Abdullah and Saud, contested long, leaving him for a while in partial control.
[4] Died Nov. 9, 1953.
[5] Died May 1, 1951.

149

mately descended, constitute the main stock of the north, and, according to tradition, are the offspring of Ishmael whose father Abraham is allegedly the builder of the Ka'ba, ancient Meccan sanctuary. To this northern wing belonged the Mudar, and their kinsmen the Nizarite Quraysh, the forebears of the Prophet.

Out of these ancient roots came the Sauds of modern times, whose house has had a chequered career comprehended in three main periods. First, there was the founder, Muhammad (+1766), petty but ambitious baron of Dar'iya, who in 1738 gave asylum to the spiritual enthusiast of Uyaynah, Muhammad ibn-Abdul Wahhab, and espoused his religious cause. Muhammad, the founder, was succeeded by his son, Abdul Aziz (1719/20-1803), and his grandson, Saud the Great (+1814). This political structure built by Muhammad and completed by his immediate successors collapsed in 1818 when, defeated on the battlefield by the Egyptian Ibrahim Pasha, Abdullah, the son of Saud the Great, was beheaded at Constantinople. Next, there arose Turki, founder of a new Saudi regime, who established his capital at Riyadh. Although he was assassinated in 1834, the state was once more freed of foreign control under his son and successor, Faisal. His latter years were spent in a strenuous effort to keep the peace between his two eldest sons, Abdullah and Saud, and in constant watchfulness to ward off a rival power, that of ibn-Rashid of Hail. After these chaotic conditions wasted the power and prestige of the Sauds, Abdul Rahman, a third son of Faisal, went into exile in Kuwait, accompanied by his son, Abdul Aziz, father of the present king of Saudi Arabia, and organizer of the third state in the history of the House.

The ambition of Abdul Rahman was to re-establish the kingdom of Saud the Great and to make the Wahhabi faith universal. He taught his sons the elements of this religious belief and prescribed a Spartan life, especially for Abdul Aziz, who learned at an early age to use the rifle and perfected the

150

arts of traveling in the desert. In these accomplishments the young prince attained great proficiency, while he never relished the study of books. He rapidly grew to gigantic stature. Of a very energetic and quick-tempered disposition, he was characteristically generous and impulsive. Endowed with a retentive memory, he also possessed an admirable loyalty to friends. But he was not destined long to enjoy the happy, carefree life of a prince. At a very early age, Abdul Aziz—future political architect of Saudi Arabia—was caught in the maelstrom of Peninsular affairs, involving an agonizing struggle with ibn-Rashid of Hail and the Ottoman Turks. On an international scale, he was thrust into contact with the Germany of Kaiser Wilhelm II and the Great Britain of the closing Victorian era. In these initial stages of his career, he made a brilliant contribution to the re-establishment of the House of Saud.

Muhammad ibn-Rashid was the ruler of the Shammar tribes, his capital, Hail, being 355 miles northwesterly from Riyadh. Envious of the resources of Riyadh, he sought to annex it, taking advantage of the old rivalry between Abdul Rahman's elder brothers, Abdullah and Saud. Crowned with victory in his siege of the proud city, he installed his own governor, but allowed Abdul Rahman and his family to remain in the palace in deference to the latter's prestige among the Wahhabis. As head of the family of Saud, when his two elder brothers had died, Abdul Rahman could not long endure ibn-Rashid as master, and tried his utmost to arouse the neighboring tribes on behalf of a Saudi restoration. Learning of these machinations, ibn-Rashid instructed his agent, Shaikh Salim, Governor of Riyadh, to eliminate Abdul Rahman and the House of Saud. But with characteristic Saudi resourcefulness, Abdul Rahman forestalled the plot by annihilating Salim's bodyguard and making him a prisoner. The townspeople of Riyadh then joined the loyal forces in driving out the representatives of ibn-Rashid. With his superior numbers, ibn-Rashid laid siege to Riyadh and after a period of valiant resistance, Abdul

151

Rahman fled with his household and faithful retainers. He first lived on the bounty of the Ajman tribes of whom Hithlain was the Shaikh, but later decided to take his family into the safety of the remote oasis of Jabrin where the primitive Murra tribes were in control. In this rustic environment, the family of Saud dwelt. Here Abdul Aziz, accompanied by his cousin Abdullah ibn-Jiluwi, a lifelong friend and supporter, shared the life of the Murra, receiving rigorous training in the Bedouin arts of fighting and survival in the desert. From the Murra he learned the value of mobility and surprise attacks, practiced in raids over immense distances.

Ottoman Turkey had long viewed with alarm the growing power of ibn-Rashid. Hafiz Pasha, the Turkish Governor of Hasa, had recognized the value of the House of Saud as the logical opponent to ibn-Rashid and had, therefore, requested Shaikh Muhammad of Kuwait to extend an invitation to Abdul Rahman, promising the Sauds a monthly subsidy as long as they continued to reside in Kuwait. It was an atmosphere in great contrast to that of life among the Murra tribes into which Abdul Aziz was thrown in 1891, when he accompanied his father to Kuwait, largest port on the northwestern side of the Persian Gulf. Through here passed the wares of India and the East on their way to Najd, Syria, and points west. Less rigorous physically, life here offered him an opportunity to develop his intellectual faculties as he came in contact with men from India, Java, and Malaya, as well as from Iran, Iraq, Syria, Turkey, and the interior of Arabia. In spite of the comparatively dissolute life of Kuwait he retained his religious piety, and married at the age of fifteen. In 1897, when news was brought that Muhammad ibn-Rashid had died and that the inhabitants of southern Najd would welcome Saudi leadership, he tried to throw off the yoke of the Rashids and to recover Riyadh. However, the tribes did not rally around him and he returned to Kuwait bitterly disappointed.

In the meantime, a series of incidents had materially altered the situation in favor of the House of Saud. In 1897 Mubarak removed his brother Muhammad, Shaikh of Kuwait, by the sword, and gradually became one of the outstanding Arab personalities of his age. Kaiser Wilhelm II of Germany, seeking an outlet on the Persian Gulf for the Berlin-Baghdad Railway, had planned to make Kuwait the eastern terminus. When the Germans failed to drive a bargain with Mubarak they asked the Sultan of Turkey to depose him. Learning of these movements, the British, who for years had concluded treaties with the sultans of the Trucial States, placed the interests of Kuwait under their protection. The Germans countered, acting again through the Ottoman authorities, by urging the Rashids to attack Mubarak. In planning for the defense of his territory, Mubarak sent Abdul Aziz southwest to assault Riyadh as a diversionary measure. Only twenty years old, Prince Abdul Aziz gathered a group of daring men around him, including his intrepid cousin Abdullah ibn-Jiluwi, who later became Governor of Hasa. Disappointed in his first encounters with the Rashidi forces, he withdrew to Jabrin where in a fifty-day conference with his aides he laid down his plan of operations. In 1901 Abdul Aziz entered Riyadh by night. A life-and-death struggle left him the master of the city, and at the great mosque and in the presence of the religious leaders and notables, he was formally proclaimed by his father, Governor of Najd and Imam (head) of the Wahhabis.

The successes of the Wahhabi leader worried the Turkish Sultan, Abdul Hamid, who, with German connivance, had formed a dream of pan-Islamic unity, with Arabia—the heart of the Islamic world—under his caliphal jurisdiction. With the support of a Turkish contingent, the Rashidi forces sought to avenge their defeat, but were scattered in battle during the war of 1904. The death of the Rashidi leader, Abdul Aziz ibn-Mut'ib, in 1906 left ibn-Saud master in the home of his forebears. Confusion followed in his rival's camp and, though not without serious problems in his own domain, Abdul Aziz ibn-Saud had by 1907 achieved so great a security for the House of Saud that a new day in Peninsular Arabia was dawning under its aegis.

12. The Rise of the Saudi State

THE period from 1901, when ibn-Saud was proclaimed Governor of Najd and Imam of the Wahhabis, to 1907, when the House of Saud had recovered its former ascendancy, may be described as the restoration. A foundation had thus been laid for the rising Saudi state, a new structure in the society of nations, forged on the anvil of adversity and inner conflict. Adversity was encountered in the changing pattern of contacts with the Turks, the British, and the adjoining states. Inner conflict stemmed from the rivalry of the powerful Hashimites, the still burning embers of Rashidi hostility, and the proverbial defection of the Bedouins. Through it all, the cementing zeal of the Wahhabi movement, the astute character of ibn-Saud, and, perhaps, the readiness of Arabia for a new order are discernible.

In 1908 ibn-Saud learned that an Arab-Turkish official, Husain ibn-Ali of the Hashimite family, had been appointed Sharif of Mecca. This governor claimed jurisdiction over Hijaz, including the Ataiba tribes on the eastern edge of Hijaz, a region which was under the authority of ibn-Saud. As he was preparing to defend this territory against Husain, word came of a rebellion led by sections of the Ajman and Hazazina tribes, instigated by his cousins, the sons of Saud. Having made peace with Husain, ibn-Saud hurried south where, at the village of Hariq, he met and defeated the conspirators. He proceeded to Laila, capital of the Aflaj district, where he tried and pronounced death sentences upon the nineteen captured leaders. Having executed eighteen by the sword in public, ibn-Saud pardoned the nineteenth, ordering him to go and inform his friends both of the clemency and stern justice of ibn-Saud. The story of Laila spread with good effect throughout the country.

During the comparatively peaceful interval up to 1913, ibn-

Saud dispensed justice, eradicated raiding, and established safety of life and property. While he was stabilizing his realm, his enemies were planning and plotting. Sharif Husain had the ambition of extending his domain; the Young Turks wished to consolidate the Ottoman Empire; Mubarak of Kuwait was filled with envy and jealousy; the Rashidi family wished to regain their former position; and the Germans had not abandoned their aspiration for a port on the Persian Gulf. When the Turks were defeated at Tripoli, they withdrew many troops from the Arab world, giving ibn-Saud the opportunity he craved. Resorting to his favorite surprise tactics, he marched on Hofuf with seven hundred picked camel cavalrymen who crossed the moat, scaled the wall, killed the sentries, stormed the main fort, and had the Governor captured—all within six hours. From Hofuf ibn-Saud proceeded to the coast of the Persian Gulf, 45 miles to the east. He quickly captured the seaports of Oqair, Khobar, Dammam, Qatif, Jubail, and villages up the coast to Kuwait, appointing his cousin Jiluwi as Governor of Hasa. Hardly did the Turks have time to bestir themselves when World War I was upon them.

As the gigantic struggle developed between Great Britain and her Allies on the one side, and Germany and the Central Powers on the other, each of the main contestants sought the support of the Arab rulers who controlled the land athwart the strategic line of communications leading to the prize of India and the Far East. These rulers consisted primarily of Husain ibn-Ali, Sharif of Mecca and King of Hijaz; ibn-Saud, Sultan of Najd and Hasa; Mubarak, Shaikh of Kuwait; ibn-Khalifah, Shaikh of Bahrain; the Sultan of Muscat; and the Imam Yahia of the Yemen. The British had in 1914 very able representatives in Sir Percy Cox and Captain W. H. I. Shakespear who made bids for active friendship. Captain Shakespear was killed in 1915 while fighting at the side of ibn-Saud's forces. It soon became clear to ibn-Saud, however, that the British were making terms with Sharif Husain to the west, whereas the Germans, acting through the Turks, had a friendly understanding with the Rashidi and Shammar tribes to the north. With Colonel T. E. Lawrence, Prince Faisal, the eldest and ablest son of Sharif Husain, was fighting the Turks, in return for which Husain was promised a throne from which to rule over all Arabia. Meanwhile the British sent H. St. John B. Philby, accompanied by Lord Belhaven, to visit ibn-Saud and take stock of the situation. Receiving this mission at Riyadh in 1917, ibn-Saud promised to observe neutrality. In view of the British deal with Husain, he could not side actively with the Allies, and devoted himself to the pacification and organization of the Saudi state. In 1915 Britain had officially recognized it.

By the spring of 1918, Sharif Husain had become convinced that he had been largely responsible for driving the Turks back northward and that consequently he was the most important figure in the Near East. He proclaimed himself "King of the Arab Countries," and wrote to ibn-Saud demanding recognition, and asking him to abandon any claim of jurisdiction over the Ataiba tribes. In response, ibn-Saud sent Wahhabi *mutawwi's* (missionaries) to convert the Ataiba to the puritanical faith. Khurma, a town near the edge of Hijaz that had accepted the Wahhabi message, was now attacked by Husain, whose forces, however, were repulsed. Meanwhile the position of Great Britain toward the internal feud of Arabia was inscrutable. The India Office backed the Wahhabi rulers, the Arab Bureau at Cairo gave support to Sharif Husain, and the Foreign Office signed treaties with the French regarding matters detrimental both to ibn-Saud and Husain. Ibn-Saud faced the dilemma of honoring his pact of friendship with Britain and at the same time of resisting the ambition of Husain, who also was an ally of Britain.

Ibn-Saud had just crushed the Rashidis, incited to war against him by Husain, when General Allenby captured Damascus and General Marshall took Mosul. Shortly thereafter Ottoman Turkey petitioned for an armistice, and on November 11, 1918, World War I ended with the armistice signed by Germany. Khurma was now attacked by Abdullah, the son of Husain, whose column was scattered by ibn-Saud. Warned by the British, at the request of Husain, not to invade Hijaz, ibn-Saud returned to Najd after installing a garrison at Khurma and receiving the fealty of the Ataiba. In the meantime the British continued to favor Husain, following the advice of Colonel Lawrence, and sent Sir Percy Cox to confer with ibn-Saud in 1920. But in the early spring of 1921, the ruler of the Rashidis was murdered and his followers were left in utter confusion; then the death of Sultan Salim of Kuwait removed another barrier to the growing aspirations of the Saudi House. Ibn-Saud was able, therefore, to enter Hail, capital of the Rashidis, in triumph. On his return to Riyadh he was acclaimed as "Sultan of Najd and Its Dependencies."

With the march of events King Husain became increasingly egotistical. He quarreled with the British, demanding that the French relinquish their mandate over Syria and that the Balfour Declaration promising the Jews a national home in Palestine be rescinded. Lawrence was sent to reach an agreement with him but failed. The British tried again without success to reach a reconciliation with him late in 1923. His own subjects plotted against him, and his unpopularity at home and abroad sank to a new level on March 6, 1924, when he proclaimed himself Caliph of Islam three days after the Turks had abolished the Ottoman Caliphate. Resentment flared up in the Moslem world, and the Wahhabi Arabians were incensed to fury. Having received a measure of encouragement from India's Moslems, and with the concurrence of important Islamic leaders, ibn-Saud now embarked upon the conquest of Hijaz—Holy Land of Islam—which he ruled as a trust till the inhabitants themselves chose him as their king after the capture of Jidda in December 1925. Husain abdicated on October 5, 1924, and a week after his arrival in Jidda he sailed first to Aqaba, whence in July 1925 he was conveyed by a British warship to Cyprus. There he lived at Nicosia till a few days before his death. In 1926 the inhabitants of Asir—lying between Hijaz and the Yemen—petitioned ibn-Saud for admission as a dependency of Najd. In the same year, at a solemn assembly, over which Abdul Rahman, the venerable father of Abdul Aziz presided, ibn-Saud was asked to be King of Najd, an honor he accepted, without the elaborate ceremony of coronation, in a manner in keeping with the austere practices of the Wahhabis.

On June 6, 1926, at the time of the annual pilgrimage, when an assembly of Moslem delegates from distant parts were considering means for raising the standards of hygiene and social life in the Holy Places, in order to make Hijaz a credit to the name of Islam in the world, an incident occurred which cast a shadow over the relations between the two great Moslem states—Saudi Arabia and Egypt. In connection with the yearly visit to Hijaz, Egyptians had for centuries brought a litter (*mahmal*), reputedly the same one on which their Queen Shajar-al-Durr rode into Mecca when she performed the pilgrimage in the mid-thirteenth century. Surrounded by an armed escort and to the tunes of a bugle march, the litter was thus paraded through the holy centers of worship. Offensive to the austere Wahhabis, who regarded the *mahmal* as an idol and the musical accompaniment as lurid mockery of the true spirit of Islamic piety, the entire ceremony was denied a place in the holy pilgrimage rites. Upon this occasion sharp words led to stone-throwing and ended in shooting. The upshot was that twenty-five persons were killed and many were wounded. But for the personal intervention of Hafiz Wahba, Amir Faisal, and the King himself, the Egyptians might have been wiped out. Asked to render an apology, the Egyptian government balked, and ibn-Saud imposed sanctions strictly prohibiting the armed escort from entering the Hijaz again and suspending the *mahmal* ceremony until 1936. Repercussions in the diplomatic sphere followed inevitably and cooperation between the

159

two countries was seriously hampered until 1940, when the incident was finally closed.

While foreign relations, save the unhappy incident with Egypt just reviewed, were progressing favorably, Russia having been the first to accord King ibn-Saud recognition, followed by Great Britain, France, Germany, Italy, and other nations, extremely serious trouble was brewing internally. Dawish, strong Shaikh of the Mutair tribe, joined by ibn-Hithlain, Shaikh of the Ajman tribes near Kuwait, and Shaikh Bijad, chief of the Ataiba, formed a powerful opposition within the militant Wahhabi community to the policies and practices of ibn-Saud. Acknowledged as the brains of the insurrection, Dawish rose to challenge the orthodoxy and religious efficacy of the Saudi administration. He denounced the laxity of ibn-Saud, judged by Wahhabi standards, attacking him for taxing the pilgrims, levying a tax on tobacco—a prohibited article—and fostering the use of the telephone, telegraph, radio, and motor car—instruments of the Devil. Above all, he deplored the King's intercourse with the "infidel" British and other foreigners, demanding that a holy war (*jihad*) be declared at once against the unbelievers. Most of these doctrinal issues were referred by ibn-Saud to the conclave of divines (*ulama*), while he sought desperately to moderate the crisis by resort to diplomacy or the sword as the case required.

This already dangerous condition worsened in 1928. The British, who then held a mandate over Iraq, had found it necessary to employ planes and motorized artillery in quelling the marauding tribesmen of Dawish, who had violated Iraq territory. Police posts and desert forts had been established on the Iraq-Najd border without ibn-Saud's consent. Military action against the followers of Dawish necessitated the invasion of Saudi territory, and against his wishes and interests ibn-Saud was brought into direct conflict with the British forces and the government of Iraq. Sir Gilbert Clayton, High Commissioner in Iraq, worked assiduously for a settlement but failed to reach an agreement with ibn-Saud, who vehemently repudiated the right of Iraq to construct fortresslike police stations on the frontier with Najd. Adding to the discomfort of the Saudi House was the attempt of Imam Yahia, King of the Yemen, to drive a wedge between Idrisi, ruler of Asir—a dependency of Najd—and the Saudi throne. With characteristic determination and vision, ibn-Saud seemed to grow stronger as his troubles multiplied. Ever his mainstay, the *Ikhwan* of the Wahhabi faith rallied around him, ready to defend the Saudi state. Contingents began to pour in from every quarter until an army of about 15,000 men had been recruited. Again and again, the Saudi forces assailed the recalcitrant Dawish—the main source of national disorder—until the rebels were crushed, Dawish captured wounded, and his son killed. With Bijad and Dawish securely interned, and ibn-Hithlain dead, the country began to breathe more easily again. The King of Hijaz, Najd and Its Dependencies, sat on his throne more securely than ever before.

Although King Abdul Aziz ibn-Saud was devoutly religious and the regaining of the kingdom of his fathers was due to the zeal of his Wahhabi followers, he was not bigoted. He delighted in discussing religion with Dr. Dame, of the Bahrain Dutch Reformed Church. The King did not hesitate to send for missionary physicians and nurses when there were serious illnesses. Many, many treatments were given to members of the royal household during the twenty-five years prior to his death. Dr. Paul W. Harrison and Dr. Storms, with their wives and nurses as well as Dr. Dame and Mrs. Dame, have been wonderful American ambassadors of good will. They have always responded to requests for services outside their medical duties. This attitude was always greatly appreciated.

One incident which is indelible on my memory occurred some years ago, before airplane service, about 1938. I arrived at Riyadh early one afternoon after a four-day crossing of the desert from Jidda. I was dusty and dirty so, when I had been shown to my rooms, I immediately went into the bathroom and commenced emptying cans of water over myself from a huge Ali Baba type of jar. Suddenly I heard a voice asking me to come to the outer room. I thought it must be someone with a message. I draped the oversize bath towel about myself, went out, and, to my astonishment, there was His Majesty! He laughed and thought my costume a great joke. We sat down and chatted, but my knowledge of Najdi Arabic was limited. The King ordered his guard-servant to bring the *hakim sitt*, lady doctor, the American nurse who was accompanying Dr. Dame on his visit to the Riyadh harem. She came, and the three of us talked together for half an hour—I, all the time, in my bath towel! The incident is an excellent example of the simple friendliness of a great man and the kind helpfulness of a sincere missionary lady.

There are no permanently established missions in Saudi Arabia, but the mission hospitals along the Persian Gulf, in Iran and Turkey, have done untold good to the people and have been of tremendous benefit to American prestige and enterprise.

13. Saudi Arabia in the Modern World

In the early thirties, despite his growing power, other trials were in store for ibn-Saud. Hasan al-Idrisi, ruler of Asir, persisted, with the encouragement of the Yemenite dynasty and the connivance of Fascist Italy, in an endeavor to secede from his authority. After a period of uneasiness, ibn-Saud took the step in February 1934 of inviting the Imam Yahia, ruler of the Yemen, to meet him at Abha, capital of Asir. Nothing of value was accomplished, and the Yemen reverted to its chronically hostile attitude even after ibn-Saud had dispatched his final appeal and ultimatum. Two Saudi armies, commanded by Crown Prince Saud and Amir Faisal, Viceroy of Hijaz, moved quickly into the Yemen, everywhere defeating Yemenite opposition. While Saud advanced on the plateau through Najran, Faisal proceeded along the Tihama plains down to Hodeida, the chief port of the Yemen. There the British cruiser *Enterprise* arrived in time to inform the Italian naval forces that Britain was confident in the ability of Faisal and the Saudi Arabians adequately to protect the property and lives of foreigners.

In this fashion the protest with which imperialist Italy had sought to secure a foothold in Arabia was frustrated. Mussolini had long dreamed of acquiring such influence in the Yemen as, in conjunction with the colony of Eritrea, would enable him to dominate the southern end of the Red Sea. With that done he might cut the short route between Britain and India. In seven weeks, however, the war was won and the Imam Yahia sued for peace, sending an emissary to sign the terms at Mecca. Ibn-Saud accorded the Yemenite envoy every honor and courtesy, and received him with great hospitality. Against the counsel of his advisors, the Saudi monarch imposed no indemnity and presented no territorial claims. As a result of this farsighted policy toward a conquered enemy, it might be extremely difficult to arouse Yemenite feeling any more against the Saudi regime.

Negotiations were initiated at this time for the conclusion of friendship pacts with Egypt, Iraq, Iran, and the Yemen. Ibn-Saud fostered Pan-Arab understanding along religious, cultural, and commercial, but not political, lines. His judgment of British power was astute. Great Britain had recognized him as an independent sovereign, and she had sent a Minister Plenipotentiary and Consul General to his kingdom. Many of the rabid *Ikhwan* still urged him to attack Aqaba and Kuwait but, realizing the value of British protection over these parts, he wisely refused to antagonize the British, although he continued to press his claims through the appropriate diplomatic channels. He wished peace, solemnized in treaties of friendship, with King Faisal of Iraq and his brother Amir Abdullah of Transjordan.

In nearby Palestine a crisis was developing of vital interest to ibn-Saud and the world of Islam. Palestine had been an Islamic country from A.D. 635 to 1918 when the Turks were expelled by the victorious Allies and for 900 years prior to this it was ruled successively by Greeks and Romans. During those centuries, Arabs, Jews and Christians dwelt together in relative harmony. In their intercourse with Great Britain, the Arabs had accepted at its face value the pledge of T. E. Lawrence, made in good faith, that there would be a self-governing pan-Arab state after the victory of the Allies. The mandating of Syria to the French and of Iraq, Palestine, and Transjordan to the British brought a widely felt disappointment. Distrust and contempt for the promises of Europeans replaced the former respect that many peoples of the Near East had held for Westerners. Under the Balfour Declaration, 400,000 Jews had settled in Palestine by 1934. With the help of capital provided in Europe and America the Jews bought many of the most choice lands of Palestine at high prices. Subsequently the Jewish organization making the purchases stipulated that only

Jews might be employed on such lands, and leasing of them was open only to Jews.

Great resentment flared up among the native Arabs of Palestine, leading to bloody outbreaks. British troops did a magnificent job in an attempt to preserve order, but there were riots in Jerusalem and other centers of population. The British government then took the initiative in calling a conference of "Arab Kings." Iraq, Transjordan, Saudi Arabia, and the Yemen were represented. Of the rulers, ibn-Saud was the only one of international importance, a highly influential figure in the Moslem world. He was represented at the conference by his son, Prince Faisal—Viceroy of Hijaz and Minister of Foreign Affairs. Held in Cairo, the conference contributed little toward a solution of the problem posed, though some constructive suggestions were made by the Saudi delegation. Matters drifted along with little change. The British government, through a statement of policy in 1937 and its White Paper of 1939, brought about a slightly more friendly response from the Arab side.

King Abdul Aziz ibn-Saud was always intensely concerned with the Palestine problem. He issued a statement conveying his views on the subject, which was published on May 31, 1943, by *Life Magazine*. In no uncertain terms, he stated that he knew of nothing that justified Jewish claims to Palestine as their commonwealth, for the Jews had not ruled it since the Roman period, while the Arabs seized Palestine over a thousand and three hundred years ago. Furthermore, he felt that since the Jews were impelled to seek a place in which to live, there were many places in America and in Europe more fertile and more spacious, where they might settle without conflict. He also proposed that the Arabs guarantee, with the support of the Allies, the interests of the Jews native to Palestine.

The Saudi king felt toward Palestine, I believe, much as most Americans would feel if, say, France or Russia insisted that the United States should receive 800,000 foreign refugees

165

(and subsequently more) into the state of Vermont, which is about the size of Palestine. Palestine, moreover, has at least 40 per cent less arable land than Vermont.

Ibn-Saud remained a steadfast friend to the Allies throughout World War II. During the dark days of 1940, when France fell and Italy entered the war on the side of Germany, he officially maintained strict neutrality and openly declared that he was a friend of Britain and was sure she would not be defeated. Practically all his *Majlis* (council) disagreed and were convinced that Germany would be victorious. The King's judgment was of course vindicated in the end and his great prestige and reputation for farsightedness and wisdom were increased.

The influence of ibn-Saud in the Moslem world was undoubtedly unique. His power was derived not only from his rule over Hijaz, the heart of Islam, with its sacred Moslem cities, Mecca and Medina, but also from his record of accomplishment and compelling personality. Had he so desired, he could have directed the Moslems of Egypt, Palestine, and Syria to cut British lines of supply and communication to such effect that British troops, sorely needed at al-Alamain, would have had to be diverted for policing. Thus the victory of the Eighth Army, won by a narrow enough margin, would have been seriously endangered. Instead, ibn-Saud sent his son, Amir Mansour, to Egypt before the battle of al-Alamain to speak to the Moslem Indian troops. The presence of Mansour was concrete evidence of the friendship of ibn-Saud to the Allies in this military crisis.

In Iraq the Germanophile Gailani gave Britain serious concern, but ibn-Saud frowned upon this rebellion and tried to dissuade Gailani and his followers. Had ibn-Saud encouraged the Iraqi rebels it is quite conceivable that the Germans would have flown many troops to Iraq for the short distance around Turkey and over Syria. Turkey might then have been influenced to become a German ally. With this accomplished, Hitler's forces could have reached the rich oil deposits of Iraq and Iran, and advanced to the Suez Canal to join forces with the Afrika Korps.

The following excerpts from a letter of H. E. Shaikh Hafiz Wahba, Saudi Ambassador to Great Britain, give evidence of the faith of ibn-Saud in the ultimate victory of the Allies, and show his attempt to discourage the Iraqi rebels at a time when Germany seemed to be winning the war:

"In the first place Sayed Rasheed Ali fomented trouble against the British without consulting any of his neighbors. He never consulted even King ibn-Saud, although there is a Treaty between the two countries signed in 1940, which compels both countries to consult one another on any subject relating to any Arab question.

"Perhaps Sayed Rasheed thought that his forces could beat the British forces without any help from his neighbors. But after a short time he found out that his army could not stand long against the British, which had unlimited resources. He then sent the late Nagy Pasha Al Sowedi, one of his cabinet ministers—whose family, as well as himself, have personal friendly relations with H. M. King Abdul Aziz—to Riyadh; but the King told him straight away that they had blundered and made a big mistake in fighting Great Britain at such a critical time, and that any difference of opinion between themselves and Great Britain should have been solved by peaceful means. His Majesty told him also that they are indebted to Great Britain for their independence, for Great Britain had conquered Iraq in the last World War but they [the British] found it better, from their own point of view, to grant Iraq her independence.

"His Majesty went on to say to Nagy Pasha—'In the second place I am a staunch friend of Great Britain, inheriting this friendship from my grandfather, Faisal Ibn-Turki. When a friend is in duress, then, for the sake of friendship, one does not act against him. Personally, if I had sufficient armaments I would have gone to the help of Great Britain and not acted against her. With the exception of the question of Palestine, Great Britain did nothing against the Arab interests and the present war is one of life or death. So our duty is, if not able to help Great Britain, to be neutral. This is the least I can do. I believed that from the very beginning of your insurrection it would be a failure. You also know that, Nagy. For that I advise you to cease hostility against Great Britain and negotiate with her if possible.'

"Naturally, Nagy Pasha defended Sayed Rasheed's policy and gave his reasons for it, as was his duty as a member of Rasheed's Cabinet."

Having declared war on March 1, 1945, against Germany and Japan, Saudi Arabia joined the United Nations Organization and was represented at the San Francisco World Security Conference. For the kingdom of ibn-Saud this meant wider international recognition and was bound to draw the country into new and closer relations with the rest of the world. The simple dignity of H.R.H. Prince Faisal, his personal grace and alert mind, won him the esteem of the other delegates. As chairman of his country's delegation, Prince Faisal was accompanied by two key figures in Saudi Arabia's diplomatic service: H. E. Shaikh Hafiz Wahba, Ambassador to Great Britain, and H. E. Shaikh Asad al-Faqih, then Minister to Iraq and since Ambassador to Japan. The latter diplomat also served in the capacity of delegate to the United Nations Committee of Jurists, which met in Washington, D.C., during the month of April 1945.

The King showed great wisdom in initiating the movement for the settlement of the Bedouin *Ikhwan* in selected areas of Najd and Hasa. He induced preachers to accept life on a farm or in newly constituted villages. Living in fixed homes and cultivating the soil have gone against the grain of Bedouin character, yet the King tried to carry out the permanent settlement of about one-third of the former nomads under his jurisdiction. Among the successful settlements are those of the Haleet district, northwest of Duwadami; Fawara district, to the southeast of Hail; and Oglat al-Suqhour, on the Wadi ar-Rumma to the east of the road between Medina and Hail. Though many of the former Bedouins still despise the pursuit of agriculture, much of the future prosperity of the land lies along this path.

King Abdul Aziz with his usual foresightedness took steps to see that his successor would be a suitable one. He chose his eldest living son, Saud ibn-Abdul Aziz. He had the powerful religious council—the Ulema—consider this selection, and they confirmed it. Furthermore, he called upon his adult sons to swear allegiance to their brother, if and when he became their ruler. They obeyed. Consequently when on November 9, 1953, King Abdul Aziz ibn-Abdul Rahman Al-Faisal al-Saud died, the designated heir took over the reins of government of Saudi Arabia without the slightest argument. There were only the simplest of ceremonies.

One of the first acts of King Saud ibn-Abdul Aziz al-Saud was to appoint his eldest brother, Prince Faisal, as Heir Apparent holding the portfolios of Prime Minister and Minister of Foreign Affairs.

King Saud was born January 12, 1902, in Kuwait on the Persian Gulf, and was the second son of King ibn-Saud. (The eldest Turki had died.) By a royal decree he was appointed Heir Apparent on May 11, 1933, after confirmation by the Consultative Assembly. The succession to the throne is not automatic nor necessarily inherited. Saud was commander of the Saudi Army in Asir during the brief war with the Yemen. He led and directed the forces going toward Sanaa along the high plateau while Prince Faisal conducted the campaign down the Red Sea coast. Both were successful. Saud was appointed Commander-in-Chief of all Saudi Arabian forces and Faisal Viceroy of Hijaz. The Council of Ministers was formed

169

in 1953 to facilitate government administration and to distribute responsibilities. Saud was made its first President.

For many years Saud acted for his father in dealings with the interior, especially with the tribes of Najd, who had formed the nucleus of ibn-Saud's forces with which he had regained the kingdom of his father and had added to it. These Najd tribes with their shaikh chieftains are the puritanical Wahhabis, very independent in their views and not at all averse to expressing these opinions to their king.

His past experience is proving valuable to King Saud in his present broader contacts with Middle East neighbors and with the world powers. His attitude during his visit to the United States in January 1957; his friendly counsel and aid to King Hussein of Jordan, a member of the former enemy Hashimite family; his stand against Communism—all have demonstrated a mature judgment, strength of character, and farsightedness that promise well for the stability of his country and provide a beneficial influence in all the Middle East.

In appearance King Saud is a striking figure, 6 feet 2 inches tall, broad in proportion, weighing about 200 pounds, with strong features which are lightened by the captivating smile inherited from his father. Like him, Saud has to wear glasses and take particular care of his eyes. The Saudi costume accentuates his commanding appearance. It consists of a camel's hair or woolen cloak called a *mashlah* in Saudi Arabia or *abba* in Lebanon and Syria. In winter it is made of heavy material; in summer, it is of almost transparent weight for the summer heat. The cloak is worn over a white cotton shirt called a *thoub*. The head covering is of three parts: the *kufiya* or small, close-fitting, usually quilted, skull cap; over this is a head shawl called a *gutra*, which is folded into a triangle and is most effective in protecting the back of the neck. The *gutra* is also useful when folded across the face as protection against wind, sand, and sun; it is held in place by the third part of the head covering, a head rope called an *iqal*. This varies in material: the royal family uses *iqals* made of woolen cords nearly covered by gold threads; the usual *iqal* is of black woolen or camel's hair. Various localities in the Arabian Peninsula can be determined by their characteristic *iqals*.

Although during his childhood and youth King Saud was not compelled to suffer the hardships of his father, his was far from an indolent life. He was born soon after his father, at the age of 20 years, had recaptured the ancestral capital city of Riyadh. He was educated in Kuwait and at the age of seven began his studies. Within four years he had memorized the Koran. When 13 years old he was sent by his father to capture the leader of a tribal revolt. He succeeded. Near the end of World War I he fought at the side of his father against the Shammar tribes and finally defeated them and their allies, the house of ibn-Rashid. This consolidated the rule of ibn-Saud. The influenza which followed the war claimed his elder brother, Turki, and one of his younger brothers as victims.

While ibn-Saud and his son were performing their religious rites in the Great Mosque in Mecca on March 15, 1935, an attempt was made by three pilgrims with daggers to assassinate them. Saud successfully defended his father, but was slightly wounded himself. During this same year he visited the Netherlands and two years later went to Iraq, where he strengthened the alliance of the two countries. In 1937 he represented King ibn-Saud at the coronation of King George VI in London. He also visited Italy, Switzerland, France, Belgium, and the Netherlands after leaving England. As Crown Prince, he travelled extensively over the United States during 1947, at first as the guest of President Truman and subsequently of Aramco. He received the Legion of Merit from the President.

Since his ascension to the throne in 1953 King Saud has visited all members of the Arab League to cement his friendship and to obtain intimate knowledge of the various rulers and governments. In addition he visited Kuwait in 1954, as well as Bahrain and Pakistan; during November 1955 he was a guest in India and in Iran. At the invitation of President Eisenhower he visited the United States during January 1957. Following this he was the guest of Generalissimo Franco in Spain during February and travelled extensively. A Moslem country for many centuries, Spain was especially interesting to him. He made calls in Tunisia and Libya after leaving Spain.

Due to various circumstances King Saud decided to turn over to his brother, Heir Apparent Faisal, most of the administration of the affairs of his kingdom. This was formalized by the Royal Decree which he issued on March 23, 1958. Further details of Faisal's role are given in the next chapter under the heading "Internal Administration."

14. Political Administration

DISTINCTIVE problems of political organization must of necessity arise in a country greater in area than the British Isles, Germany, France, and Italy combined. When one bears in mind that Saudi Arabia has previously had little contact with the outside world, practically no experience in modern political administration, and hardly any tradition of self-government on a broad national scale, the rapid strides taken by her administrators toward efficiency and order are little short of miraculous. Within the limited confines of this chapter, some aspects of the governmental structure will be delineated, in order to suggest the nature and operation of the Saudi Arabian system of control.

A preliminary statement might serve to show the present-day trend toward modernization. Ibn-Saud was fully aware of the importance to the progress of the nation of modern military and technical equipment. His Minister of Finance, Abdullah Sulaiman, bought from the Marconi Company fourteen complete wireless stations through the good offices of H. St. John B. Philby, to whom a concession was granted to import Ford cars. Whereas in 1926 there had probably been less than a dozen cars in the entire country, a total of 2,316 in 1956 were used by Aramco alone, and some 8,000 were estimated to be owned by the government, government-sponsored companies, and private owners. Handsome profits accrued to the automobile owners who offered their services in the transporting of pilgrims between Jidda and Mecca-Medina.

Ibn-Saud organized a small regular army, furnished with modern rifles and machine guns. The force was trained, in the early stages, by former Turkish officers. Shortly after its formation, this military machine was tested on the field of battle, subduing the rebellion of the Harb tribes south of Mecca. A competent elderly Turk served as commander of the regular troops. But for the past several years there have been American and British military missions at Taif. As a result of the British-French-Israeli invasion of Egypt, diplomatic relations were severed and the British military mission was withdrawn. The American mission was transferred to Dhahran.

There has been some training assistance by the United States under the Dhahran Airfield Agreement of June 18, 1951. This aid is being considerably expanded under the 1956 exchange of notes with Washington. It will result in the establishment of a United States Military Training Mission with army, navy, and air-force branches. Modern arms have been provided by the United States under a reimbursable agreement of the above date. A military academy has been established at Riyadh which can train 600 officers annually. The Ministry of Defense recently announced a five-year plan which calls for the induction of 58,000 men into the regular armed forces of Saudi Arabia.

The history of the U.S. training school at Dhahran is of interest, for it bears on the American defense policy as well as that of Saudi Arabia, and is mutually beneficial. The origin of this important project was the concept of Colonel Harry R. Snyder in 1943 for a U.S. air-base on the western shore of the Persian Gulf to facilitate the movement of U.S. forces between Europe and the Far East. In March 1945 negotiations between King ibn-Saud and Colonel Snyder, with Minister Colonel William A. Eddy and Colonel V. H. Connor, resulted in permission being granted to make and use an airport in eastern Saudi Arabia on the condition that competent training in aviation should be given Saudi Arabs.

Dhahran was chosen as the air-base location. Construction commenced on January 2, 1946 and was completed March 15, 1946—a remarkable feat by the U.S. Corps of Engineers. After delays in implementing the training program, Colonel Snyder, with invaluable assistance from the U.S. Ministers to Saudi Arabia, Col. Eddy and Mr. J. Rives Childs, sent a group of 28 air-force instructors to Dhahran in June 1947. King ibn-Saud

174

appointed 50 candidates for training; from them 31 students were selected by Mr. Harlan Clark representing the U.S. government. Actual training commenced in September 1947. The officer in charge was enthusiastic about the quality and character of the initial Saudi Arabs.

The following courses are included in the curriculum for the six-week training periods: administration, aircraft maintenance, operations and weather, air installations, supply, communications, automotive maintenance, English, mathematics, geography, physical fitness, safety and sanitation, hotel and food services.

Education

Remarkable progress in establishing schools has been made. While in 1951 there were 226 educational institutions staffed by 1,217 teachers for the total of 29,887 pupils, the number reported by the Saudi Arabian Consulate in New York on July 31, 1957 was 73,779 students taught by 3,240 instructors, located in 557 institutes of learning.

The Saudi government has made a logical division of the various classes and types of education, as may be seen in the following tabulation:

Type of Institution	Pupils	Teachers	Buildings
Elementary	64,000	2,700	518
Secondary	8,800	400	32
Institutes	532	55	2
Colleges	127	19	2
Industrial or vocational schools	320	66	3

The presentation by King Saud of ten of his palaces to the Ministry of Education emphasizes his intense interest in schooling of all kinds. In the budget for 1957 the sum of $8,148,000 was allocated on account of the building of 50 schools.

To quote from *The Kingdom of Saudi Arabia* by Dr. Omar Khadra, Saudi Delegate to the United Nations: "No fees are charged to students who elect to enroll in the schools and all institutions are wide open to all Saudi citizens. The government selects students to study abroad and contributes to their expenses. No less than one thousand students are seeking knowledge and learning in the best universities of Egypt, Beirut, Syria, Europe, and the United States. In this country (U.S.A.) there are one hundred pupils dispersed in the best educational institutions at a varying level of intellectual attainment. A number of them are working on advanced degrees in universities such as Harvard, Cornell, and Chicago. It is expected that those students studying either in the States or Europe would eventually return to their homeland and assist in developing their country in whatever tasks called upon them to do by the government. . . . Last year [1956] the amount of 128,174,066 Saudi *riyals* ($34,606,998) were spent by the Ministry on the various facets of education. This represents an increase of 400 per cent over the amount appropriated for education in the preceding year."

Health

In the matter of public health and sanitation, great strides have been made since the days when the hot branding iron was a cure-all and the goats of Jidda constituted a considerable portion of the Sanitation Department of that city. During the ensuing twenty or thirty years the government has accomplished outstanding results in both the handling of the annual flood of pilgrims and in reaching the remotest parts of the realm by mobile clinics.

It is the policy of the government to prevent epidemics by injections, inoculations, and vaccinations. Pilgrims come from all parts of the globe. Practically all the seaborne ones arrive at the port of Jidda and have to pass through a quarantine center examination. In April 1956 King Saud opened the modernized quarantine station which can accommodate approximately 3,000 persons. This station cost roughly $3,000,000 and is considered one of the largest and most modern of its kind: "No pilgrim is allowed admission into the country prior to supplying Saudi Arabian consulates and missions abroad with adequate evidence that meet with the requirements of the Ministry of Health. It is an established rule of the government that no person be granted permission to either leave or enter the country unless he receives the necessary medical injections required by law." (*The Kingdom of Saudi Arabia* by Dr. Omar Khadra.)

For the year 1957 the sum of $5,129,874 was budgeted for the Ministry of Health; in 1956, $32,500,000 was spent; in 1955 the sum was $7,500,000.

It is reported that there are over 7,000 beds in the various hospitals operated by the government and in Jidda there are several privately owned and run nursing homes. "The Ministry of Health's program, ranging over a 3-year period beginning in 1955, calls for the construction of 22 hospitals providing 5,372 beds, 60 clinics, 23 mobile units, and a serum-manufacturing plant. . . . In operation at the end of 1956 were: 65 government-sponsored hospitals, 10 private hospitals, 3 military hospitals, 78 clinics, 21 mobile units." (Information by the courtesy of Aramco.)

Internal Administration

Shortly before his death in November 1953, King ibn-Saud ordered that a Council of Ministers be formed to divide the responsibilities in the governing of his rapidly developing state. His son King Saud followed this plan. There are at present nine Ministers and five Counselors. Heir Apparent Faisal combined the offices of Prime Minister and Minister of Foreign Affairs. There is a Minister of Defense, Minister of Communications, Minister of Education, Minister of Health, Minister of Finance, Minister of Commerce and Industry, Minister of Agriculture, and Minister of Interior. This group is scheduled to meet at least once monthly.

On August 17, 1957, the Council of Ministers of King Saud was composed of the following members of the royal family and prominent Saudi Arabs:

Prime Minister and Minister of Foreign Affairs, His Royal Highness Prince Faisal

Education, H. R. H. Prince Fahad bin Abdul Aziz

Communication, H. R. H. Prince Sultan bin Abdul Aziz

Defense and Aviation, H. R. H. Prince Fahad Bin Saud

Interior, H. R. H. Prince Abdullah àl-Faisal

Finance and National Economy, His Excellency, Shaikh Mohamed Surour al-Abban

Agriculture, H. E. Shaikh Khalid al-Sudairi

Health, H. E. Dr. Rashad Pharaon

Commerce and Industry, H. E. Shaikh Mohamed Alireza

The advisers in the council were:

Chief Adviser to His Majesty King Saud, His Royal Highness Prince Abdullah Bin Abdurrahman

Adviser to His Majesty and Deputy Foreign Minister, His Excellency Shaikh Yusuf Yassin

Adviser to His Majesty, H. E. Shaikh Khalid Gargoni Abu Al-Walid

Adviser to His Majesty, H. E. Al-Sayed Jamal Al-Husaini

Adviser to His Majesty, Shaikh Ibrahim Bin Mohamed

Adviser to His Majesty, His Royal Highness Prince Mishal Ibn Abdul Aziz. (Information from the Royal Saudi Arabian Embassy, New Delhi, India.)

Throughout Hijaz, local councils were formed under ibn-Saud to assist the governors of the five leading towns: Mecca, Medina, Jidda, Yenbo, and Taif. In the country as a whole, the governors were largely drawn from the loyal Najdi constituency, aided, however, by the advice of councils of prominent citizens representing the local population. To his assistance ibn-Saud called men of competence and fidelity. He was not limited to men of Arabian origin but frequently employed upright Moslems of Arab stock regardless of their original country. Some of the highest officials in his government came from outside Saudi Arabia. Shaikh Hafiz Wahba,

178

Ambassador to Great Britain and for many years Chief Counselor, is an Egyptian of Najdi ancestry. Yusuf Yassin, long a Chief Secretary and in 1957 Deputy Foreign Minister, is a Syrian from Latakia. Shaikh Fuad Hamza, for several years Acting Minister of Foreign Affairs, Minister to France and later to Turkey, was a Druze from Lebanon; he died in 1952.

As might be anticipated, the great increase in revenues has caused rapid expansion of all activities of the government, and various new departments have been established. The activities begun by the late King Abdul Aziz have been amplified by King Saud. On ascending the throne, he appointed his brother, Heir Apparent Faisal, the Prime Minister. Faisal has long been intimately connected with foreign affairs. He has made extended visits to America as well as to Great Britain and has firsthand knowledge of these countries. During the summer of 1957 he was successfully operated on in New York. His recovery after years of intermittent illnesses has enabled him to assume actively the responsibilities which had long been his on paper.

On March 23, 1958, King Saud issued a royal decree detailing the duties and responsibilities of his brother. These are specified as the administration of the departments of foreign as well as domestic affairs and defense, along with full powers to reorganize the details of government. Committees have been formed to study ways and means to make a reorganization with a view to greater efficiency in all departments. However, the ultimate sovereign power remains in the hands of King Saud.

The official transference of responsibilities to Faisal would seem to be decidedly beneficial to the governing of the country. By this action it is expected that the finances will be handled more efficiently and that the Council of Ministers will be delegated more duties. It is quite probable that the Council membership may be altered, as well as some of the personnel in various departments and in embassies.

In regard to foreign policy, Faisal has stated (April 18, 1958) in Riyadh that his country will *not* join either Arab bloc but that it "aims to be friends with every state that has no aggressive intentions toward us." His country will also seek to strengthen relations with the United States "owing to mutual economic interests" between them. Faisal has indicated that he is willing to resume diplomatic relations with Britain and France if with the former there is an agreement regarding the Buraimi Oasis and with the latter the settlement of the Algerian situation. Diplomatic relations were broken off in November 1956 when Britain, France, and Israel invaded Egypt.

It seems probable that a policy of neutrality will exist toward all the nations of the Middle East and a continuance of the cordial relations with the United States.

Because Mecca and Medina, the two holiest cities of Islam, are located in Saudi Arabia and because religion is so important to the Saudi Arabs, there seems little chance that Communism will gain any appreciable influence.

The country is politically organized under four major divisions, corresponding to the formerly independent kingdoms which constitute the present Kingdom of Saudi Arabia. Each political division might be visualized as the counterpart to a state in the American Union. The four states are: (1) Najd, the "heart of Arabia"; (2) Hijaz, the holy land of Islam; (3) Hasa, of which Abdullah ibn-Jiluwi, cousin of ibn-Saud and champion of the Saudi cause, was the governor until his death a short time ago when his son, Sa'd, succeeded to the rulership of the state; (4) Asir, a highland area bordering on the Yemen.

Each of the rulers of the above divisions had command over considerable military forces which serve as escorts, police, and reserves in time of trouble. Under the rulers of the states are the amirs of towns and villages. In all but the smallest administrative units, a Director of Finance works along with the amir and reports both to him and the Ministry of Finance at Riyadh.

In the larger towns there may be a member of the *ulama* (theologians) class who will give the amir counsel in religious matters. Some of the governors have *qadis* (judges) to assist in the trial of criminal cases, as well as in giving legal advice when needed, but in small places the governors act as their own judges.

Under the Ministry of Finance is the Department of Mines and Public Works, created in 1936 to deal with the oil and mine concessions. Administered until early 1944 by a Lebanese, Najib Ibrahim Salha, the department then came under the management of Sayed Izz-al-Din al-Shawa of Jaffa, member of an old and prominent Palestinian Arab family. Late in 1945, Sayed Sami Kutbi, who was born in Mecca, took over the position. That considerable progress has been made in the financial administration of the Saudi government is evidenced by the Council of Ministers' compiling and presenting budgets for the Moslem years 1376 A.H. and 1377 A.H., the latter being equivalent to the period of July 28, 1957 to July 17, 1958. The Moslem year dates from 622 A.D. and, being a lunar year, is 11 days shorter than the solar now in general use. The following details are quoted from translations of Saudi government publications:

This summary is taken from the translation made by the Arabian Research Division of Aramco at Dammam, March 28, 1957:

	Saudi Riyals*	Approximate U.S. Dollars
Ministry of Education	22,000,000	5,940,000
Ministry of Interior	1,055,725	285,046
Ministry of Communications	62,945,443	16,995,270
Ministry of Health	19,026,541	5,137,166
Ministry of Agriculture	1,902,128	513,575
Ministry of Defense and Aviation	40,000,000	10,800,000
Ministry of Finance and National Economy	3,800,000	1,026,000
General Projects	194,500,000	52,515,000
	345,229,837	93,412,057

* The Saudi *riyal* is equivalent to $0.27, U.S. Currency, as of January 1, 1957.

181

For full details the following is quoted by the courtesy of Aramco; I have computed the U.S. dollars equivalents:

"April 12, 1957, the following statement appeared in the Mecca newspaper *Al-Bilad al-Sa'udiyah*, issue No. 2408, on March 21, 1957. This translation was made by the Arabian Research Division, Dammam, March 28:

"Notice from the Ministry of Finance and National Economy on the Budget of State Public Projects for the Year of 1376 (8 August 1956 to 27 July 1957)

"The Council of Ministers, in its session held on 13 December 1956, decided, under No. 61, to appropriate the oil revenue that is received *annually* by the Treasury of the State to the account of public projects.

"Royal Order Bo. 3/10/1336, dated 1 January 1957, was issued sanctioning Decision No. 61 and ordering its implementation.

"Following are the projects which have been authorized:

	Saudi Riyals	*Approximate U.S. Dollars*
(1) *Ministry of Education,* for the account for building 50 schools	22,000,000	5,940,000
(2) *Ministry of Interior,* for the construction of the Riyadh prison, for armed launches (for the Coast Guard), and for a telegraph system for the (Directorate General of) Public Security.	1,055,725	285,046
(3) *Ministry of Communications* (itemized below)	62,945,443	16,995,270
Projects for the (Directorate General of) Roads, Bridges		
(a) For the account of the Jidda-Medina road	7,000,000	1,890,000
(b) For the account of the Riyadh-al-Diri 'yah-al-Shumasi road	4,000,000	1,080,000
(c) Khobar road	1,574,575	425,134
(d) For the account of the Yanbu-Medina road	2,500,000	675,000
(e) Roads outside Riyadh	5,855,500	1,580,985
(f) For the account of the Medina-Tabuk road	1,000,000	270,000
(g) For the account of the Riyadh-Kharj road	6,000,000	1,620,000

182

	Saudi Riyals	Approximate U.S. Dollars
(h) Heavy equipment (not specified)	500,000	135,000
(i) For studies on the Jidda-Dammam automobile road	700,000	189,000
	29,130,075	7,865,119
Projects for the Railroad	22,000,000	5,940,000

Projects for (the Directorate General of) Posts (Telephones) and Telegraphs

	Saudi Riyals	U.S. Dollars
(a) Buildings for the Siemens project	631,420	170,483
(b) Equipment for the Siemens project	3,194,217	862,439
(c) Works to be completed (not specified)	500,000	135,000
(d) Completion of the (telephone?) lines to Taif	39,827	10,753
(e) Riyadh telephone project	879,560	237,481
(f) Marine stations project	250,022	67,506
(g) Completion of the construction of the third story on the *automatic* (telephone) building, Jidda	26,100	7,047
(h) Alin (?) area project, Riyadh	78,000	21,060
(i) Mobile post offices project	500,000	135,000
(j) Cost for furnishing 12 reserve (?) centers	441,000	119,070
(k) Cost for a royal mobile telephone station	92,220	24,899
(l) Value of land for the carrier (system?) Taif, and value of land for the telephone exchanges and carrier (system?), Mecca	1,000,000	270,000
(m) Value of post office boxes for subscribers	70,000	18,900
(n) New railroad locomotives	2,000,000	540,000
(o) Barges and marine tugboat	1,600,000	432,000
(p) Buwaib road	410,000	110,700
	11,712,366	3,162,338
(4) *Ministry of Health* (itemized below)	19,026,541	
(a) The four clinics in Riyadh	658,362	177,758
(b) Shaqra hospital	275,617	74,416
(c) Buraidah hospitals Nos. 1, 2	549,209	148,286
(d) Abha and Bisha hospitals	615,508	166,187
(e) Unaizah, Hayil, and Jaizan hospitals	1,173,358	316,806
(f) Completion of al-Majmaah hospital	331,169	89,416

183

	Saudi Riyals	Approximate U.S. Dollars
(g) Construction of second story to al-Sadad hospital, Taif (see item "j" below)	550,683	148,684
(h) Furnishing the rest of the hospitals (in the kingdom)	8,716,688	2,353,506
(i) For (hospital perimeter) walls and for hospital roads; for additional buildings to the nine hospitals (unidentified); and for landscaping work to the grounds on which the nine hospitals (unidentified) were built	3,000,000	810,000
(j) For the rest of the first story of al-Sadad hospital (see item "g" above)	633,182	170,959
(k) Completion of basic works for the Jidda quarantine (station)	451,605	121,933
(l) Last payment to the account of the Riyadh hospital	2,044,160	551,923
	18,999,541	5,129,874
(5) Ministry of Agriculture (as itemized below)		
(a) Costs of completion of Akramah dam	183,528	49,553
(b) For the Riyadh dam project	1,718,600	464,022
	1,902,128	513,575
(6) Ministry of Defense & Aviation	40,000,000	10,800,000
(7) Ministry of Finance & National Economy (itemized below)	3,800,000	1,026,000
(a) For the account of aerial photography	1,500,000	405,000
(b) For the account of customs warehouses	800,000	216,000
(c) For the account of enlarging Jidda port	1,500,000	405,000
	3,800,000	1,026,000
(8) General Projects (itemized below)		
(a) Religious institutes	1,000,000	270,000
(b) The Prophet's Mosque (Medina)	4,000,000	1,080,000
(c) The Holy Mosque (Mecca)	60,000,000	16,200,000
(d) The pilgrimage and the pilgrims	4,000,000	1,080,000
(e) Riyadh projects	23,000,000	6,210,000
(f) Mosques	2,000,000	540,000

		Saudi Riyals	Approximate U.S. Dollars
(g)	The Eastern Province (Hasa)	6,000,000	1,620,000
(h)	Medina projects	2,000,000	540,000
(i)	Desert roads (in tribal areas?)	1,000,000	270,000
(j)	For the (Directorate General of) Broadcasting (Press & Publications)	1,000,000	270,000
(k)	Water projects	3,000,000	810,000
(l)	Government buildings	80,000,000	21,600,000
(m)	Buildings for the official offices in Dhahran airport	3,500,000	945,000
(n)	For the account of the public electric (power) station, Riyadh	4,000,000	1,080,000
		194,500,000	52,515,000
	ENTIRE BUDGET	SR 345,229,837	$93,212,056

The Saudi Arabian Budget for the 1377 A.H. (1958) Fiscal year was as follows:
The directorate general of broadcasting, press and publications announced the following Royal Decree No. 5/1/3 dated 23 Jumada II 1377 (13 January 1958): "With the help of God Almighty, We, Saud ibn-Abd al-Aziz, King of the Kingdom of Saudi Arabia, after reviewing the statements of the revenues and expenditures of the state for the fiscal year 1377, and in accordance with the Council of Ministers' decision No. 108 dated 22 Jumada II 1377 (12 January 1958) regarding the budget for 1377 (rendered) in accordance with Article 7 of the Council of Ministers Regulations, have ordered the following:

1. The estimate of the revenues of the state for the fiscal year 1377 shall be SR 1,500,000,000 ($300,000,000) in accordance with Schedule No. 1 attached to this order.
2. The expenditures of the state for the fiscal year 1377 shall be fixed at SR 1,375,000,000 ($275,000,000) in accordance with Schedule No. 2 attached to this order.
3. A surplus of SR 125,000,000 ($25,000,000) shall be added to the general reserves and allocated to the repayment of the public debt.
4. All revenues shall continue to be collected in accordance with the regulations and instructions in force and shall be deposited in the Saudi Arabian Monetary Agency and its branches for the account of Ministry of Finance.

185

ﾠ

5. Expenditures shall be paid by the Saudi Arabian Monetary Agency in accordance with the budget and instructions covering it, and in accordance with the Council of Ministers' decision.
6. Any amount of the (estimated) revenues, or any amount saved from the expenditures as fixed in this budget shall be paid into the general reserves of the state.
7. The President of the Council of Ministers shall carry out this order and notify all concerned to act in accordance therewith."

(The official value of the Saudi *riyal* is $0.267, but during the fiscal year 1377 A.H. (1957-1958) the free market value fluctuated, so the average is considered to be $0.20 and is used in the 1377 A.H. budget conversions.)

Schedule No. 1, Estimate of Revenues for the Year 1377 A.H.

	Saudi Riyals	Approximate U.S. Dollars
1. Oil revenues	375,000,000	75,000,000
2. Income tax	866,000,000	173,200,000
3. Zakah	1,600,000	320,000
4. Customs	126,000,000	25,200,000
5. Harbor fees	4,500,000	900,000
6. Port fees	500,000	100,000
7. Quarantine fees	7,506,000	1,501,200
8. Government press	1,100,000	220,000
9. Saudi airlines	32,000,000	6,400,000
10. Railroad and Damman port	36,000,000	7,200,000
11. Services of development companies	5,276,000	1,055,200
12. Posts, telephones, and telegraphs revenues	6,500,000	1,300,000
13. Residence permits	1,500,000	300,000
14. Passports	1,600,000	320,000
15. Vehicle license plates	1,500,000	300,000
16. Drivers' licenses	500,000	100,000
17. Stamps	4,500,000	900,000
18. Airport fees	1,500,000	300,000
19. Road tax	5,000,000	1,000,000
20. Ministry of Agriculture services	1,500,000	300,000
21. Nationality booklets	16,000	3,200
22. Commercial registry and trademarks	1,000,000	200,000
23. Company registration fees	10,000	2,000
24. Certification of Deeds	35,000	7,000
25. Rental of state property	1,500,000	300,000
26. Government sales	2,500,000	500,000
27. Refund of payments	750,000	150,000
28. Pensions	10,000,000	2,000,000
29. Miscellaneous income	2,607,000	521,400
30. Revenues from previous years	2,000,000	400,000
TOTAL	SR 1,500,000,000	$300,000,000

POLITICAL ADMINISTRATION

Schedule No. 2, Estimate of Expenditures for the Year 1377 A.H.

	Saudi Riyals	Approximate U.S. Dollars
1. (a) Appropriations for HM the King and the Royal Family	70,000,000	14,000,000
(b) The Royal Cabinet budget	8,000,000	1,600,000
2. (a) The Council of Ministers administrative staff	2,380,000	476,000
(b) The Secretariat General of the Council of Ministers	1,650,000	330,000
(c) The Grievance Board	1,670,000	334,000
(d) The Office of the Comptroller General	2,570,000	514,000
(e) The Consultative Council	900,000	180,000
3. Ministry of Foreign Affairs	20,000,000	4,000,000
4. (a) Ministry of Defense and Aviation	280,000,000	56,000,000
(b) Saudi airlines	27,000,000	5,400,000
(c) Civil aviation	3,000,000	600,000
5. Ministry of the Interior and its agencies	86,700,000	17,340,000
6. Ministry of Education	87,000,000	17,400,000
7. Ministry of Communications and its Agencies	109,600,000	21,920,000
8. Ministry of Agriculture	21,000,000	4,200,000
9. Ministry of Finance and its agencies	35,000,000	7,000,000
10. Ministry of Health	44,700,000	8,940,000
11. Ministry of Commerce	3,000,000	600,000
12. Royal Guard	16,000,000	3,200,000
13. National Guard	60,000,000	12,000,000
14. (a) Allocations for Tribes and Mujahidin	192,000,000	38,400,000
(b) Royal guests and public expenses	30,000,000	6,000,000
15. Intelligence	5,000,000	1,000,000
16. (a) Judiciary of the Hijaz and dependencies	12,000,000	2,400,000
(b) Judiciary of Najd and dependencies	6,000,000	1,200,000
17. (a) The Office of the Mufti, Institute and dependencies	500,000	100,000
(b) (Religious) institutes	10,500,000	2,100,000
18. (a) Committees for Public Morality in the Hijaz	4,000,000	800,000
(b) Committees for Public Morality in Najd and dependencies	5,000,000	1,000,000
(c) Imams and Muezzins in Najd and dependencies	1,500,000	300,000
19. Amirates of the (Najd) dependencies	18,000,000	3,600,000
20. Broadcasting, press, and publications	6,000,000	1,200,000
21. Labor Department	2,000,000	400,000
22. Department of Electricity	4,000,000	800,000

		Saudi Riyals	Approximate U.S. Dollars
23.	Schools, orphanages, and homes for old people	7,330,000	1,466,000
24.	Secondary projects and public expenditures	14,000,000	2,800,000
25.	Pensions and severance allowances	2,000,000	400,000
26.	Miscellaneous expenditures	23,500,000	4,700,000
27.	Refund of revenues	500,000	100,000
28.	Expansion of the two holy mosques and general projects (see itemized list below)	76,000,000	15,200,000
29.	Emergency expenditures	75,000,000	15,000,000
	TOTAL	SR 1,375,000,000	$275,000,000

List of Projects Approved in the Budget for the Year 1377 and Allocations Therefore

Details of Item No. 28	Saudi Riyals	Approximate U.S. Dollars
Holy Mosque	30,000,000	6,000,000
Prophet's mosque	5,000,000	1,000,000
Medina projects	1,000,000	200,000
Mosques	2,000,000	400,000
Religious institutes	1,000,000	200,000
Government buildings	10,000,000	2,000,000
Eastern Province projects	6,000,000	1,200,000
Water projects	5,000,000	1,000,000
Government employees housing project in Riyadh	8,000,000	1,600,000
Riyadh electricity	4,000,000	800,000
Broadcasting	4,000,000	800,000
TOTAL	SR 76,000,000	$15,200,000

Radio Mecca commented as follows on the budget:

"With the publication of the Royal Decree on the State Budget for 1377 A.H. (28 July 1957 to 17 July 1958) and the details of the budget itself, the financial situation in the country should become stable. The passing phases of the financial crisis began with the aggression against Egypt and Saudi Arabia's decision to stop oil exports to the countries responsible for the aggression. King Saud further assisted Egypt during her economic crisis and gave other financial assistance to many Arab countries. In addition to that, development projects in

188

the country consumed a large part of the state revenues. Under these circumstances, expenditures rose above revenues.

"To meet this financial situation, King Saud, several months ago called for an economic and financial Congress which met in Jidda. As an outcome of the Congress, import committees were formed and were authorized to issue permits for allocating hard currency for necessary imports. Several weeks ago, King Saud solicited the assistance of world-famous economists to study the financial situation under his immediate guidance.

"As a result of these measures it was found necessary to reduce state expenditures and withhold a part of the state income to settle government debts. His Majesty began with himself and reduced his personal expenses. The expenditures which were estimated at more than SR 2,000 million were thus reduced to SR 1,375 million; while the state income was estimated at SR 1,500 million. The surplus of SR 125 million will be allocated to the Saudi Arabian Monetary Agency in the form of dollars and other hard currency which will back Saudi currency. The Agency will receive in the next few months additional sums of money for this purpose.

"New regulations have been set forth for the Monetary Agency and they shall be applied in accordance with the general budget. On the basis of these measures and within the next few months, the restrictions imposed on currency and on imports will be lifted. The rate of the Saudi Riyal then, will be fixed at the official rate as approved by the International Monetary Fund. The Riyal will thus have an internationally recognized purchasing power." (Radio Mecca, 13 January 1958)

The foregoing is evidence that the often repeated criticism of the enormous sums spent by King Saud and the royal family for personal pleasures only is not entirely justified. There is no doubt that much of the annual income from oil is spent on lavish living by the prodigious royal family, but it is also true that a very real beginning has been made to spread expenditures systematically for the benefit of the whole country.

To support this statement, the following is quoted from a letter of the Saudi Arabian Ambassador, Shaikh Abdullah Al-Khayyal, Washington, D.C., March 5th, 1957: "In the matter of health His Majesty has approved a five years' project to raise the health standards in his country. Hospitals are being constructed in all large and small cities. In 1955 fifteen new hospitals were erected. Mobile health units provide Bedouins and tribes in isolated areas with medical treatment and vaccination—hospitalization, surgery, analysis, and medicine are provided free to all Saudi Arabians.

"Education is being stressed in Saudi Arabia. There are over 560 modern schools in Saudi Arabia—primary and secondary, in addition to five colleges. Construction is now underway on a new university in Riyadh.

"It is estimated that at present there are approximately five hundred students specializing in various educational and industrial fields abroad, at the expense of the Saudi Arabian government.

"The government is now in process of constructing a railway 600 miles long between Riyadh and the Red Sea, linking the cities of Riyadh, Medina, Jidda, and Mecca.

"An agreement has been reached by the three governments of Saudi Arabia, Jordan, and Syria to repair and put into operation the old Hijaz line between Medina and Damascus, which links with the eastern express trains of Europe. His Majesty gave two million Syrian liras to pay the cost of preparing plans and technical details of this project.

"Last year His Majesty opened the new Jidda-Medina road measuring 350 miles.

"There are experimental farms under construction in Kharj and Jizan. Modern mechanical reapers, harvesters, and other machinery and spare parts are sold to the farmers at a nominal reduced price, which can be paid in small installments.

"Expert advice is supplied to the farmers through printed

pamphlets, press publications, and the radio, as well as by direct contacts between members of the free Advisory Service and farmers in agricultural districts.

"Further, agricultural missions are sent abroad in order to broaden the scope of farmers and acquaint them with the most recent methods in agriculture and to teach them to operate modern farm machinery."

This lengthy quotation is made to emphasize the attempts being made by the new monarch with his recently appointed Council of Ministers to use much of the fabulous oil revenues to develop and benefit his country.

As with our own foreign aid programs there are bound to be cases of inefficient administration, but the efforts are well worth greatest commendation.

The political divisions of the nation are hereunder listed on the authority of Col. Gerald de Gaury, *Saudi Arabia Notebook,* Cairo, 1943:

NAJD (Administered from the capital, Riyadh)
 I. *Province of Najd*
    (a) Hauta
    (b) Hariq
    (c) Wadi Dawasir
    (d) Washm
    (e) Sudair
    (f) Mihmal
    (g) Khurma, including Turbah and neighboring oases
    (h) Bisha
        Bedouin divisions attached direct to headquarters of the Najd province
    (i) Subai and Suhul
    (j) Ataiba
    (k) Duwadami, including Sha'ara and numerous Ikhwan settlements

191

(l) Qahtan

(m) Mutair, with headquarters at Artawiyah

II. *Province of Qasim* (headquarters at Anaiza)
   (a) Anaiza
   (b) Buraida, including villages along Wadi Ruma
   (c) Rass, including Qasr ibn-Uqail, Subai, and Naibaniya

III. *Province of Jabal Shammar* (headquarters at Hail)
   (a) Hail
   (b) Taima
   (c) Khaibar
   (d) Mutair (*see i-m above, when not attached to Riyadh*)

HASA (Headquarters at Dammam)
   (a) Hofuf, which includes Jash and Mubarraz
   (b) Qatif, including Sofwa, Awamia, Dammam, Sinabis, Darain Island, Tarut, Ruffiya, and islands off the Hasa coast near Qatif
   (c) Jubail including Ainain
   (d) Bedouin divisions of

Murra	Mutair
beni-Hajir	Manasir
beni-Khalid	Awazim
Ajman	Rashaida

ASIR (Headquarters at Abha)
   (a) Abha
   (b) Shahran, including Suk ibn-Mushait or Khamis Mushait
   (c) Qahtan
   (d) Rijal Al Ma
   (e) Najran
   District of Asir Tihama (Headquarters at Jizan)
   (a) Sabya, including Darb and Baish
   (b) Jizan
   (c) abu-Arish

HIJAZ (Administered by the Viceroy, Headquarters at Mecca)

(a) Qariyat al-Milh, including Qat and Minwa
(b) Jauf (formerly under Jabal Shammar province of Najd and its dependencies, including Sakaka)
(c) Tabuk, with jurisdiction over the bani-Atiya and Huwaitat
(d) al-Ula with jurisdiction over the Hutaim and wuld-Ali
(e) Duba, with jurisdiction over Tuqaiqat and Hawaitat (Tihama)
(f) Wejh, with jurisdiction over the Billi
(g) Umluj
(h) Yenbo
(i) Medina, with jurisdiction over the greater part of the Harb
(j) Rabigh
(k) Gadhima
(l) Jidda
(m) Mecca
(n) Taif
(o) Ghamid and Zahran
(p) beni-Shehr (headquarters at Numas)
(q) Lith
(r) Kunfida
(s) Birka, with jurisdiction over the beni-Hasan

Foreign Affairs

Representing H.R.H. Amir Faisal—Prime Minister, Viceroy of Hijaz and Minister of Foreign Affairs—is an Acting Minister of Foreign Affairs stationed at Jidda. This important office has been filled by Shaikh Yusuf Yassin—a native of Latakia—since 1939, when its former occupant, Fuad Hamza, was sent to Paris as Saudi Arabian Minister. His Royal Highness Prince Abdullah Faisal has been appointed Minister of Health and

Interior. H.R.H. Prince Mishal has replaced his brother Prince Mansur, who died in 1951, as Minister of Defense. Shaikh Yusuf Yassin is Deputy Minister of Foreign Affairs, spending much time in Cairo as a leader in the Arab League. Fuad Bey Hamza was in Riyadh as one of His Majesty's most valued advisors, until his death in 1952. Rushdi Bey Melhas—a long time member of the royal palace entourage—usually welcomes guests arranges their audiences and accommodations.

The following is a list of diplomatic representatives as of August 17, 1957:

EMBASSIES OF SAUDI ARABIA

Afghanistan	Kabul, 1289 I. Shepur; ambassador to be appointed
Egypt	Cairo, 2 Midan Al-Rimaha, Giza, Shaikh Ibrahim Sulaiman
Ethiopia	Addis Ababa, Shaikh Omar Sakaf
France	Paris, 7 Rue Ante Pascal, Diplomatic relations broken off since November 1956 by invasion of Egypt by France
India	New Delhi, 6, Hardinge Avenue, Shaikh Yusuf Alfozan
Iran	Tehran, Hedyat Avenue, Sayed Hamza Goths
Iraq	Baghdad, Waziria, Shaikh Ibrahim Al-Suwayel
Japan	Tokyo, Shaikh Asad Al-Faqih
Lebanon	Beirut, Rue Verdun, Shaikh Abdulaziz Al-Kuhaimi
Libya	Tripoli, Shaikh Ibrahim Sulaiman (also accredited to Egypt)
Morocco	Shaikh Khair El-Deen Zerekli
Pakistan	Karachi, Talpur House, Dipch and Ojha Road, Bunder Road Extension, Shaikh Abdul Rahman Al-Bassam

POLITICAL ADMINISTRATION

Spain	Madrid, Calle Marquesdel Riscal 12, Dr. Midhat Shaikh Al-Ard
Sudan	Khartoum, Shaikh Abdul Rahman Hulasi
Syria	Damascus, Shaikh Abdul Aziz Bin Zaid
United Kingdom	London, 24 Kensington Palace Gardens, W. 8, (Shaikh Hafez Wahba) Diplomatic relations broken off since November 1956 by invasion of Egypt.
United States	Washington 8, D.C., 2800 Woodland Drive, N.W., Shaikh Abdullah Al-Khayyal

LEGATIONS OF SAUDI ARABIA

Indonesia	Djakarta, No. 3 Djalan Imam Sondjol, Shaikh Abdul Rouf Al-Sabaan
Italy	Rome, Lungo Tevere Delle Nav 19, Shaikh Mowafack Al-Alusi
Jordan	Amman, Shaikh I. Khami
Switzerland	Berne, Hotel Bellevue Palace, Shaikh Fakhri Shaikh Al-Ard
Tunisia	Tunis, Shaikh Ali Awad
Turkey	Ankara, No. 12, Kazi Mustafa Kamal Bulvard, Shaikh Ibrahim Islam
West Germany	Bonn, Shaikh Jawad Zikri
Yemen	Taiz, Shaikh Ibn Ibiqan

UNITED NATIONS DELEGATES

New York City	(Office) 3117 Chrysler Building, Shaikh Ahmed Shukairy, Dr. Omar Khadra and Shaikh Jamil M. Baroody

CONSULATES

Egypt	Cairo, 2 Midan Al-Rimaha, Giza, Shaikh Abdul Aziz Dagistani

195

Egypt	Alexandria, 232 26th July Avenue, Egypt, Talat Nazir
	Suez, 46 Saleh El-Din El-Ayobi Street, Egypt, Abdu al-Askary
Iraq	Basrah, Shaikh Mohamed Al-Shubaili
Jordan	Jerusalem, Shaikh Ali Al-Sugair
United States	New York, 405 Lexington Avenue, Room 3103, Shaikh Ibrahim Bakhur

It was often asked what would happen to the Saudi Arabian government after the founder was gone. In answer one must bear in mind that Crown Prince Saud had been designated by his father as the successor to the throne. Both the *Ulama* (theologians) and the state council elected Amir Saud, confirming his succession. I have been informed that all his brothers who were of age swore allegiance to Amir Saud in case of the death of their father.

King Saud has in turn given his brother Faisal, his Prime Minister, powers to reorganize the government as well as to have complete charge of foreign affairs, internal affairs, and finances. The close family allegiance seems to have continued to the present.

III. The Position of Saudi Arabia in World Economy

15. Contact with the West

Diplomatic-Consular Relations

SAUDI ARABIA was long a land closed to the Western peoples, principally because it is the heart of Islam. Religious taboos and not inhospitality have prevented free travel in the country, especially in the provinces of Hijaz and Najd. All foreigners require special permission to enter Saudi Arabia, the usual ports of entry being Jidda and in Hasa. Where there are no Saudi Arab representatives, the granting of the visa is deferred until one arrives at Cairo, Beirut, Baghdad, or Bahrain. Here a visa is issued if entry is approved by the Saudi Arabian government.

Foreign embassies, legations, and business firms are located at Jidda. Members and employees of these, except of the oil and mining companies, are not allowed to go without special government permission beyond the prescribed limits of the city, 60 miles north and south, and 18 miles eastward. The soldier escort provided by the government for travel outside these limits is either paid a previously agreed-upon salary, or is given a substantial gratuity. Since life and property are perfectly safe throughout Saudi Arabia today, ibn-Saud having abolished banditry, the function of an escort consists in evidencing the King's approval of a foreigner's presence, and in providing whatever personal aid and guidance may be necessary.

Established in Jidda are Afghan, American, British, Chinese, Egyptian, French, Indonesian, Iranian, Iraqi, Turkish embassies and legations. The American Embassy, first as a Legation, was established in May 1943. The first full-time resident minister, Colonel William Eddy, was born of missionary parents in Sidon, Syria, spent many years in Arabic-speaking countries, and made a brilliant record in Arabia. In mid-1946 he was succeeded by J. Rives Childs, till 1951; then by Ray Hare, followed by George Wadsworth.

The Saudi government is kept in touch with the representatives of foreign powers through an Acting Minister of Foreign Affairs, stationed permanently at Jidda. Having conferred with foreign agents, Shaikh Yusuf Yassin who has occupied this office since 1941, submits synopses, accompanied by his own views, to H.R.H. Amir Faisal, Secretary of State for Foreign Affairs, who has residences in Jidda as well as Mecca. The latter informs the King of all major matters and is governed by the views of his brother, whose decisions are final.

Amir Faisal comes to Jidda whenever foreign questions demand his presence or a foreign representative arrives who is of sufficient rank to merit his personal welcome and reception. In that event the Amir resides in Kazam Palace at Nazla, a mile east from Jidda, where all foreign representatives are officially received by him. As a rule the King visits Jidda twice every year, once after the great pilgrimage holiday, and at some other occasion. Generally the important figures of Jidda are received in audience by the King in this order: first, Saudi Arabian government officials, leading businessmen, and other distinguished citizens; second, foreign diplomats, for whom part of a day may be set aside; third, foreign firms, including executive heads of concessionaire companies, the representatives of foreign banking, shipping, and other firms, to whom a period of time is definitely given in advance.

Concessionaire Companies

There is at present only one concessionaire company in Saudi Arabia. This is the Arabian American Oil Company (Aramco), which holds two concessions, signed May 29, 1933, and May 31, 1939, respectively. This company employs 13,213 Saudi Arabians, 3,541 other Moslems, and 2,878 Americans.

Another concessionaire company was a metal mining company, the Saudi Arabian Mining Syndicate, Limited. This concession was signed December 24, 1934. There were 800 to 925 Saudi Arabians employed and a staff of 30 to 35 Americans, British, and Russians. After seventeen years of operation, the last of the profitable ore was mined, milled, and the mine closed down. The company was liquidated in 1954.

Banks

Although some of the banking facilities have been mentioned in the descriptions of the cities of Riyadh and Jidda, these data will be included here.

The bank with by far the longest history in Saudi Arabia is the Netherlands Trading Society of Holland. In its former Jidda office, an old wooden structure of many years ago, the counting and handing over to the Saudi government of the first loan of the oil company consisting of 30,000 gold sovereigns was made during the torrid heat of a July afternoon in 1933 and is an unforgettable memory—there was no air conditioning in those days. This bank handled the accounts of the oil company and the mining company for many years. There is now a branch at Dammam.

During the early days—that is, prior to 1930—the British Westminster Bank, Ltd., represented by Gellatly, Hankey & Co. Ltd., served many business firms as well as the Saudi government, but I have received information that it is no longer functioning.

The French bank of Indo-Chine was the next foreign financial institution to establish an office in Jidda. It now has a branch on the Persian Gulf.

The National Monetary Agency was founded to work out a currency stabilization plan. This was accomplished by the aid of Point Four under the direction of Dr. Samuel S. Stratton, commencing in 1952. This agency is practically the official Saudi Arabian government bank. It has done a remarkable feat in a country using gold and silver coinage from time immemorial to successfully introduce a paper currency called "receipts." Naturally many commercial transactions are greatly facilitated by this innovation.

There is a new Bank of Riyadh located in that city. Its capital is largely local.

There is a National Bank of Saudi Arabia which has branches in all the Middle East states.

In addition there are the other Middle Eastern banks, as follows—Bank of Lebanon, Bank of Pakistan, Arab Bank, Cairo Bank, and Bank of Egypt (the Bank Misr).

There is but one United Kingdom representative, the British Bank for the Middle East.

Only lately have any American banks established offices in Saudi Arabia, although the Guaranty Trust Company of New York has long conducted an extensive business through its correspondent, The Netherlands Trading Society. The National City Bank of New York has founded branches in Jidda and in Dammam. The American Express Company has established a branch in Jidda. It conducts banking as well as its usual travel and express business.

Steamship Agencies

Outside of Jidda on the Red Sea coast there are no steamship agencies except those of the Khedivial Mail Line located at Yenbo and Wejh. Among the steamship agencies represented at Jidda, the following are the most important:

Agent	for	Lines
1. Ali Reza Zainal		Mogul Lines
		Isthmian Line
		Turner Morrison, Ltd.
		Halal Shipping Co.
		Cowasji Dinshaw Co.
2. Bank Misr		Misr Steamship Line
3. Fazil Arab		Hansa Line
4. Gellatly, Hankey & Co., Ltd.		Represented a large number of British and Continental shipping companies and was Lloyd's agent for 80 years. Recently discontinued.

5. Netherlands Trading Society Dutch Lines, including
    Holland-Lloyd
    Blue Funnel
    Lamport and Holt

Mercantile Firms

Trade transactions in the international field were under Allied control during World War II and little free enterprise was possible until 1945. The following are the principal firms dealing in exports and imports:

Firms	*Nationality*
Anglo-Arab Construction Co.	Saudi Arabian
Ajaji Bros.	" "
Al-Qusaibi Bros.	" "
Arabian American Trading Co.	" "
al-Jabir Bros.	" "
E. U. Juffali Bros.	" "
Ali Reza Zainal	" "
Fazil Arab	" "
Gellatly, Hankey & Co., Ltd.	British
(Recently discontinued)	
Husain Uwaini & Co.	Saudi Arabian
Mitchell Cotts Ltd.	British-Dutch
Netherlands Trading Society	Dutch

New foreign and local companies are now doing international business in and with Saudi Arabia. This is facilitated by a chamber of commerce.

A royal decree was enacted and published in the newspaper *Umm al-Qura* (the official organ of the Saudi government) at Mecca on January 18, 1946, for the formation of a Chamber of Commerce at Jidda. A committee of thirteen leading merchants was formed which elected Mohamed Alireza as its first president, with Ahmed Mohamed Saleh vice-president. One of the first rules enacted was to give foreign companies established in Jidda the right to membership. There were initially 51 members divided into three classes: 28 first class, 16 second, and 7 third. An official publication was inaugurated with articles by members, and others copied from foreign commercial magazines.

The happy results of the activities of the Chamber of Commerce along with the Ministry of Commerce and Industry are shown by the establishment of the following enterprises: ammunition, auto service and repair facilities, cement and block manufacture, fishing and fish cannery, ice, iron foundry, leather goods, tanning, pearls, pottery, printing, rug making, sheetmetal working, soap manufacture, tile and marble production.

To convey an idea of the importance of International Trade other than oil, I quote from data compiled by the Research Department of Aramco:

Imports	1955
Foodstuffs	$44,500,000
Textiles	22,900,000
Vehicles and machinery	62,300,000
Pharmaceuticals, tobacco, confections	11,100,000
Construction material	12,600,000
Aramco	50,000,000
Others	37,600,000
Total	$241,000,000

This is an impressive increase from five years before, when the total imports (1950) were valued at $101,000,000.

Exports (other than oil), Estimated at $1,000,000. These consist principally of dates, pearls, and charcoal, but it may be noted that the Mahad Dhahab Mine, of the Saudi Arabian Mining Syndicate, Ltd., closed down in July 1954 after having exported 769,631 ounces of gold and 1,003,130 ounces of silver with a total approximate value of $32,000,000.

Foreign Contracting Companies

Under novel and at times difficult situations due to heat,

desert conditions, inexperienced native labor, and foreign language problems, the foreign contractors have shown tremendous accomplishments. Herewith is a brief synopsis of these:

(1) International Bechtel Corporation of 220 Bush Street, San Francisco 4, California;

For the Saudi Arabian government:

Rebuilding Jidda-Mecca highway, 46 miles

Construction Jidda pier, 5,500 feet of causeway and 1,845 feet steel trestle

Construction of Jidda airport, including all terminal offices and shops, two asphalted runways (6,000 and 6,500 feet long) equipped with lights for night operation

Survey of highway route from Jidda to Medina, 239 miles

Construction of diesel power plant at Jidda

Construction of diesel power plant at Riyadh

Construction of airport at Riyadh

Construction of landing field at Hofuf

Completion of Dammam port, including a 5-mile causeway and 2-mile steel trestle, with pier-head 744 by 84 feet all carrying government standard-gauge railway. (The British firm of Thomas Ward, Ltd., commenced the causeway.)

For Aramco

Refinery at Ras Tanaura, approximately 250,000 barrels per day

Construction of pier at Ras Tanaura 3,750 feet long with two "T" arms of 600 feet

Construction (1957) of a 15,000-barrel-per-day plant for reducing sulphur content in diesel oil

Construction of 10 gas-oil separating plants

Construction of hundreds of houses of several types

Construction of 142 miles of 22-inch pipeline and related facilities to bring the Safaniya Off-Shore Oil Field into production

For Tapline

Construction of Ras Mishaab terminal and facilities including a "Skyhook" line 15,000 feet long with an island of steel pile for discharging ships in 45 feet depth of water

Surveying and construction of 854 miles of 30- and 31-inch Trans-Arabian Pipe Line

(2) Williams Brothers Overseas Company, of San Francisco, California: construction of 213.8 miles of 30- and 31-inch pipe for Tapline

(3) John Howard & Co., Ltd., London: construction of warehouses on Jidda pier

(4) Thomas Ward & Co., Ltd., of Sheffield, England: construction of initial section of Dammam pier causeway, construction of some miles of Jidda-Medina paved highway.

(5) Michael Baker, Jr., Inc., of 1604 "K" Street, N.W., Washington 6, D.C.

Construction of marine railway and wharfage extension at Jidda pier

Construction of Jidda power-plant extension to a total of 3,300 kilowatts in 1953

Construction of office and apartment buildings in Jidda

Remodeling and air-conditioning building of the Saudi Arabian Monetary Agency

Construction of wharf for landing of small boats with pilgrims at Jidda

Construction of Nasrieh power house at Riyadh for 2,200 kilowatts

Construction of streets in Jidda and in Riyadh

Making plans and commencing construction of Saudi Arabian military base at Kharj

(6) Brown and Blauvelt, 468 Fourth Avenue, New York City, N.Y.: Survey, estimates, and recommendations for the rehabilitation of the Hijaz Railway from Medina to Maan, Jordan, 522 miles

(7) Burns and Roe, Inc., of 160 West Broadway, New York City, N.Y.

For the Saudi National Company provided management services for the expansion and operation of the company's utility system

Construction, design, and supervision of installation of power plant of 1-5,000 kilowatt gas turbine generator with provision for two more similar units during period January to June 1955

Surveyed and submitted recommendations for present and future electrical requirements for Jidda

Planned and specified lighting for Medina airport

Examined gypsum deposit near Yenbo for Shaikh Mohamed Bin Ladin. In 1955 specified and recommended plant for 100 tons per day output of plaster. (This confirms my recommendations of 1947 when I located and examined this project.)

King Saud as well as his father and ministers, have repeatedly expressed their desire for closer relations with the West, in particular with the United States. Their experiences with the oil and mining companies, cordial throughout, have also been extremely beneficial to the country. The King sent his sons, Prince Saud, Prince Faisal, Prince Khalid, and Prince Mansour to Egypt, England, and America to create better understanding with these countries. The first visit to America by a Saudi prince was made in the autumn of 1943. On that occasion, Prince Faisal and Prince Khalid, accompanied by Shaikh Ibrahim Sulaiman and Shaikh Abdullah Balkhair and Shaikh Hafiz Wahba, Saudi Arabian Ambassador to London, and a bodyguard of two Arabs, were the guests of the U.S. Department of State. They were received at Washington first, then in New York and Princeton, after which they visited New Mexico and Arizona, and went on to California. They saw American methods of ore treatment and smelting in New

Jersey, agricultural and animal husbandry methods in the semi-arid southwestern states, and oil production and refining in California. That was the beginning of a very practical American diplomatic policy which may pay huge dividends of international peace and prosperity, not only in our contact with Saudi Arabia but with other countries as well.

With the objectives of cementing diplomatic relations and furthering the general development of Saudi Arabia, a new Standard Technical Assistance Agreement was signed on February 17, 1957, by M. Perez-Guerrero, Representative of the Technical Assistance Board, and Shaikh Ali Awad, Acting Under Secretary, Ministry of Foreign Affairs on behalf of the government of Saudi Arabia.

This agreement was for giving advice, making available services of experts, organizing seminars, training programs, demonstration projects, and expert working groups; awarding scholarships and fellowships, and making arrangements for candidates nominated by the Saudi Arabian government to study or receive training outside the country; preparing and executing pilot projects, or research, in such places as may be mutually agreed.

During the coming year it is expected that U.S. aid to Saudi Arabia will consist of assistance in the improvement of the port of Damman and the construction of a civil air terminal at Dhahran. Both result from the exchange of notes of April 2, 1957, which extended the Dhahran Air Field Agreement. Detailed plans are still in the preliminary stage. For the Damman project some $20,000,000 of grant aid will be required and for the air terminal $5,000,000. Negotiations are under way for the necessary economic assistance agreement and project agreement.

Point Four

"Point Four" work was carried on from 1950 to the fall of 1954. The first work was undertaken by the Geological Survey Mission, which subsequently became a part of TCA. Its purpose was the development of the water resources; a great deal was accomplished in locating sources, drilling wells, and giving pertinent advice.

In 1952 advisers regarding financial, customs, and budget matters arrived. They assisted in the establishment of the Saudia Arabian Monetary Agency and the creation of the new Customs Tariff Law.

During 1953 the following were accomplished: completion of the survey for the Jidda-Riyadh railway; training in the United States of a number of Saudi Arabs; surveys and reports made in the fields of agriculture, public health, and education; exploratory survey for economic minerals; assistance in the organization and establishment of the Ministries of Communications, Agriculture, and Education.

In mid-1954 the Saudi Arabian government decided, while it had before it several special project agreements, that it no longer wished the type of technical assistance offered by United States—at least for the time being, but the subsequent 1957 agreement may resuscitate the above projects, or some of them.

The Buraimi Dispute

A serious situation has developed in the southeastern part of Arabia, which includes the Buraimi Oasis. This oasis has an area of only 15 square miles and an estimated population of perhaps 10,000. It is a small part of a large desert territory—approximately 30,000 square miles—which was made subject to international arbitration in 1954. Since records show that the resident tribes have paid taxes to rulers of Saudi Arabia for over one hundred years, the late King Abdul Aziz claimed this as a part of his kingdom. By virtue of their treaties with the Trucial States, the British government disputed this claim, although the Admiralty Handbook of 1920 stated that this territory was outside the authority of either the ruler of Abu Dhabi or of the Sultan of Muscat, on the Persian Gulf.

Since it is a part of the Rub al Khali, the "Empty Quarter," a huge desert, there was little interest shown until the developments by Aramco indicated that oil structures might extend into this area. To settle the dispute, King Saud and the British government agreed to arbitrate, an agreement concluded in Jidda on July 30, 1954. The first meeting of the arbitration tribunal was held at Nice, France, January 22, 1955. The tribunal consisted of five members, including Sir Reader Bullard, representing Britain, and Shaikh Yusuf Yasin, representing Saudi Arabia. The others were called neutral members.

After days of hearing witnesses, the neutral members proposed to meet on September 16 of that same year to render a decision. The evidence indicated that this would be in favor of the Saudi claims. Sir Reader Bullard chose this date to resign, walking out before the decision could be announced.

On October 26 a British note was delivered to the Saudi Arabian government, stating that its forces had taken over the Buraimi Oasis, and warned Saudi Arabs not to cross the line they had established. Prime Minister Anthony Eden announced this fact in the House of Commons on the same day.

On November 9, 1955, Saudi Arabia made a formal protest and proposed a resumption of arbitration proceedings. To date, the British government has not agreed to reopen such proceedings. It has maintained forces to protect the operations being conducted by the Iraq Petroleum Company. On August 20, 1957, Saudi Arabia in the United Nations Security Council protested the British government's use of Buraimi.

In April 1958 Prime Minister Prince Faisal issued the statement that his country was willing to renew the diplomatic relations that had been broken off with Britain in 1956, due to her joining France and Israel in the invasion of Egypt. Since British forces have now been withdrawn, Saudi Arabia is ready to renew relations, provided Britain agrees to resume the suspended arbitration proceedings regarding Buraimi.

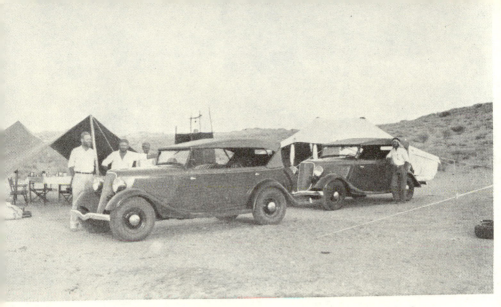

Dhahran, September 1933. The first camp of American oil geologists

Dhahran, today. The headquarters of Aramco, where most of the approximately 3,000 American employees live

Aramco has developed gardens and air-conditioned homes, like these in Dhahran, for its Senior Staff employees

Both Arabs and Americans are given excellent treatment at the Aramco hospital at Dhahran

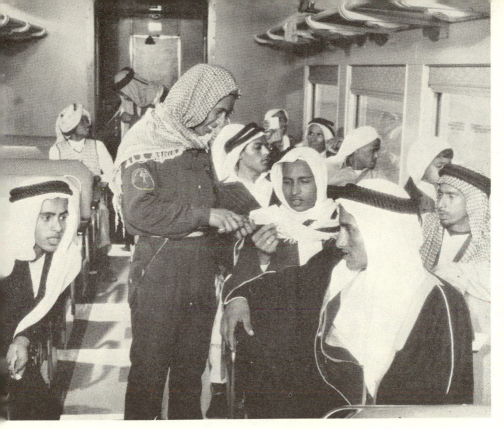

Interior of passenger train on the Saudi Arab railway

Work train during the construction of the 357-mile railway from Dammam
(Persian Gulf) to Riyadh

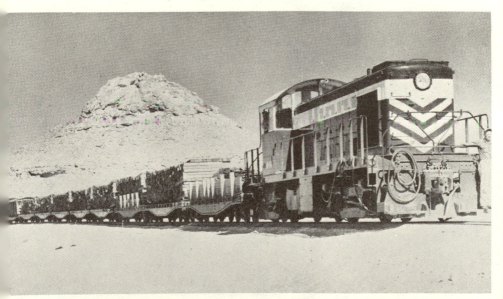

Mahad Dhahab (Cradle of Gold) mine, showing workings of 2,000 years ago, a possible source of a considerable amount of King Solomon's gold. It was the plant of the Saudi Arabian Mining Syndicate from 1935 to 1954

Mahad Dhahab mill, where 200 to 300 tons of ore per day were treated by the cyanide process

New hydroformer in the Ras Tanura 189,000-barrels-per-day refinery

One of the supply bases in the Ghawar oil field. This geological structure of 140 miles is the world's longest yet developed

This 400-ton drilling rig, 1
feet tall, was moved across 2
miles of desert from Rub
Khali to the Uthmaniyah a1
of the Ghawar field

Aramco motor caravan commencing trip into the Rub al-Khali. Formerly
only camel caravans traversed this area

Welding 30-31-inch pipeline to convey 450,000 barrels of oil per day (1958) over 1,000 miles from Saudi Arabia to the Mediterranean

Ras Tanura pier, where tankers load to transport oil to world ports

Drilling one of the 28 offshore wells in Safaniya, the new submarine oil field in the Persian Gulf. Its length of 20 miles is the world's largest submarine oil structure yet developed

Laying the 137-mile pipeline to connect Safaniya with the refinery at Ras Tanura

16. Oil and Mines

Early Dealings with King ibn-Saud

SAUDI ARABIA is presumably the only country in the world whose development of oil and mining resulted from purely philanthropic sentiment. The late Charles R. Crane of New York, onetime United States Minister to China, acquired a lifelong devotion to the Near East, dating back to his early sojourn in Egypt as a young man. Subsequently, he served on the King-Crane Commission which in 1919 reported to President Woodrow Wilson on the Syrian-Palestinian situation. He educated several Syrian Arabs in America and was a director of Robert College in Istanbul. His desire to help the Arabs prompted him in the winter of 1926-1927 to visit the Imam Yahia, ruler of the Yemen—and he was, incidentally, the third American ever to visit the Yemen's capital city, Sanaa. Genuinely impressed by the cordiality of Imam Yahia and his endeavor to promote his country's welfare, Mr. Crane made him a startling offer. The Imam, on hearing that there were mines in his country, had expressed a desire to engage engineers who might examine the land, and give him a report on their findings. Mr. Crane volunteered to secure such experts and to provide their services as a gift to the Imam and his country. The Imam accepted this unique offer, skeptically perhaps. Upon his departure from the Yemen, Mr. Crane passed through Aden, where he related his experiences to the American Vice Consul, Mr. J. Loder Park, informing him of the proposal to provide the Imam with technical advisors.

In the spring of 1927 I passed through Aden on my return from a trip to Abyssinia. Mr. Park told me of Mr. Crane's idea and suggested a meeting between us in New York upon my arrival in America. The results of that meeting were the expeditions which took place from 1927 to 1932. My services were donated by Mr. Crane, entirely for the benefit of the Imam and his country.

In addition to an examination of mineral and mining possibilities, the work included investigations regarding roads, the establishment of experimental gardens, the gift and demonstration of hand- and animal-operated farming implements and equipment, the installation of various types of pumps and of windmills and engines—all contributed by Mr. Crane. There was also the gift and erection of the only steel truss highway bridge in Arabia, and advice on many matters relative to the development of natural resources, transportation, etc. On the first expedition I had an able assistant engineer, Mr. Lowe Whiting; the next year I took Charles Bradley, the eighteen-year-old grandson of Mr. Crane, and Mrs. Twitchell as assistants; the third season, my assistant was Harry C. Ballard, an old mining friend from the western part of the United States.

Reports of these unusual gifts reached Saudi Arabia. In the winter of 1930-1931 Mr. Crane accepted an invitation of King ibn-Saud to visit him at Jidda. Long an admirer and friend of the King, Mr. Crane was happy to discuss ways and means of rendering assistance to him and his realm. It soon appeared that ibn-Saud's principal desire was to find ample water supplies, especially flowing artesian wells in the Hijaz and Najd.

On March 30, 1931, I received a cable from Mr. Crane asking me to proceed to Jidda as soon as possible to examine the country for water possibilities, particularly in the vicinities of pilgrim routes. Engaged at that time in the construction of foundations for the highway bridge over the Wadi Laa in the Yemen, I arranged to leave the work in charge of Harry Ballard, and left the Yemen on the thirteenth of April, arriving in Jidda on April 15, 1931. Traveling over 1,500 miles through the Hijaz, I could find no geological evidence to justify the hope for flowing artesian wells. A pessimistic report had therefore to be made on the water question. Though a number of possibilities could be pointed out regarding the development of water in small units, reclamation projects on a large scale were entirely precluded. But mineral possibilities were suggested by the dead oil seeps seen at Duba and Muwailih and the ancient mines at Umm Garayat near Wejh.

The trip was arduous and Mrs. Twitchell was ill part of the time. Ibn-Saud's special representative was Khalid Bey Gargoni al-Walid, a man of high caliber who, driven out of Cyrenaica by the Italians, was given asylum by Saudi Arabia and served on the King's council for years, beginning in 1932. For a secretary-interpreter we had a brilliant young man from Lebanon, Najib Ibrahim Salha. Though the hosts did everything within their power for the comfort of our party, the small tires and comparatively poor engines of 1931 made the trip much more arduous than it would be today.

Upon receipt of the discouraging report regarding water supply, the Finance Minister, Shaikh Abdullah Sulaiman Al Hamdan, was considerably disappointed, although he expressed profound appreciation of our efforts. The meeting with him was held outside Jidda at Nazla where Kazam Palace now stands. A small wooden house served as the office and headquarters of the Finance Minister. It was evening and Persian rugs were spread out on the gravelly ground in front of the house. "Electreeks"—gasified kerosene lamps burning through mantles—gave a brilliant light. Shaikh Abdullah had read the reports carefully. After he had asked some pertinent questions he stated that the King and the Saudi government quite realized that practically all their revenue was then dependent on the annual pilgrimage to Mecca; that this fluctuated from year to year, and might become much less in the future than it had been in the past. In view of these conditions I was asked if I could suggest other practical sources of income, it being understood that my reports did not encourage anticipation of any large agricultural increase in the Hijaz.

I had prepared for such a question. Because of experience with ancient mining in Cyprus, I had noticed mining possibilities during our recent trip. I had seen the ancient workings, mine ruins and tailings at Umm Garayat—near Wejh—so I replied that there might be minerals of commercial value in this country but that I had not yet seen enough to give an adequate opinion. Shaikh Sulaiman grasped the idea immediately and asked for further elucidation. In reply I explained that mining engineers must have facilities to travel over the country, take samples, make the necessary surveys and reports. Shaikh Abdullah Sulaiman thanked me and said he would present my ideas to King ibn-Saud.

On May 25, King ibn-Saud asked me to meet him at Shumaisi, on the Jidda-Mecca road about 16 miles from the Holy City and 30 from the seaport. Large tents were erected and a banquet was provided. The King expressed gratitude to Mr. Crane for my services, for the work done in the Hijaz and the meticulous care taken in making reports. He was sorry to have his hopes of artesian and other large water supplies dashed, but he said he would carefully consider the idea presented by the Minister of Finance. Ibn-Saud was pleased with my frankness—this was typical of him. He wished to hear the unfavorable as well as the favorable side of any matter under discussion. Before leaving Jidda on May 28, I was very much surprised when Najib Bey Salha brought us a bundle from the King. It contained an exquisite memento for Mrs. Twitchell and Najdi robes, worn only by royal families and relatives, for myself.

We immediately returned to the Yemen and on completing the bridge piers at Wadi Laa left for home, stopping off again at Jidda en route to America. Two nuggets of gold had been found near Taif by a Turkish prospector. The King wished me to see the locality and verify the fact that it was native gold. That is was placer gold was confirmed, but the geology and topography were such that little chance of developing any property of commercial size was promised. However, I thought there might prove to be small areas which would be beneficial to the Saudi government or the local groups. It seemed worthy of investigation.

On July 20 and 21 I had meetings at Jidda with the Minister of Finance. I presented my reports, as well as a plan for engaging competent engineers and geologists to examine Saudi Arabia for minerals and do sufficient clearing and development work in order to obtain a fair idea as to a reasonably valuable estimate and to make a competent report on each property that might interest foreign capital. On the twenty-second a check for £700 was given me by the Saudi government to cover the initial traveling and other expenses of the engineers I was to engage on their behalf.

On my return to New York in 1931 I made complete reports to Mr. Crane. I recommended examination of the properties in the vicinity of Taif, by drilling and testing of ground water in the vicinity of Jidda, using in both cases the hand-operated Empire drill. I proposed also the erection of the highway bridge in the Yemen. We had completed the concrete piers but the steel had not all arrived from the seaport of Hodeidah when we had left the Yemen. Mr. Crane agreed to this program but stated that because of the depression this would have to be the last expedition which he could finance. The time limit was to be six months. Mr. H. R. Mosley accompanied me as assistant, and we reached Hijaz in late October of 1931.

Mosley, with an Arab, Ahmad Fakhry, who supervised the laborers, and some soldiers, spent nearly six months in drilling, pitting, and sluicing in the vicinity west of Taif. Efficiently done, the work was nonetheless disappointing. Although "colors" and fine gold were found, nothing developed which would be profitable to even local groups of Saudi Arabia. Mosley conducted all his work with great care and efficiency.

After starting the placer work I returned to Jidda to rehabilitate the city's water supply. This was called the Waziria water system, as it was said to have been built by a Turkish

Wazir (cabinet minister) some sixty years before. The water tunnels and terra cotta piping were repaired. With the efficient assistance of the late Cyril Ousman, then automotive and condenser engineer for the Saudi government, a 16-foot diameter American windmill was erected along with an auxiliary pump-jack and small Diesel engine. It raised an average of 40 gallons per minute into the water tunnel and flowed to Jidda 7 miles to the west, making an appreciable addition to the city water supply.

On the completion of this work in December the Finance Minister said that King Abdul Aziz would greatly appreciate it if I would go across Arabia to advise him on the water resources and oil possibilities in his province of Hasa along the Persian Gulf. Although this would be a thousand-mile trip over rough country, where no American had ever been, the invitation was readily accepted.

Arrangements were made for Mrs. Twitchell to take charge of the Empire drill testing for ground water east of Jidda. She did a very capable job and had the unique experience of directing a crew of twenty to thirty devout Moslem Najdis, who served her with great courtesy. She lived alone in the house assigned to us in Jidda by the government—an unusual situation for a non-Moslem woman.

Leaving Jidda for Hasa via the placer at Taif on December 13, 1931, I arrived at the camp of King ibn-Saud on the nineteenth, at Maizila, about 50 miles north of Riyadh. Here during an interview the King asked me to visit Bahrain and gave me letters to the Shaikh and to the merchant princes, the Qusaibi brothers. At this camp I met H. St. J. B. Philby, the eminent Arabist and explorer of Arabia. It was after this encounter that Philby made the second crossing (northwestern) of the Empty Quarter. Mr. Bertram Thomas had made the first and more extensive crossing (southeastern) the year before.

I returned to Hofuf via Oqair on January 10, 1932. The King had arrived from Najd on the twelfth, and asked me to call for a discussion of the trip. As always I had a most cordial interview with unexpected queries and subjects arising. Ibn-Saud asked me to arrange for oil geologists and oil-well drillers. I recommended strongly that the results of the Number 1 Well at Bahrain be awaited before doing anything regarding oil. Since no evidence of faulting or difference geologically between Bahrain and the mainland of Hasa could be seen, and in view of the fact that oil-well exploration and drilling was extremely expensive, and that if the Bahrain well did not strike commercial oil it would be unlikely that it would be found in Hasa, a definite wait-and-see policy was advocated. On the other hand, if the Bahrain well proved a success, it was logical that commercial oil would be found in Hasa, but in greater quantities, because of its much greater area. Furthermore, it seemed quite possible that American capital might be found to undertake the great expense of oil development in Hasa under conditions that would greatly benefit Saudi Arabia. After much deliberation the King decided to follow my advice. During the discussions, he said that he had a former arrangement with a foreign oil company concerning Hasa, but as they had not lived up to their terms of agreement he wanted nothing more whatsoever to do with them.

As usual, Shaikh Yusuf Yassin, Chief Secretary, and Shaikh Abdullah Sulaiman, Minister of Finance, were with the King during nearly all of these interviews. They expressed their opinions and asked questions only at separate discussions, not in his presence. Knowing that my time was limited to six months, the Finance Minister wished me to return to Jidda as soon as possible to look at some ancient mines. This I did, after a farewell interview with the King on January 17. On leaving the next day a beautiful silk Arab gown from India for Mrs. Twitchell and a *mashlah* for myself were received, again in conformance with Arab hospitality.

The reports, which had to be typed, translated into Arabic, typed in Arabic, and then checked by February 3, were completed after my arrival in Jidda on January 26. On February 8, we left with our staff for an ancient working said to be only three days' journey from Jidda. We had two Ford cars and two Ford trucks, with a total of thirty men. Gasoline, oil, spare parts and tires, as well as food, tents, and water, made each vehicle overloaded. Traveling to within a few miles from Medina, we crossed river beds, hills and lava flows, brush and desert for eight instead of the estimated three days. At the end of a trip of 426 miles, the ancient workings, called *Mahad Dhahab* ("cradle of gold"), were reached. This is the mine that was worked by the Saudi Arabian Mining Syndicate, Ltd. In contrast to that first trip, the mine road connecting Mahad Dhahab with Jidda is 246 miles long and was regularly traversed by 15-ton trucks even though a 3,700 foot summit was crossed. In a light car the time was usually about ten hours, including stops for lunch and water.

February 15-20 were spent in the examination, including surveying, photographing, and sampling of the mine. The return to Jidda was more easily made; the distance was reduced to 404 miles and accomplished in five days, with arrival in Jidda on February 25, 1932. The samples were shipped to New York and to London to be assayed and checked. Reports were written and maps plotted. The six months' period donated by Mr. Crane was about to expire and I began to wind up that part of my work. H. R. Mosley sailed for New York on March 7 and on the same day Mrs. Twitchell and I sailed for Hodeida, where we met the American Bridge Company foreman, Dennis Castongay. An expert on steel erection, he and I were the only Americans on the job. In 19 days the 122-foot steel truss highway bridge was completely erected. On April 26 we again landed in Jidda, as previously arranged with King ibn-Saud and at his expense, but with Mr. Crane's agreement. During a trip of 1,022 miles five ancient mines were examined, but none showed sufficient value or tonnage to be of interest. On May 6 the results of the assays of the samples taken at Mahad Dhahab Mine were received, indicating satisfactory commercial values of ore.

From evening till midnight of May 25 I had a discussion with the King's representatives, Shaikh Abdullah Sulaiman and Shaikh Yusuf Yassin, regarding the possibilities of developing mines, oil, and roads in Saudi Arabia. The King had sent Shaikh Yusuf to say that on account of the depression, with the lack of pilgrims and consequent fall in revenue, he could not afford to follow out the development program previously planned and agreed upon. Furthermore he wished me to try to find capital to carry out the development previously discussed. To this I replied that I was an engineer and not a promoter in any way, but that I would be glad to do my best under two conditions: first, that Mr. Crane would be consulted, his consent obtained, and participation offered him; second, that His Majesty would sign a letter authorizing and requesting me to undertake this project. Neither of the two ministers could write the letter or make the decisions, but they agreed with my views and said they would submit the matter to King ibn-Saud and write subsequently.

In July 1932 a letter of request and authorization reached me in New York. Mr. Crane also gave his consent for the use of all the data gained at his expense, but he stated emphatically that he did not wish and would not accept participation in any company, or companies, which might be formed for this work. He did not wish a statement ever to appear to the effect that there were ulterior commercial motives behind his philanthropic activities in Arabia. It is noteworthy that he carried out to the letter his decision not to share in any business venture that might grow out of his friendly aid to the Arabians. When, in due course, I informed the oil and mining companies concerned of Mr. Crane's connection with the investigations, each in turn authorized an offer of participation. But as Mr. Donald M. Brodie, office manager for Mr. Crane, will confirm, each offer was declined with his thanks.

Oil

In presenting the economic potentialities of Saudi Arabia to possible sponsors in the United States, I first turned to mining concerns, expecting them to be the most responsive. But I soon learned better when the several companies approached began to turn me down one by one. The consistent pattern of their attitude was that although the reports were interesting and the proposition seemed promising, it was too speculative a venture, since Saudi Arabia was an entirely unknown country. Some said that they thought the project should have greater appeal to British groups who are operating in Africa, India, and Asia.

In the meantime I had begun to make inquiries regarding oil companies. At the suggestion of a mining friend, R. Gordon Walker of the Oliver Filter Company, I met Terry Duce of the Texas Company. After a cordial interview he asked me to return in a few days, but when I did, I was informed that the company had decided it would not take the offer. Mr. Duce suggested that the Near East Development Company and the Standard Oil Company of California be approached on the matter.

It so happened that I called at the office of the Near East Development Company first, meeting Mr. Stuart Morgan, its secretary, and Norval Baker, geologist. They expressed considerable interest, Mr. Baker carefully going over the geological notes. Mr. Morgan promised to let me know if his company were interested, but made it clear that I was not bound in any way. He strongly emphasized that his parent company—the Iraq Petroleum Company—was the most powerful group of oil companies in the world, and that though it had been caught napping while the Bahrain oil fields were negotiated for by another organization, it would not permit itself to do so again.

Next, I had the privilege of meeting officials of the Gulf Oil Company, Mr. Guy Stevens, a director, and Mr. Ed S. Bleecker, a geologist. I went over my notes with these gentlemen in New York, and at their invitation went to the central office in Pittsburgh, where I had a cordial conference with Dr. Heald and his associates. Asked about their prior understanding with the Iraq Petroleum Company, they replied that they thought it would not interfere with this proposition but that, in any case, their legal department would report. Shortly after my return to New York I was informed, however, that their Iraq Petroleum Company obligations would not permit them separately to undertake an enterprise in Saudi Arabia.

Soon after this disappointment, Mr. A. S. Coriell, New York representative of the Standard Oil Company of California, asked me to call at his office, and arranged for a meeting with H. J. Hawley, a geologist who had just returned from South America. Mr. Hawley took notes on the Saudi Arabian geological data and expressed the belief that his company would contact me again. Shortly afterward, Mr. Loomis of the Standard Oil Company of California called on me. Two other conferences, accompanied by close communication with the head office in San Francisco, led to specific arrangements for a meeting with Mr. M. E. Lombardi in New York. There it was finally agreed that the Standard Oil Company would undertake to negotiate to an oil concession in Saudi Arabia. Mr. Guy Stevens, an official of another organization, had praised the personal integrity of Mr. Lombardi highly, and my experience fully confirmed that opinion. These oil people were very fortunate to have the assistance of a man such as M. E. Lombardi, as he persevered in urging the expansion of his company in the Near East. His farsightedness has resulted in obtaining American control of what is probably the second greatest oil reserve in the world today. In New York Mr. Lombardi had a power of attorney made out and given to me as evidence of authorization to act on behalf of the Standard Oil Company of California.

Accompanied by our son, Mrs. Twitchell and I sailed from

New York on January 13, 1933, for London, where we were to meet Mr. and Mrs. Lombardi and Mr. and Mrs. Lloyd Hamilton. Mr. Hamilton was to write the terms of the oil agreement and take care of all legal technicalities, while I was to give advice on Saudi Arabia and local conditions. This arrangement proved entirely satisfactory. I defined the boundaries, but Mr. Hamilton wrote the terms and finally signed the concessions on behalf of the oil company, while the Minister of Finance, Shaikh Abdullah Sulaiman Al Hamdan, signed on behalf of the Saudi Arabian government. The very able and simple form of this agreement is outstanding, and contributed to the reputation of Lloyd Hamilton, which was of the highest in oil circles. His untimely death was a great loss to the industry.

Negotiations for the concession were culminated at Kazam Palace in Nazla, a suburb of Jidda, on May 29, 1933. Najib Salha, an officer of the Saudi government, acted as the sole interpreter and secretary. Fountain-pen sets were given by the oil company to the various officials connected with the negotiations, and a brief case was presented to the interpreter. No money or other presents of any kind entered into the business deal with the following exception: a "reward" was given to me by the Saudi Arabian government, as they had promised, and to which Mr. Lombardi said there would be no objection. Mr. and Mrs. Hamilton left directly after the agreement was signed, but the company requested me to remain to attend to the next steps.

The first of these was the payment of a loan of £30,000 in gold sovereigns at Jidda to the Saudi Arabian government. This gold payment was a great tribute to the farsighted policy of the directors of the Standard Oil Company of California. It is especially eloquent of the vision and wisdom of Mr. Lombardi and Mr. Stoner. The depths of the depression in the United States had about been reached and the "bank holiday" just declared. Americans were suffering more severely than

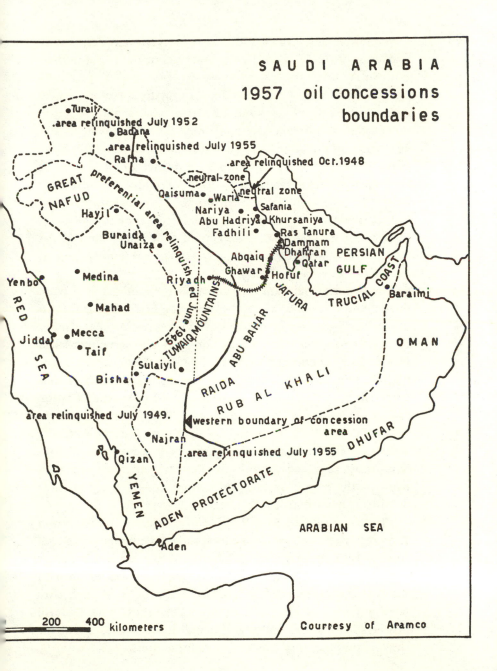

SAUDI ARABIA
1957 oil concessions
boundaries

• Turaif
.area relinquished July 1952
• Badana
.area relinquished July 1955
Rafha •
.area relinquished Oct.1948
neutral-zone
neutral zone
GREAT NAFUD
preferential area relinquished June 1949
Qaisuma•
Waria
Nariya •
Safania
Hayjl •
Abu Hadriya•
Khursaniya
Buraida•
Fadhili •
Ras Tanura
Unaiza •
Dammam
Abqaiq •
Dhahran
PERSIAN
Ghawar•
Qatar
GULF
Medina
Riyadh•
Hofuf
Yenbo•
JAFURA
TRUCIAL COAST
Baraimi
Mahad
RED SEA
ABU BAHAR
OMAN
Mecca
Jidda•
Taif
Sulaiyil•
RAIDA
Bisha•
RUB AL KHALI
area relinquished July 1949.
western boundary of concession area
Najran•
DHUFAR
Qizan•
.area relinquished July 1955
YEMEN
ADEN PROTECTORATE
ARABIAN SEA
Aden

200   400 kilometers

Courtesy of Aramco

any other people in the world: nearly everyone was despondent and pessimistic. These oil men deserve great credit for their faith in America and American enterprise.

After obtaining the concession, a company for operating in Arabia was formed by Standard Oil of California. This was named the "California Arabian Standard Oil Company"; later the name was changed to the "Arabian American Oil Company." In 1936 the Texas Company acquired a half interest in the concession. On December 2, 1948, the holdings were altered by the various financial agreements to: 30 per cent, Standard Oil Company of California; 30 per cent, Texas Company; 30 per cent, Standard Oil Company of New Jersey; and 10 per cent, Socony-Vacuum Oil Company (recently renamed "Socony Mobil Oil Company, Inc.").

The loan was paid and every sovereign counted at the bank of the Netherlands Trading Society, Ltd., in Jidda, on August 25, 1933. The terms of the concession were somewhat similar to those of the Iraq Petroleum Company and were published in the *Umm al-Qura* newspaper of Mecca which serves as the official organ of the government. After paying the loan and dispatching the receipts authenticated by the Dutch Legation at Jidda, I proceeded across Arabia to Bahrain, arriving there September 3. There the late Mr. E. Skinner, General Manager, Bahrain Petroleum Company, Ltd., had the personnel and equipment prepared for the preliminary geological examinations of the Saudi Arabian oil concessions—roughly an area of 318,000 square miles.

The first geologists were R. P. Miller, chief, S. B. Henry and J. W. Hoover. I was to introduce them to the various Saudi Arab government officials in Hasa; also to lease headquarters at Jubail and Hofuf, and assist in getting the supplies through the customs at Oqair. The new cars with 7½ x 15 inch tires were a great aid in traveling over the sands. The Qusaibi brothers had offices in all the principal towns and as agents for the oil company they facilitated many matters.

Within about a week after landing at Jubail the great dome at Jabal Dhahran had been visited and the first oil camp in Saudi Arabia established. This has now been drilled and proven to be one of the world's great oil deposits, along with the still greater fields of Abqaiq and Ghawar.

A modern oil community has been established at Dhahran, and in accordance with its usual policy the oil company does everything that is practically possible for the welfare and comfort of its staff and employees. The loyalty of the personnel is proof of the wisdom of this policy. The benefit to all Saudi Arabia is very material, as many of the Saudi Arabian employees set aside enough of their wages to purchase homes, small date groves, bands of sheep and camels, as well as spending a certain amount of money for better clothes and greater variety of food for their families. The following list of Saudi Arab enterprises in Dammam and Khobar—as compiled in 1957 by Aramco—is an amazing tribute to the ability of the Saudi Arabs as well as to the farsightedness of the oil company. The contrast between the tiny fishing villages of Dammam and Khobar—which I first visited in 1931—where limited gardens provided dates for trading, and the present thriving cities with estimated populations of 20,000 each is almost miraculous. The Aramco research report states that there are 1,145 businesses in both towns. These enterprises include 577 engaged in retail trade, 33 in wholesale, 57 restaurants and cafes, 35 bakeries, 66 units engaged in the repair of automobiles and tires, 10 manufacturers of tiles, 12 of furniture, and 15 of cement blocks, and 3 iron works.

I quote: "Aramco attempts to foster to the maximum practical extent the development of local enterprise consistent with sound economics and sound operating practices. Experience has shown that the opportunities for Aramco to utilize the services of local business are increasing." A concrete evidence of the last statement is the fact that the oil company has on hire from local owners a total of 600 light cars and trucks.

The oil company maintains a well-rounded health program at Dhahran which is having a marked effect on the nearby villages of al-Khobar and Dammam as well as elsewhere in the Eastern Province. It is also building schools which become an integral part of the government education system. Great credit is due to the management and staff of the oil company for their tact and diplomatic dealings in a strange country. The policing of all company property is done by the civilian police who operate under Saudi Arabia's Interior Ministry.

Another great ultimate benefit of the oil operations is the drilling of water wells at all the "wildcat" oil prospects. Whether oil is found or not, the water remains an asset to the country.

In addition, there is the Ghawar Field, 140 miles long, which is thought to be the second largest in the world. The northern end of this field is but a few miles westerly from Abqaiq. The 1956 Khursaniyah "wildcat" well is located 84 miles northwest of Dhahran and 31 miles northwest of Jubail (in this well five strata or "horizons" have proved productive in a total depth of 7,612 feet). The off-shore field of Safaniya has a proved commercial output. It is a great additional asset although not yet entirely delimited. The first tanker load was pumped through a new 130-mile pipeline and shipped in early May 1957 with the initial production of 50,000 barrels per day. It is planned that this field will yield 175,000 barrels per day by the middle of 1958.

The total production of crude oil in 1957 was 362,121,478 barrels (48,229,690 tons), an average of 992,114 barrels per day. Proved reserves were increased by the discovery of the Khursaniyah Field to a total of 34 billion barrels at the end of 1956.

This is an interesting contrast to the estimate of 2 billion barrels, and an indicated reserve of between 4 and 5 billion, made by the late eminent oil geologist E. I. DeGolyer in 1943.

At the end of 1957 there were 189 wells capable of immediate oil production, and during the year 17 deep wells were

SAUDI ARABIAN OIL FIELDS AND PIPELINES

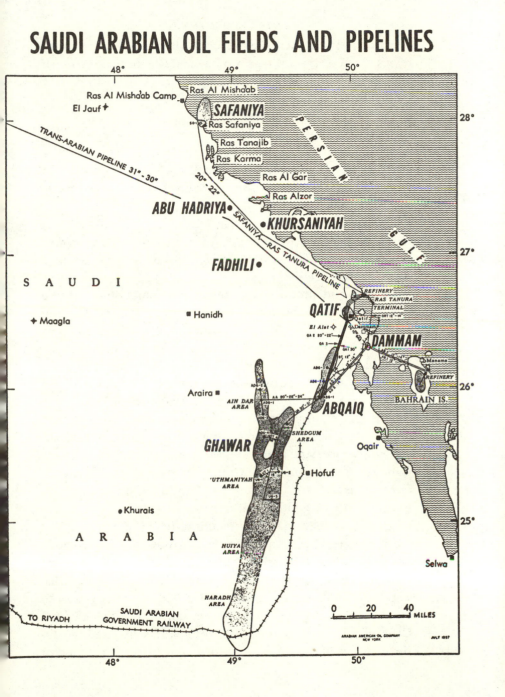

completed of which 11 were oil wells. If all the 189 wells were in production, the average would be 5,249 barrels each per day—it has been reported that the average of wells in the United States is 12 barrels per day.

Eight exploration parties carried out geological work for the purpose of creating an eventual addition to oil production. A wildcat well called Khurais No. 1 is now (September 4, 1957) being commenced after much geological study in the Dahna 77 miles westerly from Udhailiyah, or 90 miles northeast of Riyadh.

Aramco issued a statement on October 21 that this well has struck oil between 4,755 to 4,898 feet and that the indicated production is 3,000 barrels per day. A totally new oil field seems likely to be developed.

To find and produce this immense amount of oil over a land almost entirely desert has demanded special types of equipment and an enormous amount of them. Richard Kerr, who was one of the first of Aramco engineers, has been responsible for the major part of it. The following tabulation gives the status of transport at the end of 1956, but does not show the modern type of desert caravans consisting of air-conditioned trailers used for housing, cooking, machine and repair shops, seismographic equipment, light blast hole drills, and powder carriers. Huge Kenworth tractor trucks and Caterpillars serve as locomotives. One of the most spectacular of all transport is the latest technique of hauling of oil drilling rigs from one site to another without "tearing down" or dismantling—thus saving a material amount of time and expense. The accompanying photograph (courtesy of Aramco) shows a standard API drilling derrick being moved across 260 miles of desert from the Empty Quarter to the Uthmaniyah area of the Ghawar Field. This outfit weighed 400 tons; the derrick was 30 feet square at the base and 136 feet tall; it was hauled by 3 Caterpillar tractors. Out in Saudi Arabia this attracted but little attention but if transferred to America for the purpose of transporting Trinity Church spire of New York from Greenwich, Connecticut, through New York to Washington, D.C., there would be a similar distance and about the same height of load!

Tabulation of Aramco transport as of December 31, 1956

Light cars and trucks	1,112
Including 75 sedans, 180 "Land Rovers" (British type of jeep), Dodge 1-ton trucks, and Dodge Power wagons	
Light cars and trucks	500
Rented by Aramco from Saudi Arabs, consisting of cars and Ford 1-ton trucks	
Heavy-duty trucks	704
Including 250 Dodge 2-ton trucks; 150, Kenworth 5-ton; 175, Kenworth 10-ton; 100, Kenworth 15-ton; remainder are miscellaneous	
Trailers	614
Approximately half of this total are flat-bed, 30-tons capacity; approximately 30% Tankers, 2,500 to 6,000 gallons capacity; the remainder miscellaneous	
Three-wheeled scooters	137
For messengers, mechanics, etc.	
Total	3,067

In addition, the oil company has 17 planes to augment its transport.

The status of wells at the end of 1957 is shown by the tabulation below.

Without marketing, the oil and oil derivatives would be of little value. At Ras Tanura the refinery which was originally planned for 50,000 barrels per day processed an average of 192,623 during 1957. These petroleum products are shipped principally to east of Suez markets but a certain amount go to Europe. Most of the balance of the crude oil averaging 799,491 barrels per day goes to Europe and smaller quantities go to America. It is taken from Arabia by tankers and by the Trans Arabian Pipe Line—popularly known as "Tapline." During the first ten months of 1956 an average of 148 tankers per month loaded at Ras Tanura. Due to the invasion of Egypt by Britain, France, and Israel and the subsequent closing the

Field	Produc-ing	Shut-in	Obser-vation	Injec-tion	Sus-pended	Aban-doned	Drill-ing	Total
Abqaiq	50	14	2	10	0	1	1	78
Abu Hadriya	0	1	1	0	0	2	0	4
Al-'Alah	0	0	0	0	0	1	0	1
Al-Jauf	0	0	0	0	0	1	0	1
Dammam (includes 3 gas wells)	28	3	1	0	0	10	0	42
Fadhili	0	1	0	0	0	0	0	1
Ghawar								
'Ain Dar	44	5	2	0	0	1	1	53
Shedgum	14	1	1	0	0	1	0	17
'Uthmaniyah	30	13	3	0	1	2	0	49
Hawiyah	0	1	1	0	0	0	0	2
Haradh	0	7	1	0	1	0	0	9
Khurais	0	0	0	0	0	0	1	1
Khursaniyah	0	2	1	0	1	0	0	4
Manifa	0	0	0	0	0	0	1	1
Maagala	0	0	0	0	0	1	0	1
Qatif	10	0	1	0	1	1	0	13
Safaniya	16	11	1	0	0	0	0	28
Stratigraphic	0	0	0	0	0	1	0	1
TOTAL	192	59	15	10	4	22	4	306

Suez Canal, only 88 tankers were loaded during each of the last two months of 1956. In 1957 the average was 137 tankers per month. Tapline oil is discharged into a "tank farm" at Sidon, Lebanon, and from this "farm" into tankers which serve European markets. The capacity of the 1,068 mile 30-31 inch pipeline was originally 320,000 barrels per day but was increased to 450,000 barrels per day, largely through installa-tion of remote controlled auxiliary pumping units in 1957.

For additional history we must retrogress. In 1939 a supple-mental agreement was negotiated by Mr. W. J. Lenahan, who had been the Jidda representative of the oil company since September 1933. This new area included all the sedimentary formation from the original concession boundaries (on the west side of the Dahna) to the contact with the igneous rocks where oil occurrence is impossible. In these negotiations Mr. Lenahan had the opposition of the Japanese offers supported, or at least introduced, by Sr. Silitti, the Italian Minister. At the same time Fritz Grobba, the German Minister, called at Jidda. He was Minister to Iraq at Baghdad, and also accredited to Saudi Arabia. It is more than likely that he might also have tried to further the application of the Japanese. The terms offered by the Japanese were as tempting as they were fantastic. Mr. Lenahan at Riyadh told the King that such terms were not commercially practicable and that he would not attempt to match them. In conversations with the Finance Minister and Shaikh Yusuf Yassin I had no hesitation in saying that I was sure that the Japanese were after a concession principally to secure a foothold in Arabia; that their terms were political rather than commercial. I believe Mr. Lenahan at Riyadh made similar statements at his audiences with the King. After considering the matter from all points of view, King ibn-Saud stated that he preferred to continue to deal with his American friends, so the Japanese went away empty-handed. However, the map of Aramco concession to date shows that much of the above additional area has been relinquished and the present boundary is very similar to the lines laid out by me with Lloyd Hamilton.

The King's confidence has been amply justified, for the oil company at times has advanced great sums of money over and above current production royalties. This aided the government when its revenue from the Moslem pilgrims was practically cut to nothing by the war. Both the oil and mining companies made loans to the government in addition to the immense sums loaned by the British government, and by the American government through Lend-Lease, as well as the August 1946 loan by the U.S. Export-Import Bank. In addition to financial assistance, the oil company greatly aided the government through technical services and advice on water resources in Najd, the layout of irrigation systems at the Kharj, surveys of the frontier between Iraq and Najd, and counsel on a great many questions. Mr. Max Thornburg of the Bahrain Petroleum Company joined with the officials of the Arabian American Oil Company in rendering much friendly counsel.

To maintain closer relations between the oil company and the Saudi government, Mr. Fred Davies, Chairman, Mr. R. L. Keyes, President until his retirement at the end of 1957, and Mr. Garry Owen, Vice President, have taken up permanent residence in Dhahran. This is undoubtedly to the advantage of the oil company as well as to the government and should forestall disagreements and misunderstandings. Although the original concession was mutually agreed in 1933, subsequently there developed dissatisfaction. In December 1950 there resulted a new agreement giving the Saudi government and Aramco each 50 per cent of net operating income before the deduction of United States taxes. It was then estimated that the Saudi government would receive approximately $150,000,-000 per annum. But in 1956 the actual amount was $280,000,-000 and this huge revenue is more likely in the future to increase rather than decrease.

The details of the new agreement are quoted from Aramco's "Background Information" dated January 4, 1951:

"The new agreement which has been reached between the Arabian American Oil Company and the Saudi Arab government allows the government a total participation in the operation of up to one-half the company's net operating revenue.

"The government's share is inclusive of the fixed per ton royalty which Aramco is required to pay regardless of earnings. At present and anticipated levels of production, the agreement substantially increases the government's income, but from the company's standpoint, it sets a ceiling on all payments to the government—royalty, miscellaneous levies, and income taxes—of one-half the net operating revenue.

"Of equal importance is the fact that the new arrangement places all monetary transactions between Aramco and the Saudi Arab government on the basis of official, internationally accepted exchange rates. This eliminates the premium

232

gold-sovereign rate at which the company has been paying royalty.

"The terms generally follow much the same pattern as that in effect for several years in Venezuela where the government adjusts its income tax to obtain a total income, including royalty, that is equal to company profits.

"The agreement was signed December 30, 1950, in Jidda, the Saudi Arabian financial and diplomatic capital, between King ibn-Saud's ministers and representatives of the company. It embraces a revision of the original concession contract which dates from 1933. There have been several previous modifications in the contract since 1938.

"Half the remaining net operating revenue becomes the maximum limit of payments of all kinds to the Saudi Arab government, including royalty and the various miscellaneous levies now collected such as import duties, visa fees, and port charges. The Saudi Arabian income tax, the principle of which is accepted by Aramco, is adjusted to take the difference between the total royalty and miscellaneous levies and the maximum of half the net operating revenue.

"The effect of the agreement is to set a ceiling on total payments to the Saudi Arab government, at the same time assuring the government of a minimum in the fixed royalty and miscellaneous taxes now paid. These would accrue to the government even if the company operated at a loss. While the government participates in Aramco profits, it does not share any Aramco losses if they occur. Continued capital investment is the company's sole responsibility.

"The Aramco concession contract provided for royalty at four gold shillings per ton, but under a special agreement negotiated about two years ago the company has been paying on the basis of $12 as the value of the gold sovereign (20 gold shillings per gold sovereign) instead of on the $8.24 official rate. Per barrel, this is about 34 cents as against 22 cents. In addition, the riyals which the company buys from the government for paying its Saudi Arab employees and other purposes have been obtained from the government at a premium.

"Under the new agreement, all exchange is placed on the accepted international rate. Riyals are traded only within Saudi Arabia, but the company will henceforth buy this currency at the prevailing rate existing in the country.

"Aramco is given the advantage of paying the taxes imposed in any currency which it receives and in the same proportion. Under an earlier agreement with Saudi Arabia and with permission of the British exchange authorities, the company has been paying about 25 per cent of its royalties to Saudi Arabia in sterling.

"While recognizing the government's case for higher revenue, Aramco has been engaged until recently in its post-war program of heavy capital expenditures under which production has been increased to its present rate of more than 600,-000 barrels daily (the 1957 average was 992,114 barrels daily). Much of this work has now been carried out, and with the trans-Arabian pipeline system in operation, the prospects are for further increases in output.

"Last October, the Saudi Arab government decreed an income tax, the first in that country. This was drawn up with the assistance of an American advisor from the United States and provided a 5 per cent tax on all individual incomes in excess of about $5,000 and a levy on corporation profits.

"Aramco, the largest foreign enterprise in the country and the source of nearly all the Saudi Arabian foreign income, protested this corporate tax. Although admitting the taxing power of a sovereign government, the company cited Clause 21 of its original contract, which provided that the company was exempt from taxes within the country. Along with the tax, the government made a number of demands on the company, all of which were economically unacceptable.

"The negotiations which followed resulted in a new decree on December 27 which supplemented and clarified the previous tax decree, and then on December 30 in the modification of the tax article in the company's concession agreement.

"The 5 per cent tax levied on individuals and affecting many of the company's employees stationed in Saudi Arabia was unaffected by the agreement."

Having shown some facts regarding the tremendous oil production of Aramco and having described the concessions providing the areas from which the "liquid gold" is obtained, it is logical that something should be known about the organization and personnel which is operating one of the greatest American foreign enterprises.

At the end of 1956 Aramco had 20,346 employees, of whom 19,632 were in Saudi Arabia. Of these 13,213 were Saudi Arabs, 2,878 Americans, and 3,541 of sixteen other nationalities. Outside of Arabia 714 Americans carried on essential services in New York offices. The subsidiary "Aramco Overseas Company," with headquarters at The Hague, employed 121 Americans and 754 employees of other nationalities. These were engaged in engineering, purchasing, and other services in Europe, the Middle East, and the Far East. Markets and supplies are equally as important as production.

No enterprise is successful without a loyal, intelligent, and efficient personnel. All these requirements in its employees Aramco has accomplished to a remarkable degree. To the Saudi Arab employees it pays a minimum daily wage of 7½ riyals (on my first visit to Jidda in 1931 wages were ½ riyal), but it also pays nearly the same amount for welfare benefits consisting of medical services; education and training—including schooling for employees' children; community facilities comprised of food, housing, and recreation; community development; and benefit plans. The company gave cash rewards for attaining various specified levels of proficiency in the Arabic language courses. The Saudi government has sponsored a "Campaign Against Illiteracy," and some 850 employees were enrolled during 1956. It is to be emphasized that this studying was not done on company time.

Primary schools are assisted by Aramco but are under government supervision. At present there are eight such schools in the various towns close to the oil operations, and three more are scheduled. When completed, the capacity will be 3,000 pupils.

Aramco has long fostered various training courses for those employees who wish to make the extra exertion. These courses are called "Job-Skill Training" for teaching basic and then advanced skills; "Industrial Training" includes courses at higher levels; and "Supervisory Training" which gives those who are qualified opportunities to assume higher and more responsible positions entailing supervision. The company also gives advice as to financial ventures, both for purchasing their own homes and for business projects; and in some cases assists in the financing.

For the American staff there are excellent schools of all grades up to and including the ninth provided with American teachers having superior qualifications.

It is to be expected that to compensate Americans for living in a desert country there must be unusual attractions in the line of salaries, living conditions, education, and recreation. Aramco has succeeded wonderfully well in meeting these conditions.

A matter which more than any other single item brought Saudi Arabia to the notice of the American public was the proposal of a pipeline to convey Saudi Arabian oil to the Mediterranean. This was first publicized in February 1944. It was quite natural that the oil companies competing with Aramco and the Gulf Oil Corporation would not wish to see an outlet on the Mediterranean. The I.P.C. already had its pipeline discharging at Tripoli and at Haifa.

Some Americans did not wish the federal government to enter any further into private enterprise, even though the

British government had been benefited greatly by its stock holdings in the Anglo Iranian Oil Company, the Royal Dutch Shell Company, and the Iraq Petroleum Company. A fact which was not brought out during the discussions of the pipeline was the provision of a 1,000,000,000-barrel reserve for the United States Navy, to be sold to it at 25 per cent under the then market price. If this were taken at the present ceiling price of $1.11 per barrel the Navy would save a total of $277,-500,000, or roughly twice the amount the United States government proposed to advance to cover the estimated cost of the line. In addition the government was to be repaid its entire outlay within twenty-five years. This did not seem to be an unsound business proposition in any respect. Though it committed our government to a fixed foreign policy for at least twenty-five years, many people would not deem it a disadvantage to the general welfare of American enterprise. At any rate it was finally decided that on account of the political controversy the companies financed and constructed the pipeline without the participation of the United States government.

Tapline

This, one of the world's largest oil-pipe systems, was to bring the oil fields of Saudi Arabia some 3500 miles nearer to the markets of Western Europe and thereby facilitate its industries. In other words, this 1,068-mile pipeline saved approximately 7,000 miles of sailing by 65 tankers taking 20 days to make the trip to discharge oil at a Mediterranean port at the rate of 330,000 to 355,000 barrels per day (roughly 43,000 tons). Furthermore, the Suez Canal toll of 18 cents per barrel or $54,000 per day would be saved, which should yield a satisfactory profit over pipeline expenses.

The construction was authorized on March 10, 1947; welding commenced January 16, 1948; the first tankers loaded at Sidon, Lebanon, on December 2, 1950.

A company for the construction and operation of this immense project was chartered as a Delaware Corporation in July 1945 by the Standard Oil Company of California and the Texas Company—the companies owning Aramco at that time. In December 1948, when Aramco was reorganized, Tapline ownership was also split. Today it is Standard Oil Company of California, 30 per cent; Standard Oil Company of New Jersey, 30 per cent; Texas Company, 30 per cent; and Socony-Vacuum Oil Company, Inc. (now renamed the Socony Mobil Oil Company), 10 per cent. The name is "Trans-Arabian Pipe Line Company," usually known as Tapline. The operating headquarters are in Beirut. The pipeline system begins at Abqaiq—the heart of the gathering system of the Arabian American Oil Company (Aramco)—and the discharge terminus is at the Biblical seaport of Sidon, Lebanon, on the Mediterranean. The line traverses four countries—Saudi Arabia, Hashimite Kingdom of Jordan, Syria, and Lebanon. Of the 1,068 mile length, the westernmost 754 miles are operated by Tapline and the rest by Aramco.

The immense cost of some $240,000,000 was financed by the owner companies combining their resources and abilities.

Two of the leading American contracting firms accomplished the construction. International Bechtel Incorporated built 854.4 miles of the 30-inch and 31-inch main line pipe from Abqaiq and Persian Gulf westerly. This work included the installation of the four pump stations—Nariya, Qaisumah, Rafha, and Badanah.

Williams Brothers Overseas Company built 213.8 miles easterly from the seaport of Sidon and connected with the Bechtel operations. The pump station of Turaif is included in this section, but the firm of Graver Construction Company built this station as well as the tankage at Sidon.

Before work could be commenced, surveys and estimates had to be made, which were most efficiently directed by Burt E. Hull, President. Also, a great amount of negotiating was necessary for rights of way. This was ably done by Wm. J. Lenahan. Construction began in the summer of 1947.

The route going westerly from the Persian Gulf end traverses heavy sand dune country for about 100 miles, thence for 750 miles it crosses absolute desert country to the Jordan frontier. The average annual rainfall is three inches (as with most of Saudi Arabia), but as cloudbursts of one or two inches may occur, this factor had to be considered. The surface of this stretch is about equally divided among smooth gravel plains, disintegrated limestone overlying hard limestone, and level country with two to six inches of topsoil covering limestone so hard as to require blasting.

The line reaches its greatest elevation, which is 2,975 feet, in Saudi Arabia just east of the Jordan boundary. The 80-mile route across Jordan is one of great difficulty as the country rock is of hard basalt and lava—a part of the great band of volcanic action which extends over a thousand miles southerly, parallel with the Red Sea. The service road for construction, as well as the pipe laying itself, was a major operation.

The following section of 100 miles across Syria is largely a surface-graded road covered with broken limestone, but along some 45 miles there is cultivation where wheat is raised.

Thence approaching the Syria-Lebanon frontier, the line descends a steep escarpment into the Bekaa Valley and crosses several creeks, or rivers, which constitute the only running water encountered along the entire route. The line goes southwesterly to the shore of the Mediterranean over cultivated areas and descends sharply to the Sidon Terminal—the drop in the last 20 miles being nearly 1,500 feet. Submarine lines extend from the shore one mile to reach the tanker anchorages loading the ships by gravity at a rate of up to 39,000 barrels per hour.

Along the pipeline the summer temperature in places rises to 130 degrees fahrenheit. The line crosses swampy areas as well as rocky ones. These conditions were the reason for laying three-fifths of the pipeline in ditches and two-fifths on steel ring girders above the ground.

The fact that the ownership of this enterprise was hundreds of thousands of shareholders—who own the stock of the four parent oil companies—tended to influence economy and efficiency. One very notable economy was the cutting of the sea freight in half by the nesting of the 30-inch diameter pipe into the 31-inch—50 per cent of each size was used. Another example was the automatic welding of three of the standard 31-foot pipes into one 93-foot unit at Ras Mishaab on the Persian Gulf.

Specially designed Kenworth truck-tractors and trailers of 50 tons capacity hauled groups of these 93-foot units to the pipeline location, thereby saving 66 per cent in field welding or approximately 50 per cent in overland transport costs. The 15,000-foot "Skyhook" facilitating the landing of all pipe for the IBI section is still another example. Many ingenious machines and devices were invented on the ground, which added to the overall efficiency, greatly to the credit of all concerned.

At the completion of construction, 14,600 Arabs and 2,000 Americans were employed. The Arabs learned skilled work readily, and so their proportion to Americans steadily increased. The labor was satisfactory and great credit is due to the tact and teaching ability of the Americans.

The weight of this pipeline alone which had to be transported from California to Arabia was 265,000 tons—furnished by the U.S. Steel Corporation, but total of all steel used was 325,000 tons. In addition, there were the six main pump station installations. Each of these is the center of a small town, a fenced area of about 125 acres, including a radio station.

Life at the pump stations is very comfortable (infinitely more so than when I first traveled in Arabia by camel and Model T Ford with my wife, lodging sometimes in tents and sometimes none). At each station there are air conditioning and refrigeration plants, a recreation hall and infirmary, plenty of DDT for flies and bugs, free movies and shortwave radio programs. There are comfortable dwellings, mess-halls, athletic fields, and playgrounds. Except for midsummer, the weather is pleasant and nights nearly always cool. Sand and other storms do occur, but are not chronic.

In constructing the line, 50 wells were drilled to obtain water; 40 were successful. These are a tremendous boon to the livestock of the Bedouins of a great area and should greatly promote their friendliness towards Americans. In 1950 these wells supplied an estimated number of 100,000 Bedouins, 150,-000 camels, and 300,000 goats and sheep.

The date of the first tankers being loaded at Sidon was December 2, 1950. The initial capacity of the Tapline was 300,000 barrels per 24-hour day (during October 1957 the through-put was 394,367 barrels daily).

"From the above amount of oil enough gasoline can be produced to operate 2,840,000 automobiles for an average day's driving. That would take care of most of the cars in New York State. The amount of oil delivered by Tapline in a day can produce an amount of fuel oil sufficient to heat 259,000 average homes for 24 hours. That would be sufficient for the heating needs of Philadelphia for a day."

It took 4.9 million barrels to fill the pipeline before a barrel could be drawn off. To operate there must be approximately a million barrels at the Western end and other working amounts at the intermediate pumping stations.

"All in all, some 6,000,000 barrels of oil must be in the pipe and pipeline tanks at all times to keep the operation moving, and that is more than all the oil pumped daily from all the wells in the United States."

Tapline is an outstanding tribute to American enterprise as evidenced by the difficulties of terrain and climate overcome, the tonnages handled over the immense distances covered, the finances involved, the countries with whom agreements were negotiated, and the tact and diplomacy shown in

241

dealing with and training the great number of Moslems, and the ability developed by them. (Notes by courtesy and permission of Trans-Arabian Pipe Line Co., New York, from report of January 1951)

The successful conclusion of supplemental negotiations between the Trans-Arabian Pipe Line Company and the governments of Lebanon, Syria, and the Hashimite Kingdom of Jordan, regarding the sale of crude oil for the purpose of supplying requirements for petroleum products, was announced during May and June 1952 in the respective capitals of those countries.

The needs of Lebanon and Syria for crude oil for internal consumption were met by means of agreements under which Tapline would sell each government half of its annual crude-oil requirements. The other 50 per cent would come from Iraq Petroleum Company, which operates pipelines in those countries. If additional pipelines begin operations, the Tapline and I.P.C. shares will be reduced proportionately. In the case of Jordan, Tapline agreed to sell crude oil up to 100 per cent of that country's requirements as long as Tapline operates the only pipeline transporting oil through that country. The price of crude oil sold by Tapline will be at the low of competing crude oil prices posted in eastern Mediterranean ports.

Tapline further agreed to pay to each country $3 per ton on the basis of a 200,000-ton annual ceiling for products—gasoline, kerosene, stove oil, and fuel oil—consumed in each country. This would give a revenue from this source of $600,-000 each year to each country.

Tapline also agreed to a small increase in the loading fee at Sidon which, at the new rate of 2.88 pence sterling per ton, would yield an annual revenue of more than $500,000 under present operating schedules. These fees are divided equally between Lebanon and Syria.

It was also agreed that Tapline would contribute $21,000 annually to maintenance of public highways used by the company's vehicles, and also $17,000 annually to the municipalities of Beirut and Sidon, the latter payments being in consideration for municipal services.

The governments, in turn, agreed to a provision under which Tapline may make these payments in certain currencies other than United States dollars, the ratios varying in particular instances. Tapline also was granted complete freedom from any monetary exchange discriminations.

The new arrangements, which left undisturbed the main body of the concession agreements between Tapline and the three governments, were expected to add approximately $2,-000,000 annually to the combined revenues of the three countries from Tapline operations. (By courtesy of Tapline)

In 1956 Tapline further proposed a profit-sharing agreement under which the shares of the four countries through which the pipeline passes would amount to a total of 50 per cent. As of this writing, no final agreement has yet been reached to put the 50-50 offer into effect.

Mines

As the reader may have noticed, the origin of the mining enterprise was parallel with that of oil, and connected with it until December 1932, when my services were devoted entirely to the oil company. At the end of 1933, however, I terminated my connection with the oil company and went to London, where I endeavored to fulfill the second part of ibn-Saud's desire for the development of the country's natural resources, namely, the finding of suitable capital abroad for the working of mines.

In this instance, I did not go to New York, for all concerns there that were likely to be interested had already been approached without success during 1932. From January to March 1934 I met with consultants and directors of practically all mining companies whose central offices were in London, with the exception of the Chester Beatty group. To an engineer mainly concerned with facts and figures, and not with broad policies of trade and personalities, the task of finding capital to initiate mining in a country where no engineer had ever been before was a rather thankless job. Most of the officials met were extremely cordial. They studied the reports and photographs eagerly, and in a number of instances recommended the project, only to be finally overruled by their respective boards of directors. The universal opinion seemed to come close to that prevailing among the New York groups: Saudi Arabia was little known insofar as its government, transport, labor, and climatic conditions were concerned. The project was, therefore, too speculative to deserve serious consideration.

Finally, during lunch one day with an old American friend, Robert Edwards of the Anglo-Oriental, Ltd., I was relating my various experiences, but not thinking that a tin company would be interested, when Edwards requested a report and data to be brought to his office. There I met another official of that company, Gerald Hutton, an American of New Zealand origin. I was requested to return in a few days. On that occasion, after many pertinent questions were asked, Edwards and Hutton made it known that their directors, of whom Mr. John Howeson was chairman, had decided to take up this project. They planned to form a syndicate and asked me to approach all the groups to whom I had introduced this enterprise.

I proceeded to invite the groups to participate, and was pleased to discover that nearly all of them were willing to join. The shares were, in fact, oversubscribed. One American group insisted on a certain number of shares, and withdrew when it failed to receive them. It is not generally realized to what extent American and British mining companies are interdependent in personnel. The cooperation and happy relations between British and Americans in mining enterprises is a good omen for future collaboration and one which other international projects should emulate.

In May 1934 the syndicate was constituted as the "Saudi Arabian Mining Syndicate, Ltd." On June 27 I arrived at Jidda. From July 23 to November 7 I lived at Taif and the concession agreement was signed December 24 at Jidda. It was authenticated by the British Vice Consul, Cyril Ousman, December 25, 1934. The boundaries included practically all of the Hijaz, an area of approximately 110,000 square miles, the size of the British Isles, more than twice the area of the state of New York.

The negotiations were conducted with Shaikh Abdullah Sulaiman, Minister of Finance, Shaikh Yusuf Yassin, Chief Secretary to King ibn-Saud, and Khalid Bey Gargoni al-Walid, an adviser to His Majesty. The delays between meetings were about the most trying I have ever endured. Taif, of course, is restricted to Moslems except under very special circumstances. The various officials, guests of the government and other Arabians were most cordial, and called on me, but time passed very slowly.

Najib Bey Salha, who acted so ably as secretary and interpreter during the negotiations, was an employee of the Saudi government and had acted as interpreter in the oil negotiations. No presents of any kind were given to any officials or other interested persons during the transaction. The great delay in reaching an agreement was caused by the fact that no cash payment or loan of any kind was given the Saudi government. It was very difficult, in view of the loan made by the oil company, to convince the King and government that mining negotiations were conducted on a different basis, but finally this was accomplished.

On December 26 I left for Egypt, Iraq, and England. In Egypt the Ford Company gave us every facility for the special equipment and special bodies for the station wagon and three trucks which were needed to initiate the mine prospecting program. I had agreed with H. St. J. B. Philby to examine a supposed gold property in Iraq in which he was interested, provided the negotiations on mines were successful. So, after placing orders in Egypt for the cars and other supplies, I proceeded to Qaara, north of Rutba Wells, Iraq. Then at Damascus on January 11, 1935, I received a cable from the London office that the syndicate had ratified the concession agreement—the conclusion of six months of arguments, explanations and long intervals of enforced inaction.

When the mine examination at Qaara was completed, I set out for London, arriving there on January 25. After a busy time ordering prospecting and development equipment, and conferences with the Syndicate, I flew back to Egypt, leaving London February 9 and arriving in Alexandria on the eleventh and at Jidda the seventeenth. Finally the detailed examination of the mines was started on March 1, 1935. As can be imagined, it was not easy to gather personnel to man an expedition into districts where no non-Moslem and very few Arabs, except Bedouins, had been. The staff included Harry C. Ballard, originally from Denver, Colorado, who had been with me in mines in Idaho and on expeditions to the Yemen. Then W. A. George, a Britisher from Cornwall, was engaged as assayer. Byron Shanks, who came up from Australia and had had technical mining training as well as practical placer experience, was to drill to determine if there were a commercial placer in a large river bed, the Wadi Yenbo, at al-Darr. He did exceedingly good work under difficult conditions those first six months. There was also Bishopp, who had residence in Alexandria, but, I believe, was born in England. He had office experience and was engaged to look after the camp organization as well as the accounts. Another staff member was a general assistant, Arthur Van der Poll, a native of Holland who had lived in the Hijaz many years, conducting a very successful shipping agency which he had recently sold. He had been converted to Islam and spoke Arabic well, so he was of very great service in obtaining supplies and personnel. He was tireless in getting equipment through Jidda customs and up to the sites where it was needed, and during that first year was most valuable to the undertaking. The other member of the staff was Ahmad Fakhry, a British subject of Sudanese citizenship and Turkish ancestry, a monument of integrity and loyalty. He acted as interpreter and assistant to Shanks for six months. Since then he has served the mining company in many capacities. About 1946 he was appointed Director of Mines and companies. Unfortunately he died in 1954.

The terms of the mining concession agreement gave the syndicate a period of two years in which to examine an area the size of the British Isles and to select the mine or mines which it wished to develop into commercial production. Through the study by Ahmad Fakhry of ancient books in libraries in Mecca and Medina, and my reading of works by Richard Burton and other Arabian travelers, as well as through 40,000 miles of flight in our Bellanca "Skyrocket" monoplane, with ground examinations by four ground parties, a total of fifty-five ancient mines were located. Of this number only seven justified diamond drilling. It was disappointing that only one of those seven proved of sufficient size and value to justify development and equipping with a mining and treatment plant. This mine is called by its ancient name, Mahad Dhahab, "the Cradle of Gold."

There were two distinct periods of working this property, as evidenced by the ancient tailings. The older tailings underlie the modern. The age of the latter is from A.D. 750 to 1150, according to Kufic inscriptions found among them. No evidence is yet found to determine the exact age of the underlying tailings, nor is there evidence to show the lengths of time embraced in the two, or whether there were possibly several operating periods. From the general appearance of the ancient stopes in the mine mountain, as well as of the tailings, it seems not impossible that these date back to the time of King Solomon. There is a legend that Umm Garayat Mine—14 miles from Wejh—was worked by miners of King David, father of

King Solomon. As the workings of Mahad Dhahab are the largest I saw in Arabia or in the Sudan, it is a reasonable guess that this might have been a source of the gold of King Solomon. It may possibly be called one of "King Solomon's Mines."

In very ancient times gold had much greater purchasing power than at present. Furthermore, it is likely that most of the miners were slaves, receiving only their food and a pitiful bit of shelter for their labor. There would have been little overhead and no equipment, so that work could be done only during rainy seasons. The labor could then be used elsewhere. It is evident, therefore, that in ancient times there was a very substantial output and profit from workings which would not pay to operate with expensive modern equipment and technical staff.

According to the concession terms an operating company had to be formed by the syndicate upon the expiration of the two-year period. As one mine only had been developed, it was decided, with the consent of the Saudi government, to form the syndicate into a company. According to the agreement, 15 per cent of the shares of the company were allotted to the Saudi Arabian government as payment for the mining property, besides a royalty of 5 per cent of the gross value of the metals recovered and paid for. In addition, 10 per cent of the shares had to be offered for subscription to Saudi Arabian nationals and to the government. Most of these shares were taken up and paid for by them. Therefore the government and citizens had nearly a 25 per cent share in the profits and responsibilities of the company. This participation by the country and government in which natural resources are being developed and extracted, plus the participation by American, British, and Canadian interests, was an excellent example of international cooperation.

The Mahad Dhahab Mine was unique in that it had three classes of ore. First come the tailings, already mentioned. Secondly there was a certain amount of low-grade ore lying at the surface between the ancient stopes, much of which has already been cheaply mined by quarry methods. Thirdly there was the underground ore, which was prospected by thousands of feet of diamond drilling and then blocked out by drifts and cross-cuts to approximately six hundred feet below the surface.

The treatment of the ancient tailings by the milling plant included some unique problems. The ore was classed as complex because it contained the sulphides of copper, lead, zinc, and iron. But, in addition, the droppings from camels, cattle, and mankind, as well as the charcoal from their campfires, had during the past thousand years introduced elements which caused many hitherto unknown difficulties in the flotation and cyanide circuits. The mill and mine staff, with the research by the American Smelting & Refining Company and American Cyanamid Corporation, finally solved the various problems. But complexity of the ore made it necessary to produce in Saudi Arabia only cyanide precipitates which were shipped to huge smelters in New Jersey, as only very extensive plants can separate and recover in marketable form the various metals.

The mine has been of very considerable benefit to Saudi Arabia. Direct benefits came from the distribution of dividends to the government and over seventy Saudi shareholders, from the 5 per cent royalties to the government, the income tax, and 10 per cent customs duties, as well as from the distribution of wages to the thousand direct and associated employees. The indirect benefits were also considerable, including the locally mined lime, locally produced food, and sundry other supplies.

The illiterate and inexperienced Bedouins learned a certain number of English words and were taught to operate the many parts of the complicated equipment in a mining plant. The Arabs who had the higher skilled positions were usually those who formerly were drivers of motor transport. The skill with which they operated the power shovels was surprising. The very few accidents to motor transport while the big 15-ton White trucks were driven over a 3,700-foot summit, on a 500-

mile round-trip, was evidence of the amazing adaptability of the Saudi Arabian. This was also a tribute to the efficiency and patience of the members of the overseas staff.

The limits of profitable ore were found to be at 640 feet maximum depth. The first ore was milled during 1939 and the last on July 22, 1954.

A total of 293,848 tons of ancient tailings was treated, the average value of which was 0.620 ounces gold per ton ($21.70 at $35.00 per ounce, but most of the gold was sold at a premium which varied in amount). From underground 591,200 tons of ore was milled with an average value per ton of 1.089 ounces gold ($38.11), and 1,003,130.92 ounces silver were produced during the life of the property. With gold sold at an average of $40.00 per ounce and silver at $0.80 per ounce, the total value would be $31,587,780. The bullion recovery reached 95.7 per cent under Frank Cameron general manager.

Between 800 and 925 Saudi Arabs were normally employed and an overseas staff of 30 to 35. A road 246 miles long (farther than from New York to Washington) running over a 3,700 foot summit had to be built and maintained suitable for 15-ton trucks. A crew averaging over a hundred men was necessary for this work. At Jidda terminal a complete machine shop was required as each truck was thoroughly overhauled after its round trip of 500 miles.

The costs were high also because of the great distance the supplies and American personnel had to be transported. The best possible food and living conditions had to be maintained to attract American and foreign staff members. Costs were also increased by the unusually high capital outlay required to build terminal facilities at Jidda, including a 6,000 foot causeway and pier, adequate staff house, storehouse, and 246-mile road beside the usual mining camp. The small tonnage of 225 to 300 tons per day was also a factor. The cost per ton fluctuated considerably on this account, varying between extremes of $16.51 and $32.38. The average was approximately $23.11.

On October 13, 1950, the government imposed an income tax of 20 per cent on net yearly income of all companies. The Saudi Arabian Mining Syndicate concession agreement specified exemption of all taxes in return for 15 per cent share participation, the payment of 5 per cent royalty on the values recovered and paid for by the smelter, and 10 per cent customs duties. Nevertheless the government insisted on the income tax payment, thereby adding materially to the per-ton costs. But in spite of difficulties the mine paid dividends and was a profitable venture for all concerned, though especially so for the original syndicate members.

Although during the prospecting period of two years possibilities of commercial minerals were investigated, nothing of great importance was found. At Jizan, chief seaport of Asir, there is a rock salt deposit which the government mined in a very primitive way. Locally manufactured black powder was used there as the explosive. The holes for blasting were hand-churned, using one inch and 1.5-inch diameter steel bars.

After my visit to Jizan in 1940, I outlined a plan whereby a tractor-operated bulldozer and a Le Tourneau scraper could be used to remove the overburden, and a portable compressor with machine drills might increase the salt output. I emphasized, however, that an adequate market must be developed to absorb such an increased output. Rock salt usually has one per cent more sodium chloride and is less soluble than solar salt. Consequently, it is more desirable for preserving hides and skins, and so commands a certain market and a higher price. India was formerly an enormous market for the salt mined at Salif in the Yemen. In western Abyssinia salt is so scarce and highly prized that I have seen it in use as currency. Should an outlet be found for the Jizan salt, a mining industry of considerable benefit to the district might emerge.

In the Rabigh district there is a virgin deposit of barite. This would be valuable only to the oil companies for use in drilling. Investigation to date indicates that about 10,000 tons might thus be used annually. Such a demand would not of itself justify a mining and crushing plant at the present price per ton.

There is a large deposit of high grade gypsum a few miles northerly from Yenbo near the Red Sea coast. I sampled and recommended the development of this in 1947, but there has been no activity to date. Since raw gypsum has been shipped from Cyprus to the Far East, it seems logical that this Saudi deposit might be more profitable because it would not have to pay the Suez Canal dues as does the Cypriot ore.

In the Wejh district there are small ancient workings where very irregular deposits of galena had been mined, but the amount of lead obtained was very little.

There are resources of iron ores—mostly specularite—and large slag dumps at Aqiq in the vicinity of Mahad Dhahab, but no large deposit has been seen as yet. The price of iron ore precludes any lengthy transportation, and it seems probable that there is little hope of any benefit to the country from this source.

I saw mines located at Burm, south of Taif, and Nefi, north of Duwadami which are unique. At both places there were extensive stopes (workings) and dumps. Ancient books on travel had reported silver at Burm, but examination showed no silver minerals and assays gave no silver values, nor any values in rare minerals. But on the stope dumps and among the ruins there were fragments of various kinds of dishes, basins suitable for pans, and the open type of lamp. In most of Najd and highland Hijaz there is no clay with which to make pottery. There were no copper deposits or smelters for making metal pans and utensils. The alternative was the mining and cutting of this andesitic schist into shapes to serve as basins, dishes and lamps. The sizes of the ruins prove this unusual mining to have been an important and extensive industry.

In the spring of 1949 Shaikh Ahmed Fakhry, director of

mines, K. Peters, Saudi government mining engineer, and I made a 1,500 mile trip into Najd. We reexamined six ancient workings formerly visited and sampled by Shaikh Fakhry, Dirom, examining engineer of the Saudi Arabian Mining Syndicate, and myself in 1947. In addition we visited an entirely new area south of Afif and east of Muwai. Extensive ancient dumps, workings, and ruins were sampled. At least five groups of these warranted more extensive examination and possibly subsequent diamond drilling. A certain amount of equipment was ordered for this work by the government.

At the ancient workings called "Dthulm" considerable underground work as well as diamond drilling was done by the government under Peters. High gold values were erroneously reported as Richard Bogue of Point Four, a United States Geological Survey engineer, and I found by our check sampling, made at the urgent request of the Minister of Finance. The 50-ton mill erected at great expense confirmed our opinion that there was no ore of commercial value so all operations were stopped and the property closed down.

Afterword

THE birth and development of Saudi Arabia is not yet paralleled in history.

The fact that one man welded four separate provinces or kingdoms—each composed by many independent tribes—into one nation is a marvellous achievement. That this was accomplished by means of religious zeal is comparable with the founding of several of the original states of America.

The rapid transition of this nation from a poor, almost unknown area of deserts and tribal conflicts to an influential member of the world family of nations within the period of under thirty years is unique. Equally so is the transition from camel transport to the motorcar and airplane.

All of this is due to the development of one of the greatest oil productive areas in the world under a wise government and matchless oil company organization. Also unique is the fact that the oil development stemmed from the philanthropy of a single American.

That both the country and the company will continue to progress together to their mutual advantage is indicated by the policies pursued by King Saud and Aramco in their unprecedented partnership.

That serious tensions exist in the Middle East cannot be denied. These tensions have been increased by the invasion of Egypt by Israel, France, and Britain in October 1956. Why these responsible nations decided to disregard their pledges in the United Nations (which the latter two were principals in organizing) may, I believe, never be understood by the average American or true Briton.

The killing of innocent thousands of Port Said men, women, and children by the French and British air forces has added to distrust of the West. On the other hand, the constant endeavours of American Foreign Aid Policy and Point Four, though far from perfect, do contribute to lessening these tensions. The enlightened policies followed by Aramco, and the activities of private philanthropic organizations such as the Near East Foundation, American Friends of the Middle East, American Middle East Relief, Catholic Near East Relief, Church World Service, Lutheran World Relief, the Friends Service Committee, and many others, plus, especially, the American University of Beirut and the American University of Cairo, all aid enormously in decreasing present tensions. It is to be hoped that the United Nations can influence all the concerned nations to cooperate for a just solution for peace in the Middle East.

I personally believe that Prince Faisal will follow the policy of neutrality that has been established by King Saud, that he will not follow either Egypt or Russia but will maintain absolute independence. I think that King Saud and the other brothers of Prince Faisal will cooperate with him in establishing more efficiency in government administration, especially in finances and foreign affairs.

To me the future of Saudi Arabia is full of promise.

Glossary of Arabic Place and Tribal Names

Abqaiq (Buqayq, Abqayq)
Abu Arish (Abu 'Arīsh)
Abu Hadriyah
  (Abu Ḥadrīyah)
Aflaj (al-Aflāj)
Ain ('Ayn)
Ainain ('Aynayn)
Ain Burj ('Ayn al-Burj)
Ain Dar ('Ayn Dār)
Ain Darush ('Ayn Dārūsh)
Ain Dhila ('Ayn al-Dhila')
Ain Hakl ('Ayn al-Ḥaql)
Ain Haradh ('Ayn Ḥaraḍ)
Ain Heeb ('Ayn Umm Hīb)
Ain Heet ('Ayn al-Hīt)
Ain Husain ('Ayn Ḥusayn)
Ain Najm ('Ayn Najm)
Ain Rass ('Ayn al-Rass)
Ain Samha ('Ayn Samḥah)
Ain Waziria ('Ayn Wazīrīyah)
Ain Zubaida ('Ayn Zubaydah)
Ais (al-'Ayṣ)
Ajam (al-'Ajam)
Ajman (al-'Ijmān) tribe
Alamain ('Alamayn)
Alemat ('Alāmāt)
Aleppo (Ḥalab)
Amk ('Imq)
Anaiza ('Unayzah)
Aqaba (al-'Aqabah)

Aqiq (al-'Aqīq)
Arid (al-'Āriḍ)
Artawiyah (al-Arṭāwīyah)
Asaiba ('Uṣaybah)
Asfar (Aṣfar)
Ashaira ('Ushayrah)
Asir ('Asīr)
Ataiba ('Utaybah) tribe
Atiya ('Aṭīyah)
Awamia (al-'Awwāmīyah)
Awanid (Awaynīd)
Awazim (al-'Awāzim)

Badanah (Badanah)
Badia (al-Bādiyah)
Bahrain (al-Baḥrayn)
Baish (Baysh)
Beirut (Bayrūt)
Bekaa (al-Biqā')
Bir (Bi'r)
Bir Afif (Bi'r 'Afīf)
Bir al-Birka (Bi'r al-Birkah)
Bir al-Shaikh (Bi'r al-Shaykh)
Bir Dafina (Bi'r al-Dafīnah)
Bir Himaa (Bi'r Ḥima)
Bir Husainiya
  (Bi'r al-Ḥusaynīyah)
Bir Joraina (Bi'r Juraynah)
Bir Khuff (Bi'r Khuff)
Bir Qaiaya (Bi'r al-Qay'īyah)

257

Bir Rumah (Bi'r Rimāḥ)
Birka (al-Birkah)
Bisha (Bīshah)
Buraida (Buraydah)

Dafina (al-Dafīnah)
Dahna (al-Dahnā')
Dammam (al-Dammām)
Darain (al-Dārayn)
Dariya (al-Dir'īyah)
al-Darr (al-Dharr)
Darush (Dārūsh)
Dawasir (al-Dawāsir)
Dhaba (Ḍuba)
Dhahaban (Dhahabān)
Dhahran (al-Ẓahrān)
Dhat al-Okdood
  (Dhāt al-Ukhdūd)
Dhila (al-Dhila')
Dthulm (Ẓalam)
Duwadami (al-Dawādami)

Fadhili (al-Fāḍili)
Faid (Fayd)
Farasan (Farasān)
Fawara (al-Fawwārah)

Gahama (al-Qaḥmah)
Gharaine Abyad
  (Qurayn Abyaḍ)
Ghawar (al-Ghawār)

Hadda (Ḥaddā')
Hadramawt (Ḥaḍramawt)

Hafira (al-Ḥafīrah)
Hail (Ḥā'il)
Hajir (Hājir)
Hakl (al-Ḥaql)
Haleet (Ḥalīt)
Hali (Ḥali)
Hamdtha (al-Ḥamḍah)
Haradh (Ḥaraḍ)
Harb (Ḥarb) tribe
Hariq (al-Ḥarīq)
Hasa (al-Ḥasa)
Hauta (al-Ḥawtah)
Hazazina (al-Hazāzinah)
Hijaz (al-Ḥijāz)
Hodeida (al-Ḥudaydah)
Hofuf (al-Hufūf)
Horaiba (al-Khuraybah)
Howiya (al-Huway'ah)
Hummaya (al-Humayyah)
Husainiya (al-Ḥusaynīyah)
Huwaitat (al-Ḥuwayṭāt) tribe

Idrisi (Idrīsi) tribe

Jabal Dhahran
  (Jabal al-Ẓahrān)
Jabal Raoum (Jabal Ra'ūm)
Jabrin (Yabrīn)
Jafura (al-Jāfūrah)
Jash (al-Jashsh)
Jauf (al-Jawf)
Jeleed (al-Jalīd)
Jenubia (Janūbīyah)

Jidda (Juddah)
Jishsha (al-Jishshah)
Jizan (Jīzān)
Joraina (Juraynah)
Jubail (Jubayl)
Jubaila (Jubaylah)

Khafs Daghara
  (Khafs al-Daghrah)
Khaibar (Khaybar)
Khamaseen (al-Khamāsīn)
Khamis Mushait
  (Khamīs Mushayṭ)
Kharj (al-Kharj)
Khobar (al-Khubar)
Khor al-Birk (Khūr al-Birk)
Khuff (Khuff)
Khurma (al-Khurmah)
Khursaniyah (Khursāniyah)
Kunfida (al-Qunfidhah)
Kuwait (al-Kuwayt)

Laila (Layla)
Latakia (al-Lādhiqīyah)
Lith (al-Līth)

Maagala (Umm 'Uqlah)
Maan (Ma'ān)
Mahad Dhahab
  (Mahd al-Dhahab)
Madinat al-Nabi
  (Madīnat al-Nabi)
Majmaa (al-Majma'ah)
Manama (al-Manāmah)

Manifa (Manīfah)
Marrat (Marrāt)
Mastura (Mastūrah)
Medain Saleh (Madā'in Ṣāliḥ)
Mubarez (al-Mubarraz)
Murra (Āl Murrah) tribe
Musaijid (al-Musayjīd)
Mutair (Muṭayr) tribe
Muwai (al-Muwayh)
Muwaila (al-Muwayliḥ)

Nafud (al-Nufūd)
Najd (Najd)
Najran (Najrān)
Nariyah (al-Nu'ayrīyah)
Nazla (Nazla)

Oglat al-Sughour
  ('Uqlat al-Ṣuqūr)
Oman ('Umān)
Oqair (al-'Uqayr)

Qaara (al-Qārah)
Qahtan (Qaḥṭān) tribe
Qaiaya (al-Qay'īyah)
Qaisumah (al-Qayṣūmah)
Qalat al-Aqaba
  (Qal'at al-'Aqabah)
Qalat al-Sura
  (Qal'at al-Sūrah)
Qasim (al-Qaṣīm)
Qatar (Qaṭar)
Qatif (al-Qaṭīf)
Quraysh (Quraysh) tribe

259

Rabigh (Rābigh)
Rafha (Rafḥa)
Raoum (Ra'ūm)
Rass (al-Rass)
Ras Mishaab
  (Ra's al-Mish'āb)
Ras Tanura (Ra's Tannūrah)
Riyadh (al-Riyāḍ)
Rub al-Khali
  (al-Rub' al-Khāli)
Rutba Wells (al-Ruṭbah)

Sabya (Ṣabya)
Safaniya (al-Saffānīyah)
Sakaka (Sakākah)
Salif (al-Ṣalīf)
Salma (Salma)
Samira (Samīrā')
Sanaa (Ṣan'ā')
Shab al-Jaleed
  (Shi'b al-Jalīd)
Shammar (Shammar) tribe
Shumaisi (Shumaysi)
Shuqaiq (al-Shuqayq)
Shuwaik (al-Shuwaykh)
Sidon (Ṣaydā')
Sofwa (Ṣafwah)
Subai (Subay') tribe
Sud al-Jamajim
  (Sudd al-Jamājīm)
Sud Sayaud (Sudd Suyūd)
Sud Somalagi
  (Sudd al-Samlaqi)
Suhul (al-Suhūl) tribe
Suk al-Ahad (Sūq al-Aḥad)

Suk ibn Mushait
  (Sūq ibn-Mushayṭ)
Sulaiyil (al-Sulayyil)

Taif (al-Ṭā'if)
Taima (Taymā')
Tarut (Tārūt)
Thamama (Thamāmah)
Tihama (Tihāmah)
Tufaih (Ṭufayḥ)
Turba (Tarabah)
Turaif (Ṭurayf)
Tuwaik (Ṭuwayq)

Udhailiyah (al-'Uḍailīyah)
al-Ula (al-'Ula)
Umluj (Umm Lujj)
Umm Garayat
  (Umm Qurayyah)
Umm Ogla (Umm 'Uqlah)
Uthmaniyah
  (al-'Uthmānīyah)
Uwainid ('Uwaynid)
Uyaynah (al-'Uyaynah)

Wadi Abha (Wādi Abha)
Wadi Amk (Wādi 'Imq)
Wadi Dawasir
  (Wādi al-Dawāsir)
Wadi Hamdh
  (Wādi al-Ḥamḍ)
Wadi Rumma (Wādi al-Rummah)
Wadi Tathlith (Wādi Tathlīth)

Wadi Uqda (Wādi 'Uqdah)

Wadi Yenbo (Wādi Yanbu')

Wariah (Warī'ah)

Waziria (al-Wazīrīyah)

Wejh (al-Wajh)

Yamama (al-Yamāmah)

Yemen (al-Yaman)

Yenbo (Yanbu')

Yenbo Nakhl

   (Yanbu' al-Nakhl)

Bibliography

Abbott, Nabia, *Aisha, The Beloved of Mohammed*, 1942, University of Chicago Press

al-'Aṭṭār, Ahmad 'Abd al-, *Eagle of the Peninsula* (Arabic), 1937, Cairo

Antonius, George, *The Arab Awakening*, 1934, Lippincott, New York

Arabian American Oil Company, *Summary of Middle East Oil Developments*, 1952, New York

Armstrong, H. C., *Lord of Arabia*, 1934, Arthur Baker, London

Bell, Lady Gertrude, *Letters of Gertrude Bell* (2 vols.), 1927, Boni & Liveright, New York

Blunt, Lady Anne, *A Pilgrimage to Nejd* (2 vols.), 1881, John Murray, London

Boveri, Margaret, *Minaret and Pipeline*, 1939, Oxford University Press, London (privately printed)

Bowen, Richard L. J., *Arab Dhows of Eastern Arabia*, 1949, Rehoboth, Mass.

Bray, NN. E., *A Paladin of Arabia*, 1936, Kemp Hall Press, Oxford

Brown, William R., *The Horse of the Desert*, 1947, Derrydale Press, New York

Bullard, Sir Reader, *Britain and the Middle East, from Earliest Times, to 1950*, 1951, London

Burckhardt, John Lewis, *Bedouins and Wahabys* (Arabic), proverbs & travels in the Hedjaz (3 vols.). 1830, Colburn & Bentley, London

Burrow, Millar, *Palestine Is Our Business*, 1949, Westminster Press, Philadelphia

Burton, Richard F., *Pilgrimage to El Medina and Mecca* (3 vols.), 1855, Longman, Brown, Green and Longman, London
————, *Gold Mines of Midian*, 1878, Kegan Paul, London
————, *The Land of Midian* (revisited), 1879, Kegan Paul, London

Byng, Edward, J., *World of the Arabs*, 1944, Little, Brown & Co., London

Carruthers, Alex. D. M., *Arabian Adventure*, 1935, H. F. & G. Witherby, London

Cheesman, Major R. E., *In Unknown Arabia*, 1926, MacMillan, London

Cobbold, Lady Evelyn, *Pilgrimage to Mecca*, 1934, John Murray, London

Cornwall, Peter B., *Ancient Arabia; Exploration in Hasa*, 1946, The Geographical Journal (Washington)

De Gaury, Gerald, *Arabia, Phoenix*, 1946, Harrap, London

———, *Arabian Journey*, 1950, Harrap, London

———, *A Saudi Arabian Notebook*, 1943, S.A.E., Cairo

———, *Rulers of Mecca*, 1951, Harrap, London

Dickson, H. R. P., *The Arab of the Desert*, 1949, Allen & Unwin, London

———, *Kuwait and Her Neighbors*, 1956, Allen & Unwin, London

Doughty, Charles M., *Arabia Deserta* (2 vols.), 1937, Random House, New York

Eddy, William A., *F.D.R. Meets Ibn Saud*, 1954, American Friends of the Middle East Inc., New York

Erskine, Mrs. Steuart, *The Vanished Cities of Arabia*, Hutchinson & Co., London

Euting, Julius, *Tagebuch einer Reise in Inner Arabien*, 1896, Leyden

Faris, Nabih Amin, *The Antiquities of South Arabia*, 1938, Princeton University Press, Princeton, N.J.

Field, Henry, *Ancient & Modern Man in Southwestern Asia*, 1956, University of Miami Press, Coral Gables, Fla.

———, *Camel Brands & Graffiti from Iraq, Syria, Iran, Jordan, and Arabia*, 1952, American Oriental Society, Baltimore, Md.

Fisher, W. B., *The Middle East*, 1950, E. P. Dutton & Co., London

264

Graves, Robert, *Lawrence and the Arabs*, 1927

Guarmani, Carlo, *Northern Nejd; A Journey from Jerusalem to Anaiza in Qasim*, 1938, Argonaut Press, London

Hamidullah, Muhammad, *The Battlefields of the Prophet Muhammad*, 1953, Woking, England

Harrison, Paul W., *The Arab at Home*, 1924, Crowell, New York

————, *Doctor in Arabia*, 1940, John Day, New York

Hart, Liddell, *T. E. Lawrence* (*In Arabia and After*), 1934, Jonathan Cape, London

Hill, Gray, *With the Bedouins*, 1891, J. Fisher Elmwin, London

Hitti, Philip K., *The Arabs: A Short History*. Revised, 1949. Princeton University Press, Princeton, N.J. (Available in paperback through Henry Regnery Co.)

————, *History of the Arabs*, 1943, MacMillan & Co., London

Hogarth, D. G., *Arabia*, 1922

————, *The Penetration of Arabia*, 1904, Fred A. Stokes, New York

Hourani, George F., *Arab Seafaring in the Indian Ocean*, 1951, Princeton University Press, Princeton, N.J.

Huber, Charles, *Journal D'un Voyage En Arabie*, 1891, Imprimerie National, Paris

Hurgronje, C. Snouck, *Mecca*, 1931, Brill, Leiden, Netherlands

————, *The Revolt in Arabia*, 1917, C. P. Putnam's Sons, New York

Jacobs, Col. Harold F., *Kings of Arabia*, 1923

Jamme, W. F., *South-Arabian Antiquities in U.S.A.*, 1955, Nederlandsch Institute Voor Het Nabije Oosten

Keane, J. F., *Six Months in Mecca*, 1881, Tinsley Bros., London

————, *My Journey to Medina*, 1881, Tinsley Bros., London

————, *Six Months in the Hejaz*, 1887, Ward & Downey, London

Khan and Sparroy, *With the Pilgrims to Mecca*, 1905, Orientalia, New York

265

Kheirallah, George, *Arabia Reborn*, 1952, University of New Mexico Press, Albuquerque, N.M.

Kiernan, R. Hugh, *The Unveiling of Arabia*, 1937 G. G. Harrap, London

Kirk, George E., *A Short History of the Middle East*, 1949, Public Affairs Press, Washington, D.C.

Lawrence, T. E., *Revolt in the Desert*, 1926, Garden City Pub. Co., New York

————, *Secret Dispatches*, 1940, Golden Cockerel Press, London

————, *Seven Pillars of Wisdom* (2 vols.), 1946, Jonathan Cape, London

Lebkicher, Roy, *Aramco and World Oil*, 1952, Russel F. Moore, New York

Lebkicher, Roy, Rentz, George, and Steineke, Max, *The Arabia of Ibn Saud*, 1952, Russel F. Moore, New York

————, *Saudi Arabia*, 1952, Russel F. Moore, New York

Longrigg, Brigd. Stephan, "The Liquid Gold of Arabia," 1949, *Middle East Journal*, Washington, D.C.

Lowth, C. T., *The Wanderer in Arabia*, 1855, Hurst & Blackett, London

Malmiganiti, Countess, *Inner Deserts and Medina*, 1925, Philip Allen, London

Mendelschon, Isaac, *Slavery in the Ancient Near East*, 1949, Oxford University Press, Oxford

Middle East Institute, *Americans and the Middle East; Partners in the Next Decade*, 1950, Middle East Institute, Washington, D.C.

Mikesell, R. & H. Chenery, *Arabian Oil (America's Stake in the Middle East)*, 1949, University of North Carolina Press, Durham, N.C.

Miles, George C., "Early Islamic Inscriptions Near Taif, in the Hijaz (dam)," 1948, *Journal of Near Eastern Studies*, Chicago

————, *Ali B. Isa's Pilgrim Road, An Inscription of the Year*

304 H (916-917 A.D.) (At Mahad Mine), 1955, Imprimerie de L'Institut Français, Cairo.

Morton, H. V., *Middle East*, 1948, Methuen, London

Musil, Alois, *The Northern Hejaz*, 1926, American Geographical Society, New York

————, *Arabia Deserta*, 1927, American Geographical Society, New York

————, *Manners & Customs of the Ruala Bedu*, 1928, American Geographical Society, New York

Niebuhr, M., *Travels through Arabia* (2 vols.), 1792, Belfast

Palgrave, W. C., *Central and Eastern Arabia* (2 vols.), 1865, MacMillan & Co., London

Philby, H. St. John, *The Heart of Arabia* (2 vols.), 1922, Constable & Co., London

————, *Arabia of the Wahhabis*, 1928, Constable & Co., London

————, *Arabia*, 1930, Ernest Benn, London

————, *Sheba's Daughters*, 1939, Methuen & Co., London

————, *A Pilgrim in Arabia*, 1946, Robert Hale, London

————, *Arabian Days*, 1948, Robert Hale, London

————, *Arabian Highlands*, 1952, Cornell University Press, Ithaca, N.Y.

Pratt, Wallace E. & Good, Dorothy, *World Geography of Petroleum*, 1950, Princeton University Press, Princeton, N.J.

Raswan, Carl R., *Black Tents of Arabia*, 1935, Little Brown, Boston

Rida, Muhi il Deen, *Long Age* (*Biography of Ibn Saud—in Arabic*), 1950, Cairo

Rihani, Ameen, *Maker of Modern Arabia*, 1928, Houghton Mifflin, New York

————, *Ibn Saud of Arabia*, 1928, Constable & Co., London

————, *Around the Coasts of Arabia*, 1930, Constable & Co., London

Roosevelt, Kermit, *Arabs, Oil and History*, 1949, Harper & Bros., New York

Rutter, Eldon, *The Holy Cities of Arabia* (2 vols.), 1930, G. P. Putnam, New York

Sanger, Richard H., *The Arabian Peninsula*, 1954, Cornell University Press, Ithaca, New York

Seabrook, W. B., *Adventures in Arabia*, 1930, Cornwall Press, New York

Shaffer, Robert, *Tents and Towers of Arabia*, 1952, Dodd, Mead & Co., New York

Speiser, E. A., *The United States and the Near East*, 1948, Harvard University Press, Cambridge, Mass.

Storrs, Sir Ronald, *Orientations*, 1945, Nicholson & Watson, London

Taylor, Bayard, *Travels in Arabia*, 1892, Scribners, New York

Thomas, Bertram, *Alarms & Excursions in Arabia*, 1931, Unwin Bros., London

————, *Arabia Felix*, 1932, Jonathan Cape, London

————, *The Arabs*, 1937, Doubleday & Co., New York

Thomas, Lowell, *With Lawrence in Arabia*, Hutchinson & Co., London

Twitchell, Wathen, & Hamilton, *Report of the United States Agricultural Mission to Saudi Arabia*, 1943, Imprimerie Musr., Cairo

Vidal, F. S., *The Oasis of Al Hasa*, 1955, Arabian American Oil Company

Warriner, Dorothy, *Land of Poverty in the Middle East*, 1948, Royal Institute of International Affairs, London

Wavell, A. J. B., *A Modern Pilgrim in Mecca*, 1912, Constable, London

Wellstead, Lt. J. R., *Travels in Arabia* (2 vols.), 1838, John Murray, London

Williams, Kenneth, *Ibn Saud*, 1933, Jonathan Cape, London

Zwemer, Rev. S. M., *Arabia; The Cradle of Islam*, 1900, Oliphant, Anderson & Ferrier, Edinburgh

Index

275